THE
SCHOOL
BUS
LAW

THE
SCHOOL
BUS
LAW

A Case Study

in Education,

Religion,

and Politics

BY THEODORE POWELL

Wesleyan University Press

Middletown, Connecticut

Why beholdest thou

the mote that is

in thy brother's eye,

but perceivest not

the beam that is

in thine own eye?

CONTENTS

PREFACE

THIS BOOK attempts to be an objective study of the role of religious groups as a political force. It would be pretentious for an author to claim that he had succeeded in excluding all bias from his work, but a diligent effort has been made to do so here. The reader is asked to approach the following pages in the spirit of the study, to set aside bias and view the chronicle without precommitment.

The risks entailed by a scholar writing in this area have been aptly described by a former professor of this author, V. O. Key, Jr., one of the most knowledgeable observers of American politics. To discuss even in broad terms the attempts of churches to influence government action, Dr. Key states, "is a most hazardous enterprise." He adds:

> The most innocent comment about religious groups can arouse the sharpest reaction. Critical comment easily becomes bigotry or even an irreverent challenge to the work of the Lord. All of which suggests that the currents of religion run so deeply in our politics that people prefer not to talk about the topic lest discussion set off debates over questions irreconcilable because they present, at least potentially, conflicts of divergent absolutes.*

However, there has been a growing recognition by ministers, priests, and rabbis, as well as by laymen of the various faiths, that there is a need for candid, dispassionate consideration of the social and political relations of religious groups.

* V. O. Key, Jr., *Politics, Parties and Pressure Groups* (New York: Thomas Y. Crowell Company, 4th edition, 1958), p. 130.

It would be a simple matter to write a tract condemning one side or the other in this political-religious struggle. Nor would it be difficult to fashion an innocuous work that favored greater understanding and advancement of the brotherhood of man—while evading the serious problems posed by the struggle. But there would be little value in a polemic or a bromide. The author hopes that this detailed study and criticism of the political methods of Connecticut church groups will suggest how religious leaders and their followers can use their political influence without creating severe, lasting community division and without endangering the democratic process.

Such danger and division were evident in Connecticut in 1956 and 1957 during the disputes over public services for Catholic school pupils. As a staff member of the State Department of Education, the author occupied an especially good vantage point to witness many of the major events of those disputes and to observe their effects on Connecticut politics. The following account was possible in large part because of the assistance of many clergymen and political figures. Their contributions are acknowledged in the footnotes. However, some names are deserving of special mention. Frederick Pope of Fairfield, Theodore Ryan of Sharon, and Edwin O. Smith of Mansfield were especially helpful in describing the legislative struggle over the school bus bill. A number of ministers and priests, notably the Reverend William Bradley, the Reverend Harold Keir, Monsignor Robert W. Doyle, and the Reverend Loyd Worley, although not necessarily agreeing with the author's views, were most cooperative. Dr. Raymond J. Fay, Dr. Charles F. Ritch, and Dr. Maurice J. Ross, the author's colleagues in the State Department of Education, drew on their extensive knowledge of education in Connecticut to provide counsel and to suggest sources for additional information. William Horowitz, chairman of the Connecticut State Board of Education, read the manuscript and offered helpful suggestions.

The author was fortunate to have the advice of Gerald Gunther and Wallace Sayre of Columbia University. Mr. Gunther's comments on the chapter devoted to the Supreme Court's decisions prevented many errors and inadequacies. Professor Sayre's penetrating and constructive criticism gave the author a better understanding of his task and provided him encouragement during difficult stages.

The staff of the Mary Cheney Library in Manchester, Connecticut, and Virginia Knox, Public Services Division Chief of the Connecticut State Library, gave gracious, valuable assistance.

The author must also express appreciation to a number of friends and counselors: John and Elaine Mrosek of Manchester, Leo B. Flaherty of Rockville, Herbert Hannabury of Vernon, Professor James Brown of St. Joseph College, West Hartford, and Morton Feigenbaum, executive secretary of the Connecticut Anti-Defamation League, B'nai Brith, in New Haven.

To the late Ellen F. Goodsell, who provided unfailing assistance over many years, the author's debt is incalculable.

Writers are notoriously selfish in the sacrifices demanded of their wives for the sake of their work. This author is conscious that Virginia S. Powell has been so treated. It was largely her unquestioning faith in her husband that repeatedly encouraged him to overcome feelings of despair and to press on to the eventual completion of his task.

In the preparation of this work the author has sought the counsel of persons in a variety of positions and of many different viewpoints. He has tried to benefit from their advice, but he alone must, of course, take responsibility for any errors in his work and for the interpretations and conclusions he has presented.

THEODORE POWELL

Manchester, Connecticut.
April, 1960.

THE
SCHOOL
BUS
LAW

INTRODUCTION

A PUBLIC HEARING was held in the Hall of the Connecticut House of Representatives on March 12, 1957, by the General Assembly's Joint Committee on Education. The chief item under consideration was a proposed statute declaring:

> Any town, city or borough may provide for its children attending private schools therein not conducted for profit, any of the health or safety services including transportation, provided for its children attending public schools.

The news stories reporting the public hearing in the *Hartford Courant* and the *Hartford Times* described the proposal as a measure to provide public assistance to private and parochial schools. The *Courant* reported that the measure was supported by "representatives of Catholic churches, prominent Catholic laymen" and opposed by the "Connecticut Council of [Protestant] Churches and a number of Congregational ministers." [1] Two days after the hearing these news stories were criticized as a "contemptible performance" in an editorial in the *Catholic Transcript*, official newspaper of the Roman Catholic Archdiocese of Hartford. This editorial, entitled "The Hartford Papers Trick Their Readers," charged that the proposal and the nature of its support were misrepresented. The measure was intended to aid children, not schools, the editorial declared. "There were no Catholic churches represented," the editorial continued, but prominent Catholic laymen and two well-known and respected Protestants had spoken for the proposal. [2]

The views expressed in the *Transcript's* editorial were repeated in full-page advertisements appearing a few days later in the *Hartford Courant* [3] and the *Hartford Times*.[4] The advertisements were presented in the form of an open letter by thirty-one residents of the Hartford area "in the interest of full and fair reporting."

The editorial and the open letters reflected a conflict between two doctrines; the child-benefit theory and the principle of separation of church and state. Opponents of the auxiliary services bill in their arguments at the public hearing had repeatedly referred to the principle of church-state separation. Advocates of the auxiliary services employed the child-benefit theory. The reporters for the Hartford papers had not been impressed by the distinction between services to children and services to schools. They had been impressed that the division at the hearing was a religious one, Protestant against Catholic.

The public hearing on March 12 was a major skirmish in a battle which provided the most intense controversy of the regular session of the 1957 Connecticut General Assembly. Related battles had been fought in several Connecticut towns prior to the legislative session.

It is the purpose of this study to describe and analyze the struggles in four Connecticut towns and in the legislature over the issue of public services for parochial school pupils. The arguments used on both sides of the controversy will be analyzed. The role of political and religious leaders and groups will be described. An evaluation will be made of some of the techniques used in this political-religious dispute.

This study is not concerned with religious doctrines as such. This is a study of politics; specifically, the making of public policy on the question of public services for non-public school pupils.

I:

THE

GENERAL

SETTING

AIRLINE STEWARDESSES are taught to avoid discussion of four topics with passengers: sex, religion, politics, and danger. This book is devoted to discussing the last three.

Religion and politics are generally recognized as having the same potentially explosive power as alcohol and gasoline. Both stimulate strong emotional commitments. When religious forces meet in opposition in the political arena, political convictions are reinforced by religious faith. The intensity of the conflict is increased, and the usual political processes of persuasion and compromise may be abandoned. How can a religious man compromise his faith? When evangelism takes precedence, the political system is in danger.

In 1956 and 1957 a political conflict between the Protestant and Catholic clergy presented a severe challenge to Connecticut's political processes.

Some determined efforts were made locally and on the state level to obtain public services to Catholic school pupils. These efforts were led or were stimulated by Catholics. They were opposed chiefly by Protestant clergy, Protestant school board members, and Protestant legislators.

Connecticut had suffered religious-political conflict in the past.[1]

The common-school system originated in "a virtual system of [Protestant] parochial schools." In 1818 an intense battle was fought over the adoption of a constitution which deprived the Congregational Church of its favored position as the established religion of the state. That favored position had caused a number of disputes about the schools. Those disputes and the debate about the 1818 Constitution were fought among Protestant sects. Later in the nineteenth century there were new conflicts as substantial numbers of Catholic immigrants arrived. The establishment of a State Board of Education in 1833 and the centralization of educational administration had reduced church influence over the schools. However, a Congregational bias persisted in the common schools through the middle of the nineteenth century. Bible reading and other Protestant practices stimulated the growth of Catholic schools, despite attacks by nativist groups upon such schools as "divisive and un-American."

Attempts by Catholic school authorities in the second half of the nineteenth century to share in state and local school funds were generally unsuccessful. However, some local school boards agreed to assume financial responsibility for some Catholic schools while leaving religious authorities some control of the schools.

> The parochial school authorities retained some measure of supervision over the education of their Catholic pupils whom the town, in the absence of adequate school facilities, educated at public expense in parish schools. These adopted schools were governed by the same rules binding on the other public schools of the district. While the terms of agreement varied with each case, the pastor was permitted at least the right to suggest the teachers to be employed.[2]

All but two such agreements (in New Haven) had been terminated long before 1957; but conflicts over religious activities and the public schools still arose at various times during the twentieth century.

The conflicts in 1956 and 1957 were not over religion in the public school nor over public support of Catholic schools; rather, the disputes were over auxiliary services to Catholic school pupils. At least, auxiliary services were the chief subject matter of the arguments. The causes of the conflict were more complex.

There was a dispute whether existing Connecticut statutes permitted school boards to give any public services to Catholic school pupils. There was a dispute whether a law should be passed authorizing such services. There was a dispute whether such a law would violate either the Connecticut or the federal Constitution. There was a dispute over the desirability of parochial schools.

All of these disputes, however, were different aspects of a deeper conflict. One Protestant leader, commenting on these disputes, said that it was very difficult for Connecticut Protestants to accept the fact that they were rapidly losing control of the state: "We are a minority acting like a majority." [3] A Catholic priest responded, "And many Catholics are tired of being treated like an unimportant minority."

In this post-bellum exchange, the real nature of the 1956–1957 religious-political conflicts in Connecticut was clearly described. In truth, these conflicts were a major test of political strength between the Catholic and Protestant churches.

The chief forensic weapons in this test of strength were arguments—constitutional, statutory, and political—about auxiliary services to Catholic school pupils, and arguments about the desirability of Catholic or parochial schools.

Arguments challenging the existence of the parochial school were sometimes presented explicitly. The parochial school was described as unnecessary or undesirable. Often such charges were made by implication. Anticipating these charges, supporters of public services for parochial school pupils argued both in favor of services and in defense of the parochial school.

The other category of arguments included not only disputes about auxiliary services but also the extent to which government might cooperate with or aid religion—if at all. Such disputes arose out of the child-benefit theory [4] and out of differing interpretations of the First Amendment's prohibition of any "law respecting an establishment of religion." These words have been metaphorically described as erecting "a wall of separation between church and state."

The First Amendment to the Constitution of the United States declares that "Congress shall make no law respecting an establishment of religion or prohibiting the free exercise thereof." Those debating public services for parochial school pupils usually claim adherence to the First Amendment (made applicable to the states by the Fourteenth Amendment), although they may take any one of three general positions. Those three positions may be titled separation, cooperation, and child benefit.

The origination of the phrase "a wall of separation between church and state" is credited to Thomas Jefferson.[5] The meaning of the phrase and its constitutional significance have been the subject of much recent debate.[6] Separation of church and state may be defined broadly as the exclusion of one agency from participation in the affairs of the other. Cooperation can be used to mean either government aid to religion on a non-preferential basis or the use of governmental machinery for religious purposes. Thus cooperation may mean not only public assistance to parochial schools but also the promotion of religion, on a non-preferential basis, within the public schools.* The child-benefit theory has been defined by Clark Spurlock as meaning in its simplest terms "that the state's obligation to all school children in the state transcends a too-literal observance of the principle of separation of church and state." [7] The theory may be more precisely defined: Benefits may be extended by the state to all children of the same classification in order to achieve a public purpose.

These definitions of the three positions are broad. Participants in debates about auxiliary services frequently added modifications. As will be shown later, the modifications often appeared to contradict the principle asserted by the debater to defend his general position.

* A third meaning of cooperation was seldom used in these debates: state and church working together for a public purpose. There is obviously crucial constitutional difference in cooperation for a public purpose and cooperation for a religious purpose. The distinction is not always easy to make.

Some debates by national figures in recent years illustrate the policies connected with the three general positions—separation, cooperation, and child benefit; the arguments used to defend those positions; and the emotional, theological, and personal differences.

SOME NATIONAL DEBATES

Since education in America has been primarily a state and local affair, disputes about parochial and public schools most frequently occur at the state or local level. However, proposals for federal aid to education have precipitated debates in Congress and among national organizations. Such debates frequently involve figures of national prominence. A prominent name and an intensely controversial subject can combine to make a sensational news story. In the decade preceding the Connecticut conflicts, there were several such stories which gained national attention.

Non-public Schools—A Divisive Force?

Often the question of public services for parochial school pupils is not considered on its own merits, because opponents of services may base their opposition on the undesirability of parochial and private schools. Such a view was expressed in 1952 by Dr. James B. Conant, then president of Harvard University. He said that "the increasing number of private schools might result in a dual system of high school education which would threaten the democratic unity provided by our public schools." Dr. Conant acknowledged the right of private schools to exist, but he felt that their increasing number would hinder the development of an ideal "democratic, fluid society with a minimum of class distinction." Public schools served children of all faiths, he said, but some people were suggesting that tax money be diverted to private schools. This was the same as urging that "American society use its own hands to destroy itself." [8]

Similar sentiments were expressed by Mrs. Agnes Meyer at the 1952 convention of the National Education Association. She spoke of the "tensions, conflicts and animosities created by the parochial school." There were localities, she charged, "where the public school budget is kept at a minimum because of the burden of private schools on a large number of taxpayers." [9]

The response by spokesmen for the Catholic schools was immediate and strong. The executive board of the National Catholic Educational Association declared that a dual system of public and private schools was the American tradition. The first schools in this country were organized by religious groups, the board said, and a parent's right to send his child to a private school had been upheld by the United States Supreme Court.[10] Archbishop Richard J. Cushing of Boston said in an Easter Sunday sermon that Dr. Conant's statement would bring "increased boldness in pressing the campaign of secularism against independent schools, above all, religious schools." Dr. James M. O'Neill, a prominent Catholic layman, at the 1952 convention of the National Catholic Educational Association, said that the abolition of the private school would mean the end of free society in America; Dr. Conant's theory would put our nation "on the road to totalitarianism." [11]

Whether parochial or private schools are "divisive" or not, arguments about their place in American society obviously stimulate sharp language and strong feelings. These strong feelings add to the difficulty of discussing in a rational manner the issue of auxiliary services.

Non-Public Schools and Public Services

The most widely noticed debate about public services for parochial school pupils in recent years occurred in the summer of 1949 between Francis Cardinal Spellman and Mrs. Eleanor Roosevelt. In June of that year the Cardinal spoke critically of a proposal then pending in Congress for federal aid for public schools only. The aid was to be limited to current expenses, excluding expenditures for health services or for transportation. The Cardinal interpreted this bill as discriminatory against parochial schools, which he believed should have been included. He described supporters of this bill as "disciples of discrimination" and accused them of commiting "a sin, shocking as it is incomprehensible." He further accused them of advancing the "irrational, un-American, discriminatory thesis that the public school is the only true American school." [12]

On the Sunday following this speech, at each of the seven masses at St. Patrick's Cathedral in New York, the proposal was further denounced and worshipers were advised to demand that Congress defeat it. Posters near the doors of the Cathedral and in the reception hall of the rectory described the bill as "unjust, un-American and divisive."

Opposition to the bill in the Catholic press and in other Catholic churches throughout the country stimulated many thousands of letters and telegrams to congressmen calling for defeat of the bill. The National Catholic Welfare Conference news service reported that the mail received by congressmen matched the volume received during the debate on the Taft-Hartley bill in 1947 and the 1937 attempt to reorganize the Supreme Court. [13]

The week following Cardinal Spellman's speech, Mrs. Roosevelt commented in her newspaper column that the Cardinal's request for Catholic schools to share in federal aid presented to the American people a very difficult problem. Public education should not be connected with religious control of the schools, she said. Parents were free to send their children to denominational schools, of course, and these schools had a distinct contribution to make. They were free to develop new methods and to serve as "yardsticks." But non-public schools should receive no tax funds. She concluded with a warning against changing our tradition of separation of church and state. [14]

As a result of this column Mrs. Roosevelt received many letters, and in two later columns she explained that her opposition to federal aid for church schools was not due to any bias against the Catholic Church. She had not expressed approval or disapproval of any specific proposal. Mrs. Roosevelt said she had long felt that it would be desirable for representatives of the three major faiths to agree on a common body of moral and religious teaching which could be given to public school pupils. [15]

On July 21 Cardinal Spellman wrote to Mrs. Roosevelt and released a copy of the letter to the press. He accused her of condemning him for "defending Catholic children against those who would deny them their constitutional rights of equality with other American children." Mrs. Roosevelt, the Cardinal said, could have acted only from misinformation, ignorance, or prejudice, and he felt impelled to challenge her misstatements. He did not question Mrs. Roosevelt's right to differ with him, but he asked, "Why, I wonder do you repeatedly plead causes that are anti-Catholic?" The Cardinal concluded that Mrs. Roosevelt's record of "anti-Catholicism" was established by her authorship of "documents of discrimination unworthy of an American mother!" [16]

Cardinal Spellman's personal criticism of Mrs. Roosevelt obscured the position he was taking on the question of auxiliary services for parochial school pupils. He held that such benefits as milk, transportation, and immunization, if provided by the federal government, should be provided to both public and non-public school pupils. The Supreme Court, he said, had declared that health services, transportation, and non-religious textbooks given to parochial school pupils at public expense did not constitute a violation of the Constitution.* It was the charge of prejudice and anti-Catholicism that gained public attention, and it was against these charges that the *New York Times* and former New York Governor Herbert H. Lehman both defended Mrs. Roosevelt.[17]

Mrs. Roosevelt spoke in her own behalf in a letter to Cardinal Spellman. She wrote that she had supported Governor Alfred E. Smith in his campaign for the Presidency, and many other Catholics seeking public office. She had no bias against the Catholic Church and did not intend to attack the Cardinal personally. She would stand for those things which she believed to be right even though this put her in opposition to various groups. Her record, she believed, was not one of anti-Catholicism or "anti-any-religious group." In a final paragraph which revealed that Cardinal Spellman's words

* The Supreme Court had ruled on transportation and non-religious textbooks but not on health services. See below, Chapter II.

had stung her, she wrote, "I assure you that I have no sense of being an unworthy American mother. The final judgment, my dear Cardinal Spellman, of the worthiness of all human beings is in the hands of God." [18]

Less than two weeks after this reply, Cardinal Spellman telephoned and asked Mrs. Roosevelt's opinion of a statement he was giving to the newspapers. The statement said that public funds were being sought for parochial schools only for transportation, health services, and non-religious textbooks. Under the Constitution, the Cardinal wrote, "we do not ask, nor can we expect" public funds to pay for school construction, maintenance, and teaching services for parochial schools. He felt it his duty, he said, "to state in simple terms the position that Catholics, together with many Americans of other religious beliefs, are upholding." Mrs. Roosevelt described the statement as "clarifying and fair." [19] *

There were significant factors in this incident beyond the sensational ones arising from the involvement of two nationally prominent figures and the strong language employed by the Cardinal. Cardinal Spellman's position was based on the child-benefit theory. He argued for services for parochial school pupils and acknowledged that direct support of parochial schools would be unconstitutional. On this issue, which was one of public policy and not of religious doctrine, Cardinal Spellman presented himself as speaking for Catholics. He employed his church and his pulpit to rally his parishioners to support his position on a political question.

Mrs. Roosevelt said that non-public schools should receive "no tax funds of any kind," implying that auxiliary services were a contribution to the school as well as the pupil. Her opposition was based on the principle of church-state separation, although she favored public school responsibility for some religious instruction. Her position might be described as a belief in cooperation of church and state through the public schools.

---

* The personal aspects of this incident were closed a few weeks later when Cardinal Spellman, on his way to dedicate a chapel in Peekskill, made a social call at Mrs. Roosevelt's home.

The argument for auxiliary services to private school pupils and for cooperation between religion and government has been made on several occasions by the Catholic bishops of the United States in their annual statements.

In their 1955 statement the bishops declared that private and church-related schools were part of America's cultural growth and existed "not by sufferance, but by right." Church-related schools taught the "accepted curriculum" and "that which the tax-supported schools under present conditions may not teach, namely, positive religion." Parochial schools were not divisive but promoted true Christian training, the virtues of justice and charity, patriotism, and devotion to public service. Such schools had "full right to be considered and dealt with as components of the American educational system." Students of these schools, the bishops contended, were rightfully entitled to "benefit from those measures, grants or aids which are manifestly designed for the health, welfare and safety of American youth, irrespective of the school attended." [20]

The bishops were arguing both for auxiliary services and in defense of the parochial schools. By defending the schools they gave the impression they were seeking public aid for the schools, rather than services for children on an equal basis.

The bishops' 1955 statement was described as "eloquence, artifice and studied nonsense," by Glenn L. Archer, executive director of the organization Protestants and Other Americans United for Separation of Church and State. The bishops called the parochial school system a supreme example of private, cooperative effort, free of government support or control, he said, and at the same time they demanded government aid and legal recognition of those schools. Far from teaching a "Christian concept of liberty," he said, "the Catholic schools systematically exalt their 'one, true religion,' while teaching that all other religions are 'counterfeit.' " The bishops did not specify what they meant by "health, safety and welfare" benefits, Mr. Archer said, but he quoted from the *Catholic World* to show that public welfare legislation was editorially defined to include new school buildings. He commented:

Surely, if even the erection of school buildings can be termed "welfare" service, rather than "educational aid" then there are no limits to the extent of the support which the government will be expected to grant to religious schools. Will it not be claimed that payment of school electric bills, teachers' salaries, janitorial services, and the purchase of books, paper, ink, pens, pencils and all other supplies are matters of government concern because they are matters that affect pupils' welfare?

Mr. Archer recognized that medical examinations and hot lunches were health measures, but he declared that most other school services were integral parts of the school's teaching process. A school dedicated to religious propagation, he argued, was not serving a public function justifying tax support. It was revealing, Mr. Archer said, that the bishops looked back nostalgically to the days when education in America was private or church-related rather than public. It was in those times, he declared, that religious heresy was punishable by death, confiscation of property, whipping, imprisonment, and other barbarous means. The recognition sought for the parochial schools by the bishops was the same kind "which made for torture and oppression in the name of God, in the period before church and state were separated in America." The issue, Mr. Archer said, was not the right of non-public schools to exist, but the attempt of the bishops to win public support for them.[21]

Mr. Archer's forceful, unrestrained response to the 1955 statement of the bishops was to some extent irrelevant to the issue of auxiliary services. He was replying to remarks of the bishops which were irrelevant to that issue. The bishops implied that the aid was justified because the schools were performing a public service. The character of that service the bishops presented in a religious light. It is understandable that Mr. Archer, a Protestant, would question the public service value of religious teaching which in his view described his manner of worshiping God as "counterfeit." Here, as in the dispute between Cardinal Spellman and Mrs. Roosevelt and in disputes to be reported later, the debaters were not able to restrict themselves to the issue of public services for parochial school pupils.

Mr. Archer had requested a definition of auxiliary services. A partial one was supplied a short time later by Archbishop Richard Cushing of Boston in a speech on December 4, 1955. He said:

> We are not looking for any federal or government aid to build our schools. I would absolutely refuse the offer, for I cannot see how any government or state would build schools without expecting to control them in whole or in part.[22]

Archbishop Cushing emphasized that he spoke only for himself, not for the Catholic hierarchy of the United States. For him there was no alternative to the "voluntary method of financing Catholic School building." He insisted, however, that Catholic children should not be treated as "second class citizens." They were entitled to public welfare services provided to other children. Those welfare services included health services, transportation, and lunches. The Archbishop commented that Catholic relations with the public schools were ideal and without any friction. He urged his audience to avoid assuming an attitude of hostility toward the American system of government merely because of disagreement with certain policies.

Archbishop Cushing relied on the child-benefit theory for support of his position, as Cardinal Spellman had done in his statement six years earlier. They both denied any intention of advocating the use of public funds for parochial school construction. Archbishop Cushing, however, indulged in no personalities and no name-calling. The reaction to the Archbishop's statement was not one of shock. There were no political repercussions nor speculations about its effect on any candidacies. The statement received national attention, but there was no criticism of the Archbishop. He spoke for himself and did not seek to rally his parishioners in support of his position. He asked only for the support of public officials who were "fair and square to God and country in accordance with the highest ideals of American democracy."

The Catholic bishops of the United States in their annual statements have not limited themselves to arguments for auxiliary services to non-public school pupils. They have contended for both the child-benefit principle and for cooperation of church and state.

Responding to the decision of the United States Supreme Court in the *McCollum* case,* the bishops in their 1948 statement called for "a reaffirmation of our original American tradition of free co-operation between Government and religious bodies—cooperation involving no special privilege to any group and no restriction on the religious liberty of any citizen." [23] They declared that the term "separation of church and state" had become "the shibboleth of doctrinaire secularism."

The bishops' views were extended in their 1952 statement.[24] They asserted that the state should aid in the religious education of children. They criticized a "secularist trend in education," but disclaimed any intention of animosity toward public education. Because religion was important to good citizenship, the bishops said:

> The state, therefore, has the duty to help parents fulfill their task of religious instruction and training. When the state fails in this help, when it makes the task more difficult and even penalizes parents who try to fulfill this duty according to their conscience, by depriving their children of their right under our Federal Constitution to auxiliary services, this can only be regarded as an utterly unfair and short-sighted policy.

A different kind of cooperation of church and state has been proposed from time to time, chiefly by Protestants concerned about the absence of religion from the public school classroom.

They suggest that the public school can provide instruction in the essential features common to Catholicism, Protestantism, and Judaism. Mrs. Roosevelt reflected this view. She favored "separa-tion," but she also wanted agreement of the three major faiths on a "common body of moral and religious teaching" for public school pupils. She wanted both separation and cooperation.

Teaching the "common core" of American religious beliefs has

---

* In the *McCollum* case, a released-time religious education program in the Champaign, Illinois, public schools was found to be in violation of the First Amendment's prohibition of "an establishment of religion." See Chapter II.

been urged by a number of Protestant clergymen, notably by Dean Luther A. Weigle of the Yale Divinity School. He has said:

> There is nothing in the status of the public school as an institution of the state, therefore, to render it godless. There is nothing in the principle of religious freedom or the separation of church and state to hinder the school's acknowledgement of the power and goodness of God. The common religious faith of the American people, as distinguished from the sectarian forms in which it is organized, may rightfully be assumed and find appropriate expression in the life and work of the public schools.[25]

Dean Weigle's assertion that there is such a thing as a common religious faith for Americans has been challenged. Mrs. Roosevelt, while advocating the same theory, recognized the difficulty of reaching agreement on a "common core." Aside from the theological difficulties involved, this approach has been challenged as a violation of the church-state separation principle. A resolution adopted at the 1950 Mid-century White House Conference on Children and Youth recognized the great importance of religious education to the moral and spiritual health of the nation. However, the resolution concluded: "We . . . strongly affirm the principle of separation of church and state . . . and declare ourselves unalterably opposed to the use of public schools, directly or indirectly, for religious educational purposes." [26]

This "common core" approach is sometimes rejected for another reason. It is regarded as setting up a new sect, a kind of "public school" religion. This "inoffensive nonsectarian religion," Father Neil G. McCluskey declares, has no appeal for the conscientious parent. To remove the positive doctrinal elements is to suggest that religious differences are not significant. Such a bland mixture produced "a soup so thin that it pleased no palate." [27]

The most militant opposition to the views expressed by the Bishops about auxiliary services and cooperation of church and state has been that of Protestants and Other Americans United for Separation of Church and State. This group was established after a series

of conferences in 1947, apparently stimulated in part by the decision
in the *Everson* school bus case.[28]

In a manifesto adopted on November 20, 1947, the organization
declared:

> It is no part of our purpose to propagandize the Protestant faith or
> any other, nor to criticize or oppose the teaching or internal practices
> of the Roman Catholic Church or any other. . . . Our motivation
> arises solely from our patriotic and religious concern for the mainte-
> nance of the separation of church and state under the American form
> of government.

The manifesto accused the Roman Catholic Church of being
committed to "a policy plainly subversive of religious liberty as
guaranteed by the Constitution." As part of a long-range plan to win
full support of its parochial school system by tax funds, the Catholic
Church had adopted a strategy, the manifesto charged:

> . . . to fracture the constitutional principle at one point after another
> where the action can be minimized as trivial or disguised as falling
> within some other category than that of its ultimate intent. It has
> begun by demanding that certain marginal services such as bus trans-
> portation, free lunches, free textbooks, and so forth, for its parochial
> school pupils be financed by public funds raised by taxation for the
> public schools.

The document closed with a declaration of intention to acquaint
all government officials, local, state and national, "that an overwhelming body of public opinion, led by the whole of Protestantism,
is united in a common purpose" to insure preservation of the nation's
"cultural and religious democracy."

Leading Protestant clergymen were prominent in the committee
issuing the manifesto.[29]

Two months after the manifesto was adopted, the Catholic
bishops replied:

> No group in America is seeking union of Church and state; least of
> all are Catholics. We deny absolutely and without any qualification
> that the Catholic Bishops of the United States are seeking a union of

Church and state by any endeavors whatsoever, either proximate or remote. If tomorrow Catholics constituted a majority in our country, they would not seek a union of Church and state. They would then, as now, uphold the Constitution and all its amendments, recognizing the moral obligation imposed on all Catholics to observe the Constitution and its Amendments.

The bishops objected that they were criticized for seeking to have the Supreme Court reverse a decision or to influence federal legislation. Yet the signers of the manifesto openly declared their intention to attempt the very same thing.[30]

In effect, these statements issued almost ten years before the conflicts in Connecticut were a declaration of political war. The opposing sides would be led by Catholic and Protestant clergy. Theoretical positions would include:

1. Cooperation of church and state for religious education in the public schools.
2. Cooperation of the state with parochial schools for religious training.
3. Auxiliary services for parochial school pupils in accordance with the child-benefit theory.
4. Strict separation of the state from religious education.

In the decade following the exchange of clerical challenges, battles would be fought in the Supreme Court and in various states. It was to be a long, sporadic war.

The Arguments and the Groups

The arguments listed above are suggestive of the general positions taken by Protestant and Catholic groups on the relation of public and parochial schools. They also suggest the emotionalism which frequently attends discussion in this area. The arguments will recur throughout this work. It will be useful first to present them as they are outlined by Leo Pfeffer in his detailed study, *Church, State and Freedom.* Mr. Pfeffer served as attorney in a number of cases dealing with issues related to religious freedom. Generally, he seems to have represented plaintiffs who sought a strict application of the principle of separation of church and state. His book presents the development of that principle, its application in various aspects of American life, and discussions of issues concerning religious freedom. Mr. Pfeffer identifies in an objective manner the arguments most vigorously urged in support of public services for parochial school pupils as these:

1. Our democracy is based on a religious tradition.
2. Parochial schools perform a public service and make possible great tax savings.
3. Double taxation is imposed on Catholic parents who, by religious conviction, must send their children to parochial schools and hence must pay to support both the parochial and the public schools.
4. There are precedents for government aid to religion, such as tax exemptions for churches.
5. The United States is practically alone among nations in refusing to recognize financially the contribution of parochial schools.
6. It is religious discrimination to refuse welfare benefits such as health services, school lunches, and transportation to parochial school pupils.

Mr. Pfeffer summarizes the arguments most frequently used in opposition to public aid for parochial schools or their pupils as the following:

1. The principle of separation of church and state prohibits public aid to parochial schools.
2. Parochial schools divide children on religious lines. While Catholic parents have a constitutional right to send their children to parochial schools, it is a socially undesirable practice and should not be assisted by public funds.
3. Public support for parochial schools will destroy the public school system.
4. The "double taxation" argument is fallacious. Public education is for the benefit of all of society, not merely a service to parents. All taxpayers, including the childless and corporations, are taxed to support the public schools.
5. Public funds for religious schools will encourage interreligious rivalries and political divisions on religious lines.

6. Services sought initially (usually transportation) will serve as an opening wedge in a drive for public funds for textbooks, supplies, equipment, facilities, and even the salaries of lay instructors.[31]

After outlining the arguments most frequently used for and against public aid for parochial schools and their pupils, Mr. Pfeffer summarizes the positions of the various faiths and some other groups on the matter of auxiliary services and related issues.*

No Protestant group of any prominence favors any direct financial aid to religious schools, but Protestant unanimity is not as complete on welfare benefits. The National Council of Churches, and Protestants and Other Americans United for Separation of Church and State, favor medical care and dental care for all children without discrimination, if the service is provided as a health measure rather than an educational measure and if it is administered and supervised by a public agency. Protestant church groups regard free secular textbooks as an educational service that should not be provided to religious schools. The overwhelming majority of Protestant leaders take the same view of school bus service for parochial school pupils.

Not all Protestants are opposed to public school cooperation in the promotion of religion within the school. A rigid separation is urged by one Protestant group. This group includes the liberal Protestant denominations such as Universalists and Unitarians, and the

---

* Elsewhere, Pfeffer has written; "Lacking the overarching structure of an all-encompassing church, Protestant and Jewish positions are naturally less monolithic. These two faiths developed their own structures, such as the National Council of Churches and the Synagogue Council of America, less powerful and less formal than the Catholic Church, but still effective organs for the moulding of united positions and articulating united opinion. . . . On some issues, such as the meaning of separation of church and state, and religion in the public schools, Protestant opinion is more divided than either Catholic or Jewish, but even there agreement can be found among a substantial majority of Protestant groups." ("Issues That Divide," *Journal of Social Issues*, XII, No. 3, 1956, pp. 23–24.) The existence of a "Catholic position" has been questioned, (see below, pp. 23–26). However, the annual statements of the Catholic bishops of the United States may properly be regarded as the voice of the Catholic hierarchy. The bishop's agency for social welfare and educational issues is the National Catholic Welfare Conference. Pfeffer seems to have relied chiefly on statements by the bishops or representatives of the Conference for his interpretation of the "Catholic position."

liberal wings of such other denominations as Episcopalians, Congregationalists, Methodists, Baptists, and Seventh Day Adventists. Leaders of this group are often affiliated with Protestants and Other Americans United or sympathetic to its purposes. A second Protestant group will not accept a separation of church and state which means secularization of the public schools. Members of this group oppose sectarianism but want some religion in the public school curriculum. There is disagreement about how religion can be brought into the public schools without also bringing in sectarianism.

The Catholic Church, says Pfeffer, holds that the parochial school system is an equal partner with the public school system. The parochial schools are morally and legally entitled to share in public funds for education. For the present, the Catholic Church is willing to compromise and accept auxiliary benefits for parochial school pupils on an equal basis with public school children. A representative of the National Catholic Welfare Conference testified before a Congressional committee that the Catholic Church regarded the ideal system as one in which there would be no state schools at all except those that trained for military or government service. The function of the government would be limited to enforcing compulsory education laws and financing non-public schools. This is similar to the Quebec system, where Catholic and Protestant parochial schools are supported by public funds. The Catholic Church would also accept the Netherlands system, under which Catholic, Protestant, and public schools share proportionately in public education funds, Pfeffer states.

Since Pfeffer made his estimate of the Catholic position, a debate of a fundamental nature has developed among the Catholic clergy in the United States. The Catholic position on church-state relations has been given broad re-examination in the writings of the Reverend John Courtney Murray and others. These writings have inspired strong challenges by defenders of an older viewpoint.

Father Murray has contended that the Catholic Church has not faced "the problem, theoretical as well as practical, put to her by a state organized on the constitutional and political lines proper to the tradition of Anglo-American democracy." The problem of church-state relations will not be solved by Catholic doctrine formulated during "the Church's conflict with nineteenth century Continental absolutist liberalism." The vision of some European thinkers may be "obscured by the still unsettled dust of controversy or by a nostalgia for the dear dead days of the 'Catholic state' on the monarchic or dictatorial model." [32]

The First Amendment, in Father Murray's view, fundamentally declares "the 'lay' character of the state, its non-competence in the field of religion, the restriction of its competence to the secular and the moral."

While such views have received wide attention among the Catholic clergy and others, not all of that attention has been favorable. Commenting on the "self-evident" importance of this controversy, one Catholic writer has stated:

> In the event that Father Murray's teaching is true, then it would seem that our students of sacred theology and of public ecclesiastical law have been sadly deceived for the past two centuries. They have been told that the state has an obligation to worship God according to the precepts and rites of the true religion. According to Father Murray, however, the state's only permanent obligation in the line of religion is something far less exacting . . . "the liberty the Church desires apart from acceptance and profession." [33]

A Protestant theologian has commented on this controversy in response to an expression of Protestant concern about Catholic opinion:

> . . . that a very large [Catholic] majority would be justified in restricting to some extent the religious liberties of non-Catholics. The Roman Church world is deeply divided on this question and most American Catholics reject this view. A group of Catholic scholars, of whom Father John Courtney Murray is best known, are working hard to develop a Catholic doctrine of religious liberty which is consistent with the experience and needs of democratic nations. . . . This view of religious liberty, which is no mere concession to necessity, is strongly represented by the best American Catholic lay journal, *The Commonweal*. Recently there was a bitter debate between some American

Catholic leaders and some Spanish bishops, and the Pope in a carefully worded statement made full room for the American position. This is one issue on which we can expect the American Catholic laity to side with the more liberal tendencies among the hierarchy.[34]

This developing doctrine, as stated by Father Murray, seems to be at variance in some degree with the occasional assertions of the Catholic bishops that the state has an obligation to aid in the religious education of the child. Does the "lay" state, the state without competence in religious matters, have any authority to make a judgment about religious education or assume any responsibility therefore?

This controversy over the broader question of church-state relations seems not to have changed markedly the Catholic position on education and auxiliary services from that described by Pfeffer in 1950. In 1959 a similar statement of the Catholic position has been made by the Reverend Neil G. McCluskey, S.J.[35] Father McCluskey cites four reasons why Catholic laity and clergy feel direct, basic support to parochial schools is presently impossible:

1. The United States Supreme Court would find such aid to be a violation of the federal Constitution.
2. Most state constitutions prohibit such aid.
3. Government aid might well deprive private schools of their present independence.
4. Organized Catholic efforts to obtain such aid would create deep, lasting resentments.

What do Catholics want *now*?, Father McCluskey asks, and then replies: "Fundamentally, they want a sympathetic hearing for their case, public recognition of their problem, and help in working out an equitable solution." There is no "authoritative expression of a single Catholic position covering all these matters," he writes, but "there is a wide consensus among clergy and laity that Catholic energies would be best spent on achieving fuller distribution of educational items immediately related to the child benefit principle." Among these items he lists transportation, health services, testing and guidance services, special programs for the educable mentally retarded, and tax credits for those who pay tuition to private schools. There is little enthusiasm among Catholic educators for obtaining free textbooks which are inadequate for Catholic school purposes. There would be more interest in obtaining audiovisual aids, special lecturers, traveling science exhibits, and other such assistance.

As part of "a reasonable summary" of the views of Catholic parents and the Catholic clergy, Father McCluskey states:

1. Parents of parochial school pupils have a right to expect government legally to assist in financing such education.
2. Parochial school children "have every right to share in all of the state's general welfare benefits, and in any special legislation designed to develop academic and scientific leadership for the nation."
3. The Catholic . . . bishops have not asked, and have indicated they will not ask, for basic subsidy for parochial schools such as public grants for buildings, maintenance, and ordinary salaries.

These policies are based on present constitutional barriers, concern about government controls, and contemporary public opinion. While such policies are subject to change, the prevailing consensus among Catholic leaders is "that for many years it would be futile to press for full direct support for parochial school education." [36]

Pfeffer reports that organized Jewish groups, like most Protestant groups, oppose direct government financial aid to religious schools but approve non-educational welfare benefits for all children. These benefits include hot lunches and medical and dental services, but exclude transportation and instructional supplies.

Among non-religious groups, Pfeffer states, the National Education Association, the American Federation of Teachers, and the American Civil Liberties Union have all expressed opposition to the position of the Catholic hierarchy. However, the American Federation of Labor and the Congress of Industrial Organizations, with multisectarian membership, have sought some compromise between the Catholic and non-Catholic positions on auxiliary services. [37]

THE ATMOSPHERE OF THE TIMES:
1 9 5 6–1 9 5 7

The struggle in Connecticut for public services for parochial school pupils occurred at a time when similar disturbances were arising in various parts of the nation.[38] There were growing tensions between Catholics and Protestants, according to the Reverend Thurston N. Davis, S.J., editor of the Catholic weekly magazine *America*. Those tensions were "a dark cloud looming on our civic and social horizons." Protestant leaders had told him of their worry about recent deterioration of their relations with Catholics. Among the issues causing these tensions, Father Davis said, were birth control, censorship, Catholic schools, and bus service for pupils therein. Father Davis expressed these concerns in a address prepared for delivery on March 10, 1957, on a radio program, "Church of the Air." However, the officials of the network, the Columbia Broadcasting System, found this address unsuitable for that program and denied "clearance."

The network officials apparently regarded "Church of the Air" as a program that ought to be more concerned with matters spiritual than political. Doubtless they anticipated that such an address would provoke demands for "equal time" for other views to be presented.*

In late 1956 and early 1957 the Catholic-Protestant controversies noted by Father Davis were being vigorously debated in Connecticut and elsewhere.

The conflict between Catholics and Protestants over censorship was revived in late 1956 over the motion picture *Baby Doll*. Francis Cardinal Spellman in New York City denounced the film and declared that Catholics who saw it were committing a sin.[39] This denunciation was followed by a debate between Protestant and Catholic clergy about the morality of *Baby Doll* and about attempts

---

* The network officials suggested that these remarks might be given at another time, presumably when there would be opportunity for a non-Catholic response. Instead, Father Davis (possibly feeling that a radio debate would add to the tension he deplored) published his remarks as a magazine article, "A Time for Silence or a Time to Speak?", *America*, March 16, 1957.

of church groups to impose bans on motion pictures. The Reverend James A. Pike, Dean of the Cathedral of St. John the Divine in New York City, announced his opposition to church condemnation of films dealing with human problems.[40] The Reverend Donald Harrington, New York Unitarian minister, defended the morality of *Baby Doll*. It was a questionable practice, he said, to condemn a film without seeing it. "Those who did condemn the film did not understand its 'inner morality.'"[41] In Albany, Catholic Bishop William A. Scully prohibited the film for Catholics in his diocese and forbade them to attend the Strand Theater for six months. He invited those of other faiths to join this boycott to protest the showing of the film at that house.[42] His action was criticized by the American Civil Liberties Union and the American Cultural Freedom Committee.[43]

Similarly, in Philadelphia just a few days before the public hearing in Connecticut's legislature, Catholic worshipers at Ash Wednesday services were urged to "express themselves" against the presentation of *Baby Doll* in local theaters. Following a flood of telephone calls, the management of the theater chain announced the film would not be shown.[44] In Syracuse, thirty Protestant clergymen signed a petition of protest after newspapers, radio, and television stations withdrew or refused paid advertising for *Baby Doll*. A Protestant minister who gave a sermon against the "city wide blackout" was charged by a newspaper which participated in the censorship with "ignoring moral issues for denominational reasons."[45]

In Connecticut, *Baby Doll* was condemned by the Catholic bishops.[46] Strong criticism of the action of the bishops was expressed in a sermon by the Reverend Payson Miller, Unitarian minister in Hartford, on January 13, 1957. In this sermon, "Bigotry and Censorship," Mr. Miller said:

> When a church so lacking in intellectual humility and so tainted with bigotry is given a position of special privilege and authority in the state, intolerance and persecution of other religious viewpoints will be the baneful result. Separation of church and state is a very practical device for preventing any religious organization which has

fallen into bigotry from censoring the thought and practice of other religious groups and the whole community.[47]

About the same time another dispute occurred in Chicago over the film *Martin Luther*. This motion picture had been scheduled to be presented on WGN-TV in Chicago on December 21, 1956. It was canceled, according to station officials, because of "an emotional reaction." It was not reported how many people objected, but they were assumed to be Catholics.[48] Ten weeks after the cancellation, Monsignor M. Burke, speaking for the Roman Catholic Archdiocese of Chicago, said, "The honest expression of a religious viewpoint is not merely a democratic right; it is indispensable to a democracy." If a television station believed *Martin Luther* to be a positive presentation of religious beliefs, Monsignor Burke said, the Archdiocese would not protest in any way whatsoever. Despite this statement, the officials of WGN-TV announced they had no plans to schedule the film and had no further comment.[49]

Early in March, 1957, Protestants and Other Americans United filed a protest with the Federal Communications Commission against requests by Jesuit universities in New Orleans and St. Louis for television licenses. Executive Director Glenn L. Archer said that the challenge was part of a "counter-attack" against the pressure which had brought about the banning of the film *Martin Luther* on WGN-TV. Mr. Archer said, "Experience has proved that Catholic control of television means suppression of free criticism." [50]

An "unusual number" of religious conflicts were reported in the public schools of New York State in late 1956 and early 1957. Officials expressed concern about such incidents as a dispute in New Hyde Park over the question of placing a "doctored" version of the Ten Commandments in the local schools. Disputes about the observance of Christmas in public schools were also reported to the New York State Department of Education.[51]

During the week preceding the March 12 hearing in the Connecticut legislature, the Hartford newspapers carried reports of efforts to obtain bus service for parochial school pupils in Augusta,

Maine. A group of parents of these pupils declared they would send their children to the public schools if public transportation were not provided for parochial school pupils. An informal referendum of the city's voters had shown the majority in favor of such transportation, but the city government failed to accede to a request for the service. The threatened transfer of the parochial school pupils was forestalled by an agreement to seek a court test of the issue.[52]

In Connecticut, Protestant-Catholic divisions occurred over the issues of censorship, parochial school bus service, and birth control. The differences about Catholic condemnation of *Baby Doll* have been mentioned. In Stamford, early in March, a dispute was in progress over a request by the Parents Association of St. Cecilia's parochial school for public bus service for their children. A public hearing was scheduled by the Stamford Board of Education on March 13, the day following the General Assembly's public hearing.[53]

Birth control was a recurring issue between Protestants and Catholics at each session of the Connecticut legislature. Protestants attempted repeatedly to repeal the law prohibiting distribution of contraceptives. One political observer commented just before the 1957 legislative session that the issue might have unusual importance, since the Republicans had overwhelming control of both houses. He explained:

> The House, where the Republicans have always been in control, has repeatedly passed the measure, legalizing birth control in Connecticut. Just as repeatedly, the measure has met its death in the State Senate, where the Democrats have been in outright control or in strong position. And this is not because the voting has been a party matter, but because more Protestants than Catholics have usually been nominated and elected by the Republicans, and *vice versa*.

With the Republicans now in overwhelming control of the Senate, he speculated, there might be a close division on birth control. The balance of power might lie with those senators "not aligned with either major religious faith but who, incidentally, represent districts where there is a large Catholic vote." [54] The commentator foresaw a "hot, tense battle" on an issue which generated fire and feeling even when the result was completely predictable. A political division based solely on religious affiliation was "not a comforting thing to watch." Nothing could diminish the feeling on both sides that someone was trying to dictate to someone else in matters of morals. He concluded:

> There is always some touch of hypocrisy on both sides, too, with the one side loyal to the preservation of a legal ban it knows its own adherents do not all honor in practice, and with the other side *more emotionally stirred by its resentment over the legal dominance of the opposition* rather than by any conviction that birth control does not get practiced in Connecticut. (Emphasis added.) [55]

The primary cause for conflict over the birth control bill, then, was really the competition between Protestant and Catholic. The revival of the contest in the 1957 legislature would add to the tension between the two faiths. The contest would be likely to add bitterness to the struggle over the school bus bill.

References to the competition between Protestant and Catholic for "legal dominance" would be scarce in the debate over auxiliary services. But that competition would underlie other arguments that were to be used. Those other arguments would include statements about the value of the parochial school, highly charged emotional appeals and personal attacks, and some attempts at rational argument about the substance of the bill. The conduct of the conflict about the bill was to reflect in large degree the events which had occurred in local disputes during the preceding year. Those who employed rational argument in both the local and the legislative contests frequently drew their arguments from opinions of the Supreme Court of the United States.

II:

THE

SUPREME

COURT:

FIVE DECISIONS,

THIRTEEN OPINIONS

MOST OF THE arguments for and against public services for parochial school pupils heard in Connecticut during 1956 and 1957 had appeared in the various opinions of the Supreme Court of the United States in five cases dealing with public education and religious organizations. Debaters on both sides relied on the Court for legal authority and for arguments to support their policy preconceptions. In the majority and minority opinions in the five cases there was ample material for both sides to use in support of their contentions. The Supreme Court was, of course, interpreting only the federal Constitution. Partisans in the Connecticut debates, however, quoted from minority and majority opinions to argue not merely what the Constitution permitted or prohibited but to declare what the Connecticut legislature ought to do.

Opponents argued most frequently that public services for parochial school pupils was a violation of the principle of separation of church and state. Supporters of services most frequently employed the child-benefit theory, and sometimes they supplemented their argument with the principle of cooperation of church and state. All three doctrines—separation, cooperation, and child benefit—could be supported by opinions of the Supreme Court of the United States.

These three doctrines in some respects were in conflict. The Court majorities and minorities all expressed adherence to the principle of separation. Modification of the church-state separation principle (exclusion of either agency from participation in the affairs of the other) by the application of the child-benefit theory was accepted by the Court. Such modification was an indirect consequence of government action with a secular public purpose. The cooperation principle, as expounded by members of the Court, assumed that government had an interest in the promotion of religion.

The principles of separation, cooperation, and child benefit are considered in the five cases reviewed in this chapter, as is the place of the parochial school under our Constitution. These five cases, *Pierce, Cochran, Everson, McCollum,* and *Zorach,* had a dual effect on the struggles in Connecticut in 1956 and 1957.[1] First, the Court's holdings in these cases set forth some legal boundaries while leaving a great deal of freedom to the states; and second, the majority and minority opinions provided much ammunition for both sides in the policy debate.

THE *PIERCE* CASE: NON–PUBLIC SCHOOLS PROTECTED

A legal challenge to the existence of non-public schools was struck down in 1925 by the Supreme Court in the case of *Pierce* v. *Society of Sisters of the Holy Name of Jesus and Mary.*[2] An Oregon law required parents or guardians with some exceptions, to send children between the ages of eight and sixteen years to the public schools. The law has been called the product of ultranationalist elements so active during and immediately after World War I.[3]

The Sisters of the Holy Name, an order of teaching nuns operating a parochial school and the Hill Military Academy, basing their complaint on the Fourteenth Amendment, argued that the law conflicted with the liberty of parents to direct the education of their children and that it was a deprivation of their property without due process of law. The Compulsory Education Act denied parents the right to educate their children for purposes other than those of the state. Furthermore, the Act would deprive non-public schools of their students and would result in the loss of their investments.

The argument presented by counsel for Governor Pierce stressed that the Oregon act was an attempt to reduce the asserted divisive influence of parochial schools. He suggested that the law was a result of the alarm "felt at the rising tide of religious suspicions in this country." The cause of such suspicions "was the separation of children along religious lines during the most susceptible years of their lives." A mingling together of children of all creeds might be regarded as "the best safeguard against future internal dissensions and consequent weakening of the community against foreign dangers." Did not the state have the right to protect itself, he asked, against the possibility of its future citizens receiving an education inimical to the best interests of the state?

The Supreme Court of the United States upheld the complaint of the non-public schools on the grounds that the Compulsory Education Act violated the liberty of parents to direct their children's education. Furthermore, the Act would result in the destruction of the appellee's schools. This would be a deprivation of property in violation of the due-process clause of the Fourteenth Amendment. The Court recognized the power of the state to protect itself by reasonably regulating all schools, and by requiring that all children attend some school, that teachers be of "good moral character and patriotic disposition, that certain studies plainly essential to good citizenship" be taught, and that there be no instruction "manifestly inimical to the public welfare." The state's interest in the education of the child, however, did not mean he was "the mere creature of the state." A child's parents, the Court said, "have the right, coupled with the high duty, to recognize and prepare him for additional obligations." The Act was an unreasonable interference with "the liberty of parents and guardians to direct the upbringing and education of children under their control." The state was restricted by the "fundamental theory of liberty under which all governments in this Union repose."

The issues raised in the *Pierce* case were to be raised again in Connecticut in 1956 and 1957. It was to be charged that the parochial schools detracted from the democratic contributions of the inclusive public schools. Advocates of auxiliary services would argue that parochial schools existed by right and would cite the *Pierce* case to support their argument.

THE *COCHRAN* CASE: FREE BOOKS
FOR ALL PUPILS

In 1928 the state of Louisiana adopted a law permitting schoolbooks to be supplied to the school children of the state. The State Board of Education interpreted this statute as applying to children attending both public and non-public schools. The law was challenged as a use of tax funds for a private rather than a "public" purpose, and therefore a deprivation of property without due process of law as prohibited by the Fourteenth Amendment. The principle of separation of church and state, or the First Amendment restriction against government establishment of religion, was not presented in the *Cochran* case.[4] The Supreme Court had not yet recognized the First Amendment's prohibition of "an establishment of religion" as applicable, by the Fourteenth Amendment, as a restriction against actions of the states. Counsel for the appellant did employ the argument which came to be known as "the wedge argument." He contended that if free textbooks for private school children were not considered an aid to those schools but merely incidental to the state's educational system, then it logically followed:

. . . that the tuition of the children attending such schools could be paid; their transportation to and from schools could be provided; the salaries of the instructors could be paid in part or in whole; and finally, the buildings themselves could be erected,—with state funds; all of which, under the reasoning evinced in the Statutes of Louisiana, might be justified on the ground that it is in the interest of the State to see that its youth is educated.

Pursuing this line of argument, counsel contended that this diversion of public school funds for private individuals would result ultimately in parents of private school pupils paying only for private schools. The state would be deprived of power to tax for support of the public schools those who supported only their private schools. The practical result would be "the destruction of one of the free institutions under our republican form of government."

The Supreme Court rejected the contention that the distribution of books to all school pupils constituted an expenditure of public funds for a private purpose. The law did not segregate private schools nor their pupils' for these benefits. The method was "comprehensive."

The Court referred indirectly to the principle of separation of church and state. Arguing that the law had a public purpose, the Court declared that it was not "the purpose of the state to furnish religious books for the use of such [non-public school] children." The same books furnished children attending public schools were furnished to children attending private schools. "Among these books, naturally, none is to be expected, adapted to religious instruction," the Court declared. It was the Court's conclusion, however, that religion and religious schools were not aided by this law. "The school children and the state alone are the beneficiaries," the Court said. Thus the child-benefit theory was relied upon to uphold distribution of free textbooks to non-public school children. The objection that the theory logically could be extended to justify many other services was disregarded by the Supreme Court in 1930, albeit in a case where separation was not directly argued or discussed. In 1947 the child-benefit theory was again employed before the Court to justify public transportation of non-public school pupils.

THE *EVERSON* CASE: THE SCHOOL BUS DIVIDES THE COURT

In 1947 the United States Supreme Court in *Everson* v. *Board of Education* upheld a New Jersey law permitting bus service at public expense for pupils of any school except one operated for profit.[5] Pursuant to this law, the school board of the Township of Ewing adopted a resolution appropriating money out of local school funds to reimburse parents for the cost of sending their children to school on common carriers. The resolution authorized payment for transportation to public schools or Catholic schools. The law was challenged as unconstitutional on two counts:

1. It authorized taxation of some people to bestow the proceeds on others for private purposes, a deprivation of property without due process of law, as prohibited by the Fourteenth Amendment. [This was the same challenge which had been unsuccessful in the *Cochran* case.]

2. The law and the school board resolution provided for tax support of Catholic schools. This was a violation of the First Amendment's prohibition of an establishment of religion, made applicable to the states by the Fourteenth Amendment.

The Supreme Court rejected both challenges by a five to four decision. Two dissenting opinions were presented.

The majority and the minority were agreed that government could not give direct aid to religion. They disagreed on whether public transportation for parochial school pupils constituted such aid. They disagreed, too, on whether the Court could take recognition of the restrictive nature of the New Jersey law. Justice Black, speaking for the majority of five, replied to the first challenge by commenting that it was a legitimate public purpose to assist children to escape the hazards of traffic on their way to and from school.

The second challenge—that public bus service for parochial school pupils was an unconstitutional aid to religion—was denied by Justice Black on the basis of the child-benefit theory, while he insisted that the wall of separation had not been breached. He prefaced his opinion with the observation that no attack had been made against the New Jersey law because of the clause excluding schools operated for profit. (He might also have said that no attack had been made on the resolution of the Ewing Board of Education restricting reimbursement to parents of children attending public schools and Catholic schools.) The majority considered the case as though reimbursement were being made to all school children regardless of the kind of school attended. In other words, although the child-benefit theory was not followed by the New Jersey law nor the school board resolution, the *Everson* case was decided on the assumption that the theory had been followed. Justice Black's opinion employed both the child-benefit theory and the principle of separation of church and state.

Black acknowledged the difficulties posed by those two doctrines. In recent years, state courts had been faced with questions arising out of proposed state aid to church schools and proposals for religious teachings in the public schools. The state courts had remained faithful to the provisions of their state constitutions separating religion and government, but their decisions showed the difficulty of drawing a line between support for the general public welfare and support of religious institutions. Black presented a definition of the "establishment of religion" clause that was to be quoted frequently in later discussions of auxiliary services. He said:

> The "establishment of religion" clause of the First Amendment means at least this: neither a state nor the federal government can set up a church. Neither can pass laws which aid one religion, aid all religions, or prefer one religion over another. Neither can force or influence a person to go to, or remain away from church against his will, or force him to profess a belief or disbelief in any religion. No person can be punished for entertaining or professing religious beliefs or disbeliefs, for church attendance or non-attendance. No tax in any amount, large or small, can be levied to support any religious activities or institutions, whatever they may be called, or whatever form they may adopt, to teach or practice religion. Neither a state nor the federal government can, openly or secretly, participate in the affairs of any religious

organizations, or groups, and vice versa. In the words of Jefferson, the clause against establishment of religion by law was intended to erect "a wall of separation between church and state."

According to those standards the First Amendment did not prohibit New Jersey from providing public transportation to parochial school pupils as part of a general program of transportation for pupils in public and other schools. Black conceded that children were helped to get to church schools and that some children might not go to church schools if public transportation were not so provided. Depriving church schools of general government services such as police and fire protection, sewage disposal, and public highways and sidewalks would certainly make it far more difficult for the schools to operate, but clearly that was not the purpose of the First Amendment. The state was required to be neutral with groups of believers and unbelievers. The state was not supposed to be their adversary.

Justice Black cited the *Pierce* case to declare that parents had the right to send their children to a church school which met the secular educational requirements of the state. New Jersey did not contribute to or support the parochial schools. The statute provided for a general program to help parents get their children, regardless of their religion, "safely and expeditiously to and from accredited schools."

Black concluded, "The First Amendment has erected a wall between church and state. That wall must be kept high and impregnable. We could not approve the slightest breach. New Jersey has not breached it here."

By Black's definition of the purpose of transportation, the wall of separation had not been breached. The pupil was carried to the public or parochial school to get the secular education required by the state. The concurrent aid given to religious education was incidental to the public purpose. Furthermore, Black regarded school transportation not as an educational service but as a welfare benefit for the child. On the basis of these assumptions, Black was justified in concluding that a general program of school transportation was not in violation of the "establishment of religion" clause as he had defined it. The two minority opinions, while implicitly accepting his definition of that clause, rejected his assumptions. The child-benefit argument was viewed by both minority opinions as a device for circumventing the restrictions of the prohibition against a government establishment of religion.

The Jackson-Frankfurter Dissent

In a strongly worded dissenting opinion, with which Justice Frankfurter concurred, Justice Jackson argued that the majority opinion assumed a state of facts that the record did not support and refused to consider facts which were inescapably on the record. He objected that the Court closed its eyes to the restrictive nature of the New Jersey law and the school board resolution. It was the character of the school, not the need of the children, which determined the eligibility of parents to reimbursement. The Court had ignored, Jackson said:

> . . . the essentially religious test by which beneficiaries of this expenditure are selected. A policeman protects a Catholic, of course—but not because he is a Catholic; it is because he is a man and a member of our society. Neither the fireman nor the policeman has to ask before he renders aid, "Is this man or building identified with the Catholic Church?" But before the school authorities draw a check to reimburse for the student's fare they must ask just that question, and if the school is a Catholic one they may render aid because it is such, whereas if it is of any other faith, or is operated for profit, the help must be withheld.

Jackson then turned to attack the child-benefit theory itself. "The prohibition against establishment of religion," he said, "cannot be circumvented by a subsidy, bonus or reimbursement . . . for receiving religious instruction or indoctrination." Clearly, Jackson was not accepting either the child-benefit theory or the contention that transportation of a child to a parochial school served a public purpose. He chided religious groups who were quick to invoke the protections of the Constitution but who were irked when they felt its restraints.

The Rutledge-Burton Dissent

The child-benefit theory and the public-purpose argument were sweepingly rejected in the dissent offered by Justices Rutledge and Burton. Justice Rutledge wrote that the purpose of the First Amendment was not merely to prevent the official establishment of a single sect. It was intended "to create a complete and permanent separation of the spheres of religious activity and civil authority by comprehensively forbidding every form of public aid or support for religion." Daily religious education mixed with secular, Rutledge declared, is religion within the meaning of the First Amendment. Such education could not be regarded as a public purpose. It was a private matter which the state could neither forbid nor support. Transporting a pupil to get religious education was not merely a service to the child. Where it is needed, Rutledge said, transportation is an essential part of education. If the public-purpose contention justified bus service, the same argument justified public expenditure for textbooks, school lunches, athletic equipment, and writing and other materials.

Rutledge warned of the consequences of the Court's decision. The *Cochran* case had opened the way by oblique ruling for the *Everson* decision. Those two cases would make wider the breach in the wall of separation of church and state for still a third invasion. "Thus," he said, "with time the most solid freedom steadily gives way before continuing, corrosive decision."

For Rutledge, religious freedom could not exist unless religion remained free from support or interference by the state. He acknowledged the additional burden carried by parents bound in conscience to give their children religious education mixed with secular. However, public assistance to religious education would lead only to sectarian struggles and religious disunity. Nor would equal treatment of all sects satisfy the restrictions of the Constitution. The Constitution required, he said, not comprehensive identification of the state with religion, but complete separation.

Anticipating the issues of the *McCollum*[6] and *Zorach*[7] cases, Justice Rutledge concluded:

> Two great drives are constantly in motion to abridge, in the name of education, the complete division of religion and civil authorities which our forefathers made. One is to introduce religious education and observance into the public schools, the other to obtain public funds for the aid and support of various private religious schools. . . . We should not be less strict to keep strong and untarnished the one side of the shield of religious freedom than we have been of the other.

The immediate question answered by the Supreme Court in the *Everson* case was whether a state can provide transportation for non-public school pupils, including parochial school pupils, without violating the Fourteenth Amendment or the First Amendment. No challenge had been made to the restrictive characteristics of the New Jersey system. Viewing that system as a "general program," the Supreme Court majority followed the child-benefit theory and rejected the complaints that such transportation did not serve a public purpose and was an aid to religion. However, the minority and the majority opinions set forth strict interpretations of the principle of separation of church and state. Black's minimal definition of the "establishment of religion" clause excluded cooperation or non-preferential aid by government to religion. In the majority viewpoint, state power could not be used to handicap or to favor religion.

The two dissenting opinions also insisted on a strict separation of church and state. They did not accept the child-benefit theory as a justification for the New Jersey program. Jackson argued that the child-benefit theory was not followed in New Jersey and also protested that the theory circumvented the First Amendment. Similarly, Justice Rutledge rejected the child-benefit theory and described the *Cochran* and *Everson* decisions as opening wedges. "Where do you stop?" he asked; and he answered that the Constitution required "complete separation." But the principle of strict separation was accepted by all members of the Court. The majority did not regard the child-benefit theory as a circumvention. Public-welfare services could be provided to all school children, and transportation was interpreted to be a public-welfare service.

The majority revealed a logical inconsistency, and passed on a highly important constitutional point, in saying that it did "not mean to intimate that a state could not provide transportation only to children attending public schools." This suggests, although the double negative may leave a question in the reader's mind, that the parent of a non-public school pupil has no constitutional right to demand that the state provide his child the same bus service given public school pupils. But if transportation is a welfare service, not an educational assistance, what justification is there for discriminating between children according to the nature of the school they attend? If school bus service is not an aid to the school but a service to the child, is it not a violation of the religious freedom guaranteed by the First Amendment to refuse such service to a pupil at a parochial school? Or is it not a violation of the "equal protection of the laws" clause of the Fourteenth Amendment to refuse transportation to a pupil in any non-public school?

The majority opinion noted the difficulty of drawing a line between services which provided for the general public welfare and those which constituted support of religious institutions. The adoption by the majority of both the principle of complete separation and the child-benefit theory did not make it any easier to draw that line. It did provide a basis, however, for ruling out some programs of cooperation between government and religious organizations.

THE *McCOLLUM* CASE: "AN ESTABLISHMENT OF RELIGION"

In 1948 the Supreme Court in *Illinois ex rel. McCollum* v. *Board of Education* found that the manner of cooperation of the Champaign, Illinois, public school system in a released-time religious education program constituted "an establishment of religion.[8] Justice Black, speaking for the majority of eight, reiterated the statement he made in the *Everson* case that government might not aid one religion, aid all religions, or prefer one religion over another. Justice Reed, in dissent, said that American tradition showed many instances of government cooperation with religion. Justice Frankfurter, delivering a concurring opinion for those who had dissented in the *Everson* case, lauded the public school as a powerful force for social cohesion and warned against its entanglement in the struggle of religious groups for the promotion of their creeds. In a second concurring opinion, Justice Jackson objected to the sweeping nature of the Court's decision, which sustained Mrs. McCollum's complaint against all instruction and teaching of religion in the public schools. Jackson emphasized the great difficulty of separating the secular from the religious in an educational program.

The released-time religious education program in the Champaign schools was sponsored by a council of Catholic, Jewish, and some Protestant groups. The council bore the expenses of the program, but the public school authorities were responsible for some supervision of the religious teachers. Children of parents who signed request cards were required to attend the religious classes. Attendance was taken and reported as in regular classes. Children who were excused from religious instruction left the regular classroom and were sent to another part of the school building. Mrs. McCollum, an atheist, complained that her son, a pupil in the Champaign school, was excluded from his classroom and subjected to embarrassment and ridicule because of the released-time program. Her petition contended that the program violated her freedom of religion and the First Amendment's prohibition against the establishment of religion incorporated by the "due process of law" clause of the Fourteenth Amendment.

Speaking for the Court, Justice Black said that the Champaign system was unquestionably a use of the tax-supported public school system "to aid religious groups to spread their faith, and it falls squarely under the ban of the First Amendment (made applicable to the states by the Fourteenth)." Counsel for the Champaign school board asked the Supreme Court to repudiate the minimal meaning of the First Amendment as defined by Justice Black in the *Everson* case. The First Amendment was intended, it had been pleaded, to forbid only governmental preferences among religions, not equal assistance by government to all religions. The Court was also asked to overrule the statement in the *Everson* case that the Fourteenth Amendment made the First Amendment's establishment-of-religion clause applicable to the states. Black rejected both contentions and declared:

> . . . to hold that a state cannot . . . utilize its public school system to aid any or all religious faiths . . . does not, as counsel urge, manifest a governmental hostility to religion or religious teachings. . . . The First Amendment rests upon the premise that both religion and the government can best work to achieve their lofty aims if each is left free from the other within its respective sphere.

Thus, without any need to consider qualifications implied by the child-benefit theory, the Court majority rejected the assertion that this manner of cooperation of church and state was permitted by the First Amendment. In Champaign the public school buildings and the state's compulsory school machinery were being used for religious purposes. This was not separation of church and state.

The requirements of the principle of church-state separation were also spelled out by Justice Frankfurter in a concurring opinion, in which Justices Burton, Jackson, and Rutledge joined. The First Amendment prohibited "fusing functions of government and of religious sects." Praising the public school as "the most powerful agency for promoting cohesion among a heterogeneous, democratic people," Frankfurter said, "The public school must keep scrupulously free from entanglement in the strife of sects." To avoid divisive community conflicts and to relieve government of pressures by religious groups, and further to protect religion against government censorship and coercion required, Frankfurter declared, "strict confinement of the state to instruction other than religious, leaving to the individual's church and home, indoctrination in the faith of his choice." School children were imitative, and under the Champaign system there was obvious pressure upon them to attend religious classes.

Justice Jackson, in his concurring opinion, questioned if it were possible, even if it were desirable, to "isolate and cast out of secular education all that some people may reasonably regard as religious instruction." He warned against a constitutional doctrine binding all school boards in the nation "to immediately adopt and enforce rules and regulations prohibiting all instruction in and teaching of religious education in all public schools." To illustrate the difficulty of eliminating religious influences from the public school curriculum, Jackson commented:

> Music without sacred music, architecture minus the cathedral, or painting without the scriptural themes would be eccentric and incomplete, even from a secular point of view. Yet the inspirational appeal of religion in these guises is often stronger than in forthright sermon. Even such a "science" as biology, raises the issue between evolution and creation as an explanation of our presence on this planet. Certainly a course in English literature that omitted the Bible and other powerful uses of our mother tongue for religious ends would be pretty barren, and I suppose it is a proper, if not an indispensable, part of preparation for a worldly life to know the roles that religion and religions have played in the tragic story of mankind.

Nearly everything in our culture worth transmitting, Jackson said, was saturated with religious influences from many sources. He agreed that the teaching of "creed and catechism and ceremonial" should be prohibited and that proselyting in the public schools should be forbidden, but the task of distinguishing between the imparting of knowledge and evangelism was, "except in the crudest cases, a subtle inquiry."

Jackson was describing a problem the public school teacher faces almost daily. But this was not the problem before the Court. The children in Terry McCollum's school in the released-time period were not receiving instruction in art or literature with incidental references to religious themes. The released-time period was devoted to religious indoctrination. This was recognized by Jackson, and he concurred in the Court's decision. However, his warning was justified. The majority opinion had not distinguished between religious indoctrination and education with religious references.

The dissenting member of the Court, Justice Reed, was not concerned with such distinctions. For him, the constitutional restriction against an establishment of religion did not prohibit cooperation between government and religion. He believed that the meaning of the establishment-of-religion clause should be appraised in the light of the many examples of "close association of church and state in American society." Such close association he held to be a part of our tradition and our culture. The First Amendment did not "bar every friendly gesture between church and state," nor was it "an absolute prohibition against every conceivable situation where the two may work together."

In the *McCollum* case Justice Reed was a lone voice speaking in favor of the principle of cooperation as an interpretation of the First Amendment's establishment-of-religion clause. The majority of eight reiterated the separation principle expounded in the *Everson* case. However, in his concurring opinion Justice Frankfurter observed that other released-time programs might be found acceptable, and four years later the principle of separation was scrutinized again in the *Zorach* case.

THE *ZORACH* CASE: RELEASED TIME UPHELD

We are a religious people whose institutions presuppose a Supreme Being. . . . When the state encourages religious instruction or cooperates with religious authorities by adjusting the schedule of public events to sectarian needs, it follows the best of our traditions. For it then respects the religious nature of our people and accommodates the public service to their spiritual needs.

These are key words in the opinion delivered by Justice Douglas for a majority of six in the case of *Zorach* v. *Clauson* sustaining the released-time program in New York State.[9] In this 1952 opinion,

Justice Douglas argued for both cooperation and separation of church and state. Three separate dissenting opinions by Justices Black, Frankfurter and Jackson contended that the First Amendment's restriction on an establishment of religion called for separation, not cooperation of church and state.

The released-time program in New York permitted public schools to release students during the school day to receive religious instruction at religious centers away from the schools themselves. Douglas, speaking for the Court majority, distinguished between the Champaign and New York systems. He noted that in Champaign the classrooms were used for religious instruction and public school machinery was used to promote that instruction. In New York the public schools did no more than accommodate their schedules to a program of outside religious instruction. He maintained that the Court was following the *McCollum* case and declared:

> Government may not finance religious groups nor undertake religious instruction nor blend secular and sectarian education or use secular institutions to force one or some religion on any person. But we find no constitutional requirement which makes it necessary for government to be hostile to religion and to throw its weight against efforts to widen the effective scope of religious influence.

The constitutional standard, Douglas maintained, was the separation of church and state. The problem before the Court, like many problems in constitutional law, he said, was one of degree. Douglas' approach here was markedly different from Black's in the *Everson* case. Black, following the child-benefit theory, had held that separation was not violated by incidental aid to religion because of government service for the safety of children. The problem before the Court in the *Zorach* case was different in kind, not in degree. Douglas was upholding the right of government to undertake action with a religious end as its primary purpose. He was also insisting on an absolute separation of church and state. While his terms were emphatic, the total effect of Douglas' opinion was ambiguity.

Douglas' distinction between the Champaign and the New York systems, and his suggestion that rejection of that distinction reflected an anti-religious attitude, provoked vigorous and colorful dissents. In the strong language of these dissenting opinions are suggested the emotions stimulated throughout any community when the relation of church and state becomes a matter of public debate. These emotions are intensified by any suggestion that one's constitutional position is determined by his religious attitude. The dissenting Justices showed their resentment of such a suggestion.

Justice Black protested that the only difference between the Illinois system and the New York system was the use of the school building. New York was manipulating its compulsory education laws to promote attendance at religious schools. This was not separation but combination of church and state. He also objected to the majority's validation of the New York system on the basis that "we are a religious people." Judicial opinions should not make invidious distinctions between those who believe in a religion and those who believe in none. The First Amendment, Black held, meant that the religious follower and the atheist were "to be judicially regarded as entitled to equal justice under law." He could not accept the substitution of "cooperation" for "separation" as a justification for state aid to religion. He warned:

> State help to religion injects political and party prejudices into a holy field. It too often substitutes force for prayer, hate for love, and persecution for persuasion. Government should not be allowed, under cover of the soft euphemism of "co-operation," to steal into the sacred area of religious choice.

A second dissenting opinion by Justice Frankfurter expressed satisfaction that the principles accepted in the *McCollum* case were not disavowed by the *Zorach* majority, but rather disregarded. He hoped that in the future those principles would be observed by the Court. He derided the majority for its failure to recognize facts. It was not a question of the public schools closing their doors, he said, quoting Douglas, or suspending operations so the students might be free for religious instruction. Religious instruction was being substituted for regular school activity. Those who did not participate in the released-time program were compelled to attend the regular public school classes. The majority had said that if it could be shown that coercion were used a different case would be presented. Frankfurter pointed out that the New York court had denied the appellants the opportunity to present such evidence on the grounds that it was "irrelevant to the constitutional question." The Supreme Court, said Frankfurter, should have required the state court to make a canvass of all the circumstances. If coercion were not involved, Frankfurter declared, the controversy would disappear. If the promoters of religious education were content to have the public schools dismissed, letting those who wished to attend denominational classes do so, there would be no conflict. In chilling tones, Frankfurter concluded:

> The unwillingness of the promoters of this movement to dispense with such use of the public schools betrays a surprising want of confidence in the inherent power of the various faiths to draw children to outside sectarian classes—an attitude that hardly reflects the faith of the greatest religious spirits.

The biting tones of Frankfurter's comments were exceeded by Justice Jackson in his brief but challenging dissent. He too objected to the compulsory nature of the New York system. The school was being used as a temporary jail for the pupil who would not go to church. For Jackson, this was not separation but governmental constraint in support of religion. It was as unconstitutional when exerted by indirection as when exercised forthrightly. Jackson replied to the Douglas comment about hostility to religion with a personal reference:

> As one whose children, as a matter of free choice, have been sent to privately supported Church schools, I may challenge the Court's suggestion that opposition to this plan can only be anti-religious, atheistic, or agnostic. My evangelistic brethren confuse an objection to compulsion with an objection to religion. It is possible to hold a faith with enough confidence to believe that what should be rendered to God does not need to be decided and collected by Caesar.

Freedom to worship, Jackson insisted, meant also freedom for those who chose not to worship. "We start down a rough road," he said, "when we begin to mix compulsory education with compulsory godliness." The distinction made by the majority between the Champaign and New York systems was trivial "almost to the point of cynicism." The wall of separation the Court was professing to erect had become more warped and twisted than Jackson had expected. He predicted that the majority's judgment "will be more interesting to students of psychology and of the judicial processes than to students of constitutional law."

SUMMARY OF THE FIVE CASES

The protection of non-public schools set forth in the *Pierce* case was not challenged or qualified in the later decisions of the Supreme Court reviewed above. However, in the four later cases the Court relied on three principles, separation, cooperation, and child benefit, which have produced much controversy. The child-benefit theory was the basis of the *Cochran* decision. A comprehensive program to aid children to get a secular but not a religious education fulfilled a public purpose, even though the aid included parochial school pupils. The nature of the aid—schoolbooks,—was secular, and the same as that given public school pupils.

In the *Everson* case the Supreme Court was presented for the first time the problem of defining the principle of separation of church and state. The Court's initial definition of that principle, as offered by Justice Black, stated that neither the federal government nor a state could aid one religion, aid all religions, or prefer one religion over another. The First Amendment's restriction against "establishment of religion" was intended to erect "a wall of separation between church and state." But, relying on the child-benefit theory, the Court held that public bus service to aid children to get the secular education required by the state, even when mixed with the religious education of a parochial school, was not primarily assistance to religion but service to the child. While relying on the child-benefit theory, the Court insisted it was also upholding the principle of separation.

In the *McCollum* case a third doctrine, cooperation in the form of non-preferential public aid to religion, was struck down by the Court as a violation of the First Amendment. Equal aid to all religions was not separation but combination of church and state, and therefore unconstitutional. This cooperation principle seemed to be given new life, however, with the *Zorach* decision. State cooperation with religion was held to be in the best traditions of a religious people. Still, the majority maintained that the constitutional standard was separation of church and state. But separation was a matter of degree.

In these five cases the Supreme Court justices had given thirteen opinions. Only in the first two, the *Pierce* and *Cochran* cases, was the Court unanimous. The Court majorities insisted they adhered to the church-state separation principle. However, minority opinions charged that the separation principle was being circumvented in the *Everson* case by the child-benefit theory, and in the *Zorach* case by the cooperation principle.

In the majority and minority opinions there was enough variety to support many viewpoints on the relation of government and religion in education. In the *McCollum* case Jackson warned the Court against becoming a super board of education for the nation. It would seem, however, that the Court has done quite the opposite. For the most part, it has left states and school boards free to act.*

---

* The Court's willingness to leave the application of these principles with the states was reflected in *Heisey* v. *County of Alameda et al.*, 352 U.S. 921 (1956). An appeal from the Supreme Court of California was dismissed, Justices Black and Frankfurter dissenting, for want of a substantial federal question. The California court denied a federal constitutional challenge to state constitutional and statutory provisions for tax exemptions for property used for school purposes and owned by religious, hospital, or charitable organizations. A complaint that this violated the First Amendment's prohibition of "establishment of religion" was rejected. The California court said any benefit received by religious groups was incidental to achievement of the public purpose of promoting education. The Court compared the situation to that considered in the *Everson* case. Furthermore, even if religious groups were regarded as benefiting by such tax exemptions, it did not follow that the First Amendment was violated. The principle of separation of church and state was not impaired by tax exemptions granted generally to religious groups. *Lundberg* v. *County of Alameda*, 46 Cal. 2d 644, 298 P.2d 1.

The Court has set forth three principles—separation, cooperation, and child benefit—which are often in conflict. Clearly, transportation and secular textbooks could be supplied generally to school pupils without violating the Supreme Court's concept of the church-state separation principle. The doctrine of cooperation, rejected in *McCollum* and revived by *Zorach*, strongly suggests that government may act not merely to aid children and so to aid religion indirectly, but to encourage religious instruction and follow "the best of our traditions."

Perhaps the most decisive conclusion to be drawn from these five cases is that the issue of auxiliary services could be decided in Connecticut subject to very little federal restraint. The Supreme Court transferred to the states and the school boards responsibility for applying the principles about which the Justices themselves had quarreled so vigorously.

III:

THE

LEGAL SETTING

IN

CONNECTICUT

THE PRINCIPLES set forth by the Supreme Court about church, state, and education are broad and to some degree contradictory. However, the *Cochran* and *Everson* cases did leave the states free to provide to pupils of all schools (public and non-public) some non-religious services. Much of the debate in Connecticut about proposals for auxiliary services turned on the meaning of provisions in Connecticut's Constitution and statutes. There was some debate about whether auxiliary services were in violation of the state Constitution. There was more debate about whether such services were authorized by Connecticut's statutes. Questions about the application of state law to auxiliary services were rejected by the office of the Attorney General. The questions were redirected to town counsels to be decided locally. School boards had little guidance from state authority on how the statutes or the state Constitution affected auxiliary services for parochial school pupils.

RELIGION AND EDUC
IN CONNECTICUT'S (

There are three provisions of C
might be regarded as having some
services for parochial school pupils
Section Four of the First Article d
given by law to any Christian sect
Article Seventh provides that all Ch
"the same and equal powers, rights
provides that no person shall be co
classed with any religious organizatic...

States Constitution
a similar restrict
ing public f
It was a
funds
tic

The emphasis in these two provisions is on a non-preferential treatment of Christian sects. This is in contrast with the federal prohibition of "an establishment of religion." Equal aid to Christian sects by the state of Connecticut would be prohibited by the Supreme Court's holding in the *Everson, McCollum,* and *Zorach* decisions. It might also be argued that Article Seventh prohibits compelling anyone to support a religious organization. Therefore, an opponent of public services for parochial schools might contend that such public expenditure amounts to unconstitutional compulsion on taxpayers to contribute to the support of a religious organization. In refutation, of course, it could be said that the services are rendered to the pupils and not to the schools. In this respect the restrictions of the Connecticut Constitution, like that of the federal Constitution, operate only if the public service provided is regarded as an aid to the religious school.

The third provision of the Connecticut Constitution which might be regarded as having some relevance to public services for parochial school pupils is Article Eighth, "Of Education." Section Two provides that the School Fund shall remain a perpetual fund, the interest of which shall be inviolably appropriated to the support and encouragement of the public schools of the state. This restriction applies to the interest on that money which the state of Connecticut received from the sale of western lands shortly after the adoption of the United

. In the *Everson* case a contention was made that
ion in the New Jersey Constitution prohibited spend-
nds for transportation costs of non-public school pupils.
gued that the school fund moneys were mixed with other
appropriated for educational purposes, and therefore the restric-
n must apply to all public education appropriations. The New
Jersey court rejected this contention.[1]

Public services for parochial school pupils, then, are not specifically prohibited by the Connecticut Constitution. A constitutional
challenge to such services would most likely be based on the provision
in Article Seventh that "no person shall by law be compelled to join
or support . . . any congregation, church, or religious association."
The argument would turn on whether the transportation or the other
public service under dispute constituted support of a religious association. The child-benefit theory would be offered in refutation of the
church-state separation principle.

A JUDICIAL DEFINITION
OF A PUBLIC SCHOOL

Connecticut's court records provide little help in interpreting the
state Constitution as it applies to public services for non-public school
pupils. The only case bearing on the question was decided by the
Supreme Court of Errors in 1945.[2]

The case arose because the town of Torrington refused to reimburse the city of New Haven for educating children committed by the
Juvenile Court of Torrington to a county home in New Haven. These
children had been transferred from the county home to a Catholic
orphanage operated by the Sisters of Mercy. On the second floor of
the orphanage the Sisters conducted the Highland Heights School,
which was supported as part of the public school system of New
Haven. The teaching nuns were certified under regulations of the
State Board of Education, they were paid according to the same salary scale and received the same tenure and retirement privileges as
other public school teachers in New Haven. The school property was

part of the orphanage and was owned by the Catholic organization. This arrangement had been in existence since 1879.

The principal contention of the town of Torrington was that the city of New Haven had no authority to maintain a sectarian school and could not claim reimbursement for such education. The New Haven Superior Court and the Supreme Court of Errors found that the school operated in the orphanage met the two requirements of a public school; it was under exclusive control of the state (through the local school board), and it was free from sectarian education. Religious exercises were held before school and were not compulsory. The Sisters taught in their distinctive dress, but this was not found to be a significant sectarian influence.

One judge dissented. He contended that the sectarian atmosphere of the school made it, in fact, a parochial school. He asserted:

> A child receives instruction by seeing as well as by hearing. The daily routine, the physical surroundings, and the habit of their order worn by the teachers, may well prove as potent an influence in determining his religious development as would a regularly prescribed course of instruction in formulated precepts.

During each of the four years in question, the dissenting judge pointed out, the school enrolled an average of 370 pupils, all of whom were Catholics and inmates of the orphanage. To construe that the school had always been open to children outside of the orphanage was to substitute theory for reality, he said.

The complaint of the town of Torrington was denied, and the Highland Heights School, operating in the Saint Francis Orphan Asylum, continued as a part of the New Haven public school system until 1957.

This case throws no direct light on how Connecticut courts might view a challenge to public services for parochial school pupils. The declaration in the majority opinion that a public school must be free from sectarian instruction bears a similarity to Justice Black's statement in the *McCollum* case that a state cannot "utilize its public school system to aid any or all religious faiths." However, there is no indication in the majority opinion in the *Torrington* case whether school transportation or any other auxiliary services for parochial school pupils would be regarded by Connecticut's Supreme Court of Errors as unconstitutional assistance to sectarian education.

CONNECTICUT'S LAWS RELATING TO EDUCATION

In contrast to the limited treatment of education in the Connecticut Constitution and the scarcity of court decisions relevant to this study, the General Assembly has enacted many statutes pertinent to a consideration of public services for non-public school pupils. *Laws Relating to Education*, published by the Connecticut State Department of Education, contains 120 pages of laws dealing with this subject.[3] Clearly, for an understanding of public education and related services in Connecticut, one must look to the statutes rather than to the Constitution or the judicial records.

The State Board of Education

The general statutes of Connecticut give to the State Board of Education "general supervision and control of the educational interests of the state." A Connecticut court has interpreted this section as meaning something more than school instruction. The court declared that education "comprehends in its broadcast significance the acquisition of all knowledge tending to develop and train the individual and when used in this sense is not [to be] limited to the years of adolescence or to instruction in schools."[4]

The State Board of Education which is charged with such broad responsibility is composed of nine members. At least one member of the Board must be appointed from and reside in each of the eight counties of the state. One member is appointed at large. The members are appointed by the Governor for overlapping terms of six years, their terms beginning the first day of July following their appointments. Three members are appointed in the year when the General

Assembly is in regular session, this being the odd-numbered year.[5] The appointment statute seems intended to provide continuity of membership and to make the Board less subject to partisan influence than are public officials who hold elective offices or short-term appointments.

The statute describing the duties of the State Board of Education goes beyond the broad statement concerning general supervision and control. It also authorizes the Board to direct what books shall be used, to improve the methods and efficiency of teaching, to prescribe school records, and to make reports.[6] The Board is authorized to employ a secretary and an assistant secretary, as well as such subordinate agents and employees as it finds necessary to conduct its business. The secretary of the Board also serves as Commissioner of Education. The Assistant Secretary serves as Deputy Commissioner.[7] These two officials head the State Department of Education, which is the Board's agency for conducting its business. While such broad authority is given to the State Board of Education, much of this authority is delegated, not only by the Board but also by the General Assembly, to the local boards of education.[8]

Duties of Local Boards of Education

Each local board of education is directed by law to maintain "good public elementary and secondary schools and such other educational activities as in their judgment will best serve the interests of the town." The school board is permitted to secure such services in another town "in accordance with the general statutes," and the board is also directed "to give all the children of the town as nearly equal advantages as may be practicable." [9]

The broad phrase "such other educational activities" suggests a number of questions. Beyond the maintenance of elementary and secondary schools, what is an educational activity that the school board might undertake? Some of these activities are mentioned in the statutes relating to transportation, adult education courses, vocational courses, and health services.[10] But are services to anyone outside of the public schools included? The statute listing the duties of the local board of education is concerned almost entirely and specifically with duties related to the public schools. However, a board wishing to provide services to pupils of non-public schools might interpret several clauses as justifying such action. The board might say that such a service was one of "such other educational activities as in their judgment will best serve the interests of the town"; or that it was following the statutory direction "to give all the children of the town as nearly equal advantages as may be practicable"; or that such services to pupils of non-public schools were merely a reasonable exercise of their power and duty to "cause each child between the ages of seven and sixteen living in the town to attend school" as required by law. The board might go further and say that these services to children in non-public schools were "necessary to carry into effect the powers and duties" imposed upon them by law.[11]

Although the duties of the board as stated in the laws might be interpreted to include public services for pupils in non-public schools, the statute concerning the appropriations and budget of the local board of education does not specify nor imply any authority for the expenditure of the board's funds for any purpose other than "the maintenance of public schools," for which the board is directed to prepare "an itemized estimate of the cost." The same statute gives the board power to transfer funds for school purposes "to any other item of such itemized estimate." The reference to items in the itemized estimate clearly restricts such transfers of funds to maintenance of the public schools.[12]

Non-Public Schools and the Laws

Connecticut's law requires a parent to cause his child to attend regularly some public school or else show that the child is receiving instruction equivalent to that given in the public schools. This instruction may be obtained at a non-public school or at home.[13]

A non-public school must keep a register of attendance identical to that kept in the public schools and must make such reports and returns to the Secretary of the State Board of Education as do the public schools. The sole exception is that non-public schools shall not be required to report concerning finances.[14]

All private and public elementary schools must use the English language as the medium of instruction. Not more than one hour in any school day may be devoted to instruction in any language other than English.[15] Private elementary and secondary schools, like public schools, must teach their students responsibilities of citizenship.[16]

Standards other than statutory ones have been established for non-public elementary and secondary schools in Connecticut by representatives of the non-public schools and by public education officials. Except for those schools receiving tuition from public funds, approval under these standards is on an entirely voluntary basis. The procedure of approval consists of a visit by a committee (generally of three members) appointed by the State Department of Education. This committee inspects the buildings, evaluates the program, examines the facilities and equipment, inquires into the financial stability, and reviews the professional preparation of the faculty. The report of the committee is then submitted to the State Board of Education for action. Schools approved as meeting the standards are so listed in the Educational Directory published annually by the State Department of Education.

The guide to school evaluation states that:

> . . . to promote the general well-being of education in Connecticut, and in particular to establish a basis upon which the Independent Schools of this state may act, in making their contributions to this cause, these principles and procedures have been developed. . . . Co-operative effort among schools and representatives of the state helps to maintain the fine balance between the encouragement of the initiative, experimentation, and the regard for the rights for parents in directing the education of their children, on the one side, and the protection of the public, a respect for standards and the welfare of society in general and of the pupils in particular on the other.[17]

In addition to the laws of general nature discussed this far, there are more specific statutory guides for answering questions about public services for non-public schools. These include laws concerning books and supplies, school transportation, health services, and the school lunch and school milk programs.

Books and Supplies

Local boards of education are directed by statute to purchase the books and supplies necessary to meet the instructional needs of "the schools of the town or district." They are further directed to lend these books and furnish these supplies to all pupils free of charge, subject to the rules of the board concerning the care and use of the materials.[18] The reference here seems clearly to be to the schools under the direction of the local board of education—that is, the public schools. The board of education has authority to change the textbooks in the "public schools" by a two-thirds vote of the board after one week's notice of such a vote.[19]

The local board of education is also directed by statute to provide a United States flag for each schoolroom in the town as well as for each schoolhouse.[20] The statute which refers to textbooks and supplies speaks of "the schools of the town." The laws concerning the supplying of flags speaks of the schoolrooms or schoolhouses "in the town." Does the different preposition carry any great significance? A non-public school might seem to have some grounds for demanding that the local school board provide the non-public school with flags for each schoolroom and for the schoolhouse grounds.

School Bus Service

In considering Connecticut's laws affecting free public transportation for pupils of non-public schools, a distinction must be made between bus service for elementary school pupils and that for high school pupils. This distinction is necessary because Connecticut law states:

> The town board of education may provide for the transportation, to and from any high school or junior high school, of any pupil attending

such school and residing within the limits of such town, or pay the whole or part of the reasonable and necessary cost thereof.[21]

The section immediately preceding this provides for payment of tuition by a town not maintaining a high school for local children attending a high school (approved by the State Board of Education) in another town, "except if it is a school under ecclesiastical control." [22] The law quoted above does not exclude schools under ecclesiastical control. It does not, in contrast to the New Jersey statute tested in the *Everson* case, exclude schools operated for profit. The words of the Connecticut statute are inclusive regarding the school— "any high school or junior high school"—and inclusive regarding the children—"any pupil attending such school and residing within the limits of the town."

Towns which do not maintain a high school are directed by another statute to:

> . . . pay the reasonable and necessary cost of transportation of any pupil who resides with his parents or guardian in such town and who, with the written consent of the board of education, attends any high school, provided such high school be approved by the state board of education.[23]

The Attorney General of Connecticut ruled in 1945 that the language of this statute permitted a town not maintaining a high school to give public transportation service to pupils of Catholic high schools. The question was raised because the town of Middlebury, which did not maintain a high school, was furnishing bus service for pupils attending two Catholic high schools in Waterbury. The two schools had been approved by the State Board of Education. The Attorney General wrote that he was aware of the law prohibiting payment of *tuition fees* for pupils attending a school under ecclesiastical control but it was his opinion that such prohibition referred only to tuition payments. He declared:

> . . . had the General Assembly intended to make exceptions of schools under ecclesiastical control as far as transportation costs were concerned it would have said so in Section 130f, above referred to. The inclusion of the language creating the exemption in Section 202c

and the failure to include it in Section 130f clearly demonstrates that provisions of Section 130f were intended to and do apply to any high school approved by the State Board of Education whether under ecclesiastical control or not.[24]

The office of the Attorney General was asked in 1952 about the legality of free public transportation to pupils of parochial schools *within* the town. The Commissioner of Education requested a legal opinion on the following questions:

1. Are town boards of education legally obligated to transport children to attend parochial schools?
2. If town boards are not obligated to provide such transportation, may they legally do so?

In reply to these questions the office of the Attorney General wrote:

It seems to us that these questions are peculiarly within the field of administration of the school system in this State by the various local boards of education. We do not feel that the administration of the State Board of Education involves a position on this question one way or the other. With the exception of election matters or matters related to taxation, the jurisdiction conferred by statute upon the Attorney General does not cover or include advice to local officials.

We therefore advise that the subject matter involved in these cases is more properly one that should be discussed with the town counsel, and the local Board of Education should be governed by his opinion in the matter.[25]

The classification of these questions as local matters may be questioned, since the Connecticut courts have found that the local board of education is not an agency of the town but an agency of the state in charge of education in the town.[26] Furthermore, the office of the Attorney General had given advice in 1945 in reply to a question from the Middlebury Board of Education.

The opinion rendered in 1952 was not a yes-or-no answer, but it was a more definite reply than that given by the Attorney General in 1938. At that time the town of Putnam was providing bus service for parochial school pupils despite an adverse opinion by the town counsel. The Commissioner of Education in March, 1938, asked the Attorney General whether such expenditure of Putnam's public school funds imperiled payment of state aid to the town for public school operation. On April 23 the Deputy Attorney General replied that an opinion could not be given because the school board of Putnam had not yet applied for the annual state grant. He recommended that the question be submitted again after the town made such application. No further inquiry was made of the Attorney General, and his office rendered no opinion on the subject until 1952 when the Commissioner of Education was advised, as quoted above, that the question was one for local determination.[27]

Subsequently, the State Department of Education was guided by the 1952 statement in its replies to questions from local school boards about transportation for non-public school pupils. Consequently, several town counsels were asked to give opinions on the question. In 1954 opinions stating such service was illegal were given by the town counsels for Ridgefield and for New Hartford. In 1956 a new town counsel in Ridgefield advised that such transportation was not illegal. In the same year the corporation counsel for the City of Meriden gave an opinion that it was illegal.

In 1954 the Ridgefield town counsel informed the local school board that there was no statutory law "and apparently no case law" on the question of public transportation for parochial school pupils. He stated that boards of education were required by statute:

> . . . to make provision for the transportation of children where reasonable and desirable to enable the children to attend some public day school. No provision is made for transportation of school children to non-public or private schools. A Board of Education is an agency of the state and, as a general rule, has only such powers as are specifically conferred upon it by law. Thus it appears that the Board of Education is without authority to provide transportation, at public expense, to a non-public or private school. There appears to be no case law covering the specific problem at hand.[28]

The same section of the statutes was cited by the town counsel for New Hartford in his reply to a query by his school board. He observed that the board's question was restricted to elementary school pupils since the town did not maintain a secondary school and was thus required to provide reasonable transportation for pupils attending designated approved high schools. The New Hartford counsel cited the case of *New Haven* v. *Torrington* to present the distinction between a private and a public school. He stated:

> Of course, it is understood and it has been decided again and again in Connecticut that Boards of Education are agents of the law and not agents of the town, and the Board of Education has the duty of following the statute law of Connecticut as above set forth where transportation furnished by the town from funds raised by taxation is for transportation to public schools. . . .
> In view of all the foregoing, I am of the opinion and so advise the Board of Education of New Hartford, that said Board of Education could not legally furnish transportation to non-public school children or to the parochial school children as stated in your letter. Certainly, had the Legislature intended by said Section 780c, that transportation at public expense to a non-public school could be provided by the town board of education, it would have been so explicitly stated.[29]

A different interpretation of the duties of a board of education was made in 1956 by the new town counsel of Ridgefield. He advised the Ridgefield school board that he could not "find anything illegal in the Board of Education providing transportation in Ridgefield to non-public school children." He cited the statutory duty of parents to cause a child to attend a public school or to show that the child was attending an approved private school. He declared that it followed logically that since either a public school or a private school must be regularly attended, "the school board could assist the pupils to get there by means of transportation to these schools."

The Ridgefield town counsel stated:

> This does not mean that public money or property is given to aid or maintain religious schools, but that the aid is given to the pupils who are legally attending such schools, to assist them and their parents to attend an approved school for the required time.

The counsel asserted that this was the basis of law in states where such service was authorized by statute. He suggested that it "would be a proper basis for a policy for your Board to follow in allowing transportation to the non-public schools." [30]

This line of reasoning was analyzed in detail and the conclusion rejected by the corporation counsel for Meriden in an opinion given in June, 1956.

The Meriden City Council had asked for an opinion on two questions: (1) Can public funds be used to transport parochial school children; and (2) Can an appropriation for transportation of parochial school children be set up and administered by some agency of the city other than the Board of Education?

At the beginning of his reply to the first question the counsel wrote that he would assume it pertained to the "transportation of school children attending parochial elementary schools," although the question was not so limited in presentation. This assumption relieved the counsel of the necessity of interpreting the law permitting a town board of education to provide transportation "to and from any high school or junior high school." In none of the opinions reported here was this section interpreted or even referred to. No non-public high school or junior high school was maintained in Ridgefield and New Hartford. There was a parochial junior high school in Meriden, and the corporation counsel might have considered transportation of pupils of parochial secondary schools a relevant question.

The Meriden corporation counsel stated that he had discovered no Connecticut court decision "squarely on this point" and that "the Attorney General's office has not rendered an opinion on this problem." The counsel discussed the *Everson* case and pointed out that the board of education in that instance had acted in pursuance of a New Jersey statute. He then considered whether there was authority in two sections of the General Statutes of Connecticut for providing public transportation for pupils in parochial schools. The first law, Section 10–186, states:

> Each town shall furnish, by transportation or otherwise, school accommodations so that each child over six and under sixteen years of age may attend school as required in Section [10–184].

Section 10–184 in part provides that a parent or a guardian of a child over seven and under sixteen shall:

> . . . cause such child to attend a public day school regularly during the hours and terms the public school in the district wherein such child resides is in session, . . . unless the [parent or guardian] shall be able to show that the child is elsewhere receiving equivalent instruction during such hours and terms in the studies taught in the public schools.

The Meriden Corporation Counsel commented:

> It is argued that Section [10–186] imposes a duty on a town to transport school children, and that by reference to Section [10–184], that duty necessarily includes the duty to transport those who do not attend public schools but do attend such a school as would furnish equivalent instruction, which would concededly include local parochial schools. Thus, it is claimed, there exists not only the authority, but indeed the duty to transport parochial school children.
>
> A careful reading of Sections [10–186 and 10–184] leads me to the conclusion that Section [10–186] makes it mandatory on a town through its local board of education, to build or otherwise make schools available for its children, or else transport them to a location where such facilities may be had. Section [10–186] cannot be construed as a mandate to towns to furnish both school accommodations and transportation thereto. It does require that towns furnish school accommodations, and the additional phrase "by transportation or otherwise" gives the towns, and particularly the smaller ones, the opportunity to comply with this duty by transporting its school children to schools in other towns or school districts, if the town does not deem it advisable to build its own schools. It cannot be seriously claimed that cities and towns such as Meriden, which certainly furnish school accommodations, are compelled by this law to furnish transportation to such other facilities.

The counsel then declared that the authority of local boards of education to transport children was defined in the statute which presents in some detail the duties of local boards.[31] This is the section referred to in the opinion given by the Ridgefield town counsel. Among other duties there listed, boards are directed to make provision to enable the school children of the town "to attend some public day school for the period required by law and provide for the transportation of children wherever transportation is reasonable and desirable." The Meriden counsel reported:

> The provisions contained in this section, providing that the board of education shall have the care, maintenance, and operation of buildings, lands and other properties used for school purposes and providing that it shall employ and dismiss the teachers of such schools, clearly indicate that its provisions authorizing transportation of school children are limited to public school transportation.

The repeated references to public schools in many of the statutes, the counsel said, would lead a court to conclude that no authority was implied permitting public transportation of non-public school pupils. Nor did the Constitution of Connecticut or the Meriden City Charter provide such authority.

The counsel seriously doubted that another city agency could administer transportation for parochial school children. The city's public health or public welfare powers could not be so extended. The counsel concluded that further legislative action by the state was necessary to permit expenditures of public funds for such purposes.[32]

Health Services

The Connecticut statutes covering health services in schools are fairly specific in their references to public schools. Boards of education in towns with a population of 10,000 or more must appoint school medical advisers for the public schools in the town.[33] School boards in towns with a population under 10,000 are permitted, not required, to make such appointments.[34] School boards must require every public school pupil to have a health examination every three years,[35] and may appoint school nurses "for safeguarding the health of the pupils and teachers of the schools."[36] They may employ dental hygienists to "clean the teeth of school children in attendance at the public schools in such town."[37]

The State Board of Education must have prepared "suitable test cards and blanks to be used in testing the eyesight of pupils in public schools." The Board must furnish these cards and blanks along with instructions for their use, free of expense, "to each school in the state." [38]

The controlling statute in all of these provisions would seem to be the direction to the town board of education to prescribe the functions and duties of the school medical advisers "in order that the program of health protection and health supervision, as outlined by such town boards and approved by the State Board of Education, shall be carried out." [39]

In each instance the local board is directed to provide these health services for the public schools. There is no law specifically directing or permitting the board to provide health services to children not attending the public schools of the town. To justify such service a local board of education would have to rely on other sections of the statutes. The board could cite its mandate to maintain "such other educational activities as in their judgment will best serve the interests of the town," and also to "give all the children of the town as nearly equal advantages as may be practicable." This would mean categorizing health services as an "educational activity." The local board members might say that these services were "necessary to carry into effect the powers and duties imposed upon them by law." Of course, if the town meeting or town council should direct that such services be given to children other than those attending the public schools, then the board could quote the law which directed local boards to "perform all acts which may be required of them by the town."

That such general sections of the statute justify the extension of health services to non-public pupils is, of course, subject to challenge in the courts. In 1957 this challenge had not yet been made in Connecticut's courts. The advice of one town counsel had been sought by a school board, and he had stated that there was no legal authority in Connecticut law for the board to give health services to any but public school pupils. [40]

The School Lunch and School Milk Programs

Connecticut's local boards of education are permitted by statute to "establish and operate lunch services for public school children . . . such board may provide free lunches to children whose economic or health needs require such action." [41] This statute is permissive and is restricted to serving public school children.

Another statute, however, authorizes the State Board of Education, "subject to the provisions of the general statutes, to receive any federal funds made available to this State for educational purposes, except those designated for the University of Connecticut and to expend such funds for the purpose or the purposes for which they are made available." [42] Under this statute the Connecticut State Department of Education administers school lunch services to non-public schools in Connecticut.

The school lunch service of the State Department of Education is also governed by the National School Lunch Act.[43] This act declares it to be the policy of Congress "to safeguard the health and well-being of the nation's children and to encourage the domestic consumption of nutritious agricultural commodities and other food" by assisting the state in encouraging non-profit school lunch programs. The funds appropriated for this purpose are to be apportioned according to two factors: the number of school children in the state, and the state's need for assistance based on its rank in the nation according to per capita income. This act defines an eligible school as any public or non-profit private school of high school grade or under. In Section Six of the Act, another reference is made to "need" in these words: "to be distributed among the states and schools participating in the school lunch program under this Act, in accordance with the needs as determined by local school authorities."

The phrase is used again in Section Nine of the Act. Section Nine states that the lunches are to be "served without cost or at a reduced cost to children who are determined by local school authorities to be unable to pay the full cost of the lunch." Section Seven of the Act provides another description of its purpose in stating that the Secretary of Agriculture may make agreements with the state educational agency for the purpose of "assisting schools of that state" to supply food and other assistance in furtherance of the school lunch program.

Another reference to "need" is made in Section Eight of the Act, which authorizes the state agency to disburse these funds to such schools in the state which the agency, "taking into account need and attendance," determines to be eligible to participate in the school lunch program. The phraseology in this section makes it difficult to say for certain what is intended by the word "need." Since the matter to be determined is the eligibility of the school, the definition which immediately suggests itself is the need of the school. A fuller definition, perhaps, would be to say that what is intended to be measured is the need of the school for assistance in operating a school lunch program.

The declaration of policy presented in the National School Lunch Act suggests that Congress was relying on the child-benefit theory in adopting this measure. An analysis of the Act, however, suggests that Congress was conscious of extending benefits not only to children but to schools as well. In apportioning the money, the Act provides that all children in the state between the ages of five and seventeen inclusive are to be counted in determining apportionment. However, in defining "school" the Act specifies only public or non-profit private schools of high school grade or under. The exclusion of private schools operated for profit from participation in the school lunch program suggests that Congress saw some benefit accruing to the school from such participation. This is underlined by the wording in Section Seven of the Act, which declares it to be "for the purpose of assisting schools of that State." One may ask, then, whether the assistance deriving from this Act is to the school or to the child. The wording suggests that Congress felt benefit was conferred on both.

Further analysis reveals that "need" as used in the Act has several meanings. The apportionment formula described in Section Four, which includes as a factor the per capita income of the state, leads one to believe that the meaning of "need" is the state's need. However, Sections Six and Eight of the Act lead one to believe that the meaning of "need" in those sections is the school's need. In Section Nine, the Act directs that lunches are to be served without cost or at a reduced cost to children unable to pay the full cost. Here the need of the child is clearly the determinant.

A further definition of "need" is used in the administration of this act. Representatives of the United States Department of Agriculture have urged on the members of the School Lunch Unit of the Connecticut State Department of Education that some method be devised for determining the need of the community for assistance in operating the school lunch program. One method suggested is a formula which would take into account the per capita income by county. This method would provide that the state would then disburse funds to schools within a county in proportion to the county's ranking according to per capita income.

This suggested formula has not been devised by Connecticut's State Department of Education. However, Connecticut followed one definition of "need" suggested by the Act in the administration of the school lunch programs within the state in accordance with a request of the Department of Agriculture. Each participating private tuition school is required to declare that without the benefit of commodities donated by the Department of Agriculture it would be unable "to serve a nutritionally adequate meal according to the school's standards." It may be said, then, that the Connecticut State Department of Education makes the *need of the school* a requirement for participation. This requirement results in the exclusion of some non-profit schools. Those non-profit private schools which are described as "high tuition schools" are declared ineligible by the Department. Such schools obviously could not meet the requirement of school need as set down by the Department. The school lunch is an integral part of the services which such a school extends to its students. In most cases the cost of board and room is included in the tuition fee paid by the student.[44]

The school milk program administered by the Connecticut State

Department of Education is conducted under the state statute quoted above for the school lunch program, authorizing the Department to receive federal funds and expend them in accordance with the general statutes for the purposes for which they are made available. The federal act which authorizes this program is the Agricultural Act of 1949, as amended by Section 204 of the Agricultural Act of 1954. One of the purposes of the Act is declared to be to increase the consumption of milk "by children in non-profit schools of high school grade and under." Congress must have anticipated some aid to the schools from this program, since here again schools operated for profit are excluded.

The basis of apportionment of the federal funds appropriated is declared to be in accordance with the formula set forth in the National School Lunch Act. It will be remembered that this formula makes the need of the state a factor.

It can be said of the school milk program, as well as the school lunch program, that the child-benefit theory is invoked to justify these measures, but the language of the statutes makes it clear that Congress believed it was conferring benefits on the schools as well as on the children.

Despite the apparently confusing invocation of the child-benefit theory by Congress, there can be little doubt that there is sufficient legal authorization for the extension of the school lunch and school milk programs to pupils in non-public schools in Connecticut. However, the exclusion of children in "high tuition" schools contradicts to some degree the purpose of the federal School Lunch and School Milk Acts as one of "safeguarding the health and well-being of the Nation's children."

SUMMARY

It has been shown that the Connecticut Constitution does not contain a specific barrier against public services for non-public school pupils. Furthermore, there is little guidance to be found on this question in the judicial history of Connecticut.

The office of the Attorney General provided two key opinions on public transportation for non-public school pupils. One opinion declared that the statutes authorized towns not maintaining a high school to provide public transportation to an out-of-town Catholic high school if the school was designated by the local board and approved by the State Board of Education. The question of public transportation for pupils attending non-public schools *within* the town, the office of the Attorney General said, was a matter on which a local school board should seek the advice of the town counsel. Between 1952, when this reply was given, and 1956, three local school boards sought advice from their local counsel. Counsel in Meriden and in New Hartford ruled that the school board was not authorized to provide such bus service. In 1954 the Ridgefield town counsel said that the school board had no authority to transport pupils of non-public schools. Two years later a new town counsel in Ridgefield ruled that the school board "could" assist by transportation pupils attending non-public schools. His opinion was based on the child-benefit theory, the board's statutory duty to provide "reasonable and desirable" transportation, and the parent's freedom to choose for a child any school meeting the state's educational requirements.

Connecticut's laws on health services to school children all refer to the public schools. There are general statements in the statutes which might be invoked to justify the use of school funds for health services to pupils in non-public schools. The State Board of Education is authorized to extend school lunch and school milk services to non-public schools by a statute permitting the Board to receive federal funds for educational purposes and to spend those funds for the purposes for which they were made available. The federal laws governing the school lunch and school milk programs attempt to employ the child-benefit theory but actually make the need of the state, the community, and the school the standard, rather than the need of the child. In Connecticut, "high tuition" private schools are excluded from the programs by administrative decision. In this instance it is clearly the need of the school, not the need of the child, that is the measure.

Where federal funds were not involved, there was, prior to 1957, no specific statutory direction or authorization for a local school board in Connecticut to provide services to pupils in non-public schools. Such services might be justified on the basis of general statements (such as the school board's duty to maintain "such other educational activities as in their judgment will best serve the interests of the town") or by linking (as was done in the opinion rendered by the town counsel of Ridgefield) the duty of the school board to provide "reasonable and desirable transportation" with the parent's duty to educate the child in an approved school of his choice. Such authorization by reference was specifically rejected in the opinion of the corporation counsel of Meriden. Furthermore, the law covering the appropriations and budget of the local board of education does not specify nor imply authority to spend funds controlled by the local board for any purpose but "the maintenance of the public schools."

Prior to 1957 there was no authority in Connecticut law for a school board to provide any public services, except school lunch and school milk, to non-public school pupils. However, the evasiveness of the 1952 ruling of the Attorney General and the favorable 1956 ruling of the Ridgefield town counsel provided sufficient grounds for advocates of services to argue that there was uncertainty about Connecticut statutes and the transportation of parochial school pupils. This contention, coupled with a reference to the many towns then giving some auxiliary services to parochial school pupils, was frequently used as an argument for action by the Connecticut General Assembly.

IV:

THE

PRELIMINARY

STRUGGLE

THE RELATION of non-public schools to public schools was raised at a meeting of the Connecticut State Board of Education on December 7, 1955. The meeting was held at the home of the then Commissioner of Education, Dr. F. E. Engleman, in an atmosphere more relaxed than that of sessions held in the Commissioner's office. The informality disappeared, however, with the introduction of a motion by Board member Richard Joyce Smith that a study be made of the relation of public and non-public schools in the state. He made specific reference to the need for more information on the various public services provided to non-public school pupils. The sudden tension that appeared in the room was emphasized by the care with which each speaker chose his words as he commented about the subject. Everyone present seemed aware that this was a topic that could become explosive.

Mr. Smith, a lawyer and a Catholic, could discuss this issue out of years of experience connected with public education. He had served on the Fairfield Board of Education for ten years prior to his appointment to the State Board by Governor John Lodge in 1951. Although a Democrat, Mr. Smith actively supported Republican Lodge's campaign for Governor in 1950. He had served on the board of the National Citizens for the Public Schools and its successor, the National Citizens Council for Better Schools. Previously, following his graduation from Yale Law School, Mr. Smith served on the faculty there for six years. Later he took up the practice of law in New York City.[1]

After Mr. Smith presented his motion, he emphasized that he was not suggesting that the State Board of Education take a policy stand at that time. His motion was a request for information. The collection of this basic information would be important should the State Board wish at some time to make policy regarding non-public schools. The Board agreed at that meeting that the study should be made.[2]

Commissioner Engleman directed Dr. Maurice J. Ross, chief of the Bureau of Research and Statistics, to prepare a study outline to comply with the Board's request. After the outline was drafted, the Commissioner invited to his office to discuss the proposed study one representative each from the Connecticut Council of (Protestant) Churches, the Catholic dioceses of Bridgeport, Hartford, and Norwich, the Connecticut Association of Independent Schools, the Jewish rabbinate of Connecticut, and the Connecticut Association of Public School Superintendents. At a meeting on January 3, 1956, these representatives discussed the study outline and inquiry forms with Commissioner Engleman and Dr. Ross.

The study as proposed by Dr. Ross included four primary divisions: the pertinent statutes, the pertinent statistical data in the Department's files (e.g., non-public school enrollments by years, enrollments by grade and sex, and the geographic distribution of non-public schools), the services of the state and local departments of education to non-public schools, and the current condition of non-public schools. In connection with the fourth division of the study, a proposed questionnaire for non-public schools included questions concerning the administration of those schools, buildings and classroom facilities, the length of the school day and school year, subjects or courses offered, and class size.[3] An additional item concerned the professional preparation of the non-public school

faculty. Some of the representatives of the non-public schools objected to this item.

By statute and by State Board of Education regulations, teachers
in public schools must meet certification requirements for teaching
the classes or courses to which they are assigned. Non-public school
teachers need not meet these requirements.* It was Dr. Ross' conviction that faculty preparation was an important factor in determining whether a non-public school was offering its pupils, as required by
law, instruction equivalent to that offered in the public schools.
The Catholic school representatives objected that such an item of
inquiry was not pertinent to the study. Furthermore, all of their elementary schools and almost all of their secondary schools had been
approved by the State Board of Education. The Commissioner of
Education directed that this query be eliminated from the questionnaire to be sent to heads of non-public schools.[4]

A different questionnaire was proposed to be sent to public school
superintendents. Items on this questionnaire included queries about
policies of local boards of education affecting all school children
(public and non-public) and about public services or facilities made
available to non-public school pupils.

The proposed study as amended met with the approval of all
those attending the meeting. On January 12, 1956, the inquiry forms
were sent to local public school superintendents, diocesan school
superintendents, and the administrative heads of other non-public
schools in Connecticut.[5]

THE REPORT ON NON–PUBLIC SCHOOLS

The report prepared by Dr. Ross showed that non-public school
enrollments in Connecticut were increasing numerically but that the
percentage of pupils enrolled in the non-public schools of the state
had decreased slightly in recent years. This percentage in 1900 was
15.1; in 1940, 16.4; in 1945, 18.6; in 1950, 18.4; in 1955, 17.0; and

* Since three years' successful public school experience was required for a
permanent certificate, teachers with only non-public school experience could not
obtain one even if they met other requirements.

preliminary figures for 1956 showed a percentage of 17.1. The preliminary 1956 figures showed a public school enrollment of 381,543
and a non-public school enrollment of 78,923.[6]

There were one or more non-public schools in 69 of Connecticut's
169 towns and cities.[7] There were five endowed and incorporated
academies serving as public schools although governed by self-per-
petuating boards of trustees.[8] Roman Catholic parochial schools
were located in 49 of the 69 towns and cities which had non-public
schools.[9] Most parochial school pupils were receiving some public
services.

Twenty-eight towns, enrolling more than 20 per cent of the non-
public school pupils of the state, reported that they provided transportation for such pupils.[10] Three of these reports stated that the
bus service was provided if room was available. In two towns, Kil-
lingly and Plainfield, the bus service for non-public school pupils had
been voted at the town meeting.[11]

Twelve towns, enrolling more than 45 per cent of the non-public
school population of the state, reported that they provided instruction in homemaking to non-public school pupils, usually girls in the
seventh and eighth grades. In one town, Bristol, the non-public
school paid for the teacher's services. In Enfield, the instruction was
taken by the non-public school pupils voluntarily after regular
classes. Excluding Bristol and Enfield, these towns also provided instruction in industrial arts to non-public school pupils, usually boys
in the seventh and eighth grades.[12]

Two-thirds of all non-public school pupils in the state were reported to be receiving school health services from either the town
health department or the local board of education. The report commented that there seemed to be no pattern as to which agency
provided health services, either to public or to non-public school
pupils.[13]

No town reported supplying textbooks to non-public school
pupils.[14]

Examination of the basic data gathered for this report revealed
that the non-public school pupils receiving services were all parochial

school pupils. Except for pupils at one Lutheran school in Danbury, all of the non-public school pupils receiving bus service were attending Catholic parochial schools. All of the non-public school pupils receiving health and instructional services were Catholic parochial school pupils. Clearly, the issue of public services for non-public school pupils in Connecticut carried a heavy religious emphasis.

Dr. Ross' report was submitted to the State Board of Education at its meeting on May 9, 1956. It was received by the Board solely as information and not as a suggestion of any policy decision. Indeed, its author had carefully disclaimed any policy implications. He was reporting on information he had gathered, and he stated:

> . . . the existence of any policy, condition or practice to whatever degree does not necessarily make that policy, condition or practice right or wrong, desirable or undesirable. Suggestions or proposals for policy are outside the scope of this study.[15]

There was no suggestion in the Board's discussion of the report that any policy action was necessary, and none was taken. On Mr. Smith's motion, the Board voted to have the report published and distributed to local school boards, non-public school administrators, and other residents of Connecticut.[16] The desirability or the legality of providing public services to non-public school pupils might well have been a question that the State Board felt was better left in the hands of local school boards or the legislature. Indeed, seven months later the Board was to recommend that the legality of such services be clarified by legislative action.[17] However, there was one item in the report that was clearly within the Board's jurisdiction, and that indicated a violation of a State statute, but no official recognition was taken of it.

Connecticut law required public schools to be in actual session 180 days each year.[18] Children attending non-public schools were to receive "equivalent instruction during such hours and terms in the studies taught in the public schools." [19] Of the 234 non-public schools reporting, 35 reported a shorter school year than 180 days.[20] These were not parochial schools but boarding schools. The 180-day school year is a requirement maintained with strictness for public schools, and the State Board of Education must pass on each exception granted for unavoidable emergencies. At the May 9 meeting the Board was called on to approve shortened school years for eleven towns hit particularly hard by August flood and winter blizzard.[21] The State Board of Education, charged with "general supervision of the educational interests of the state,"[22] and its agency, the State Department of Education, were not moved to respond to reports that Connecticut children in 35 non-public schools were not complying with state law. This is indicative of the sometimes distant and cautious relations between public education officials and the non-public schools. Throughout the public debate and the legislative struggle that were to follow the publication of the report on the relationship of public and non-public schools, public education officials were to be conspicuous by their silence.

While the State Board of Education was noncommittal and public education officials were silent or guarded in their remarks, public interest began to be reflected in the letters published in the newspapers.

"The Voice of the People"

There was no editorial comment in the Hartford newspapers on the report submitted to the State Board of Education. This editorial silence was probably a product of division within the newspaper managements and apprehension about the strong division of opinion among the readers.[23] Comments about the issues involved were presented in letters-to-the-editor columns. The letters were evenly divided, pro and con, suggesting editorial selection to demonstrate the neutrality of the newspapers.

Letters in favor of public services for non-public school pupils embodied such arguments as: Religious schools are a part of the American tradition; in the early eighteenth century Protestant religious schools were supported by public funds; the purpose of the First Amendment was merely to prevent the national government from imposing *one* religion on the people of the nation; the First Amendment does not prohibit the states form assisting in the religious education of children; denial of health and transportation services to independent schools is discrimination; parents of children in non-public schools pay their share of taxes; independent schools save taxpayers millions of dollars in the operation of public schools; limited aid to independent schools is not a threat to public education; the services of independent schools, performed without expense to the community, are the only safeguard against financial chaos in our education system; and the Committee for the White House Conference on Education recommended that children in independent schools should receive all the medical, nursing, dental, and body-building care that is now given to children attending public schools.[24]

One letter written in opposition quoted a resolution of the American Jewish Congress. This resolution referred to the principle of separation of church and state as one of the foundations of American democracy and stated that religious education was the exclusive responsibility of the home, the church, and the synagogue. Therefore, the American Jewish Congress expressed its opposition to religious education in the public schools in any guise and explicitly opposed released-time and dismissed-time religious education programs. The resolution quoted in the letter also opposed any government aid for religious education, directly or indirectly. However, the resolution favored "the granting of genuine welfare benefits, such as medical and dental care and hot lunches to all children in whatever schools they attend, public, private or parochial, but we consider transportation to schools, textbooks and school supplies as educational and not welfare services." [25]

Another letter quoted the opinion of the Supreme Court in the *Zorach* case to state that "a government may not finance religious groups nor undertake religious instruction nor blend secular and sectarian education, nor use secular institutions to force one or some religion on any person." The letter writer observed that the constitutionality of financial assistance from tax funds for parochial schools had never been decided by Connecticut's Supreme Court of Errors. He advised, therefore, that expenditure from public funds for any assistance to parochial and independent schools should await a decision by that Court.[26]

These arguments were to be repeated as the debate proceeded. The child-benefit theory and the *Everson* decision were to be used frequently by those pressing for services. Opponents rejected the child-benefit theory and sometimes pointed out that the *Everson* decision was supported by only a bare majority of the Supreme Court.

The School Board Member and Non-Public Schools

Two conflicting viewpoints about the responsibilities of a board of education member were made public on June 21, 1956, when the *Catholic Transcript,* the official newspaper of the Hartford Archdiocese, published an exchange of letters between Sigmund Adler, member of the Rocky Hill board of Education, and State Board member Richard Joyce Smith. Their dispute grew out of a speech by Mr. Smith at the annual meeting in April of the Connecticut Association of Independent Schools.

The Smith speech contained detailed recommendations for policies on public services to non-public school pupils and public assistance to non-public schools. The speech was delivered prior to the submission of Dr. Ross' report to the State Board of Education in May. Although he had recommended that study as a possible basis for policy making by the State Board of Education, Mr. Smith's proposals made it clear that it was not always necessary to have all the facts before one reached a conclusion on policy. This was not unusual in the debate that was getting under way. A good many people on both sides had their minds already made up, presumably on the basis of what they would call principle, and the facts they later obtained served only to fortify a predetermined conclusion.

Mr. Smith began his case for services to non-public school pupils by relying on the child-benefit theory as enunciated by the United

States Supreme Court, and on the recommendation of the Committee for the White House Conference on Education. But, as he proceeded to expand his recommended list of public services and assistance, the child-benefit theory became subsidiary. The basis of the latter part of his argument appeared to be that these schools should be publicly aided because they were performing a public purpose.

What kind of aid should be given, Mr. Smith asked, to independent schools? He gave the answer to his question in several parts. Most generally accepted were health and welfare services, as suggested by the Committee for the White House Conference on Education. Among such services Mr. Smith included physical examinations by a school doctor, school nurse services, dental examinations, hot lunches, athletic facilities, and services of physical education teachers. Presumably Mr. Smith intended that the teachers would be on the faculty of the non-public school but would be paid by public funds. So, too, athletic facilities would be established on the grounds of the non-public school at public expense.

Where the size of the independent school justified it, Mr. Smith said that public funds could provide for remedial reading, psychological testing, and guidance services.

Moving on, Mr. Smith declared that every town and city should be required to provide transportation where feasible and desirable. He would exclude bus service to a handful of scattered children attending a small private kindergarten, for example, as not a feasible service. However, pupils of a large private or parochial school which served a reasonably integrated district were deserving of the same bus service as public school pupils.

Mr. Smith saw many possible patterns for providing free textbooks on standardized subjects to children of independent schools, and he believed that a pattern could be found that would not violate constitutional doctrine or a community's sense of propriety.

The proposal that public funds should be expended for non-public school buildings was usually greeted, Mr. Smith acknowledged, by gasps of surprise. But if the Hopkins Grammar School in

New Haven, a private, endowed academy, the Kingswood School in West Hartford, a private school, or the Roman Catholic Diocese of Bridgeport should undertake to build a high school for several hundred students, thus relieving the city of a substantial educational cost, would it not be reasonable to have the city bear the cost of health rooms, cafeteria, gymnasium, and athletic fields? If it was appropriate for the services to be provided at public expense, should not the state or the community also contribute to the physical plant devoted to supplying those services?

Dissenting in the *Everson* case, Justice Rutledge had protested that if the educational service of a religious school were acknowledged as a public function, he could see no possible basis for denying full public support of private religious schools just as was done for public schools. Mr. Smith developed this line of thought not as a protest but as an assertion of the right of independent schools to public support. He then proceeded to his final point, the payment of tuition. Connecticut law provided, he stated, that a town not maintaining a high school should secure high school opportunities for its children by payment of tuition at public or private high schools in adjacent communities, except schools under ecclesiastical control. Mr. Smith declared that similar treatment could be provided for elementary school opportunities where such were not available. He saw no constitutional barrier to removing the restriction against making public tuition payments for students attending schools under ecclesiastical control.

He was urging recognition of the independent school as an integral part of our educational system, Mr. Smith said. He was confident that a fair, constitutional, legal, and workable program of state aid could be established. The readiness of Connecticut families to spend millions of their own savings on the development of independent schools, he declared, was the only safeguard against financial chaos in our educational system. The fact that aid was given to students of church-related schools could not possibly create divisive religious animosities unless "organized pressure groups" were intent on promoting division.[27]

While Mr. Smith may have been confident that a fair, constitutional, legal, and workable method could be established, he was obviously proposing something more than the two services (textbooks and bus service) passed upon by the Supreme Court. He was urging not one or two services for children but "a program of state aid" for independent schools. The consequence of wide adoption of his proposals would be a vast change in our educational system. These proposals, coupled with his declaration that independent schools were the only safeguard against educational financial chaos, convinced Mr. Smith's opponents that he was campaigning for the diversion of public education funds to private schools.

These radical proposals about the school system by a member of the State Board of Education would seem to have considerable news value, but the daily newspapers paid scant attention. The *Catholic Transcript* complained that the press gave little space in its news columns and none in its editorial columns to Mr. Smith's proposals. In an editorial entitled "The Voice of Reason on a Major Matter," the *Transcript*, which printed Mr. Smith's speech in full, asked that the services of independent schools be recognized. Such schools discharged a substantial part of the community's educational responsibility. The Supreme Court, said the *Transcript* quoting Mr. Smith, had approved the provision of medical, nursing, and dental services and body-building care for non-public school pupils at public expense.[28] The great merit of Mr. Smith's speech was its "direct and objective address to matters too often deliberately ignored." The editorial concluded, "He has spoken with the calm voice of reason— may others do likewise." [29]

The *Transcript* was correct in anticipating that the dispassionate tone of Mr. Smith's address would not be maintained as the discussion of this issue proceeded. Opponents would argue that such proposals constituted an attack on the public schools and a violation of church-state separation, and would make similar statements in strong terms. The replies to these charges were to be insistent, indignant, and passionate. In succeeding months the comments of the *Transcript* itself became increasingly strident and aggressive. There could be little doubt that this was a religious division; animosities quickly became apparent.

It was not "an organized pressure group," as Mr. Smith had predicted, but a Rocky Hill school board member, Sigmund Adler, who felt obliged to challenge his proposals. Mr. Adler wrote a personal letter to Mr. Smith expressing "real concern" that a State Board of Education member was pleading the cause of non-public schools by suggesting that public money be appropriated to them.

Mr. Adler, like Mr. Smith, could discuss this issue out of long experience in public education. He had been on the faculty of Hartford High School for twenty-five years, serving as a teacher and as Dean of Boys. He was a founder of the Connecticut Vocational Guidance Association and had served as legislative chairman for the Parent-Teachers Association of Connecticut. After his retirement as a teacher, he was elected in 1949 as a Republican member of the Rocky Hill Board of Education. Subsequently he had served also as secretary and as president of the Connecticut Association of Boards of Education. In Rocky Hill he had held the post of park commissioner and other local offices.[30]

In his letter Mr. Adler asserted that the State Board of Education was concerned by law solely with the public schools. He also asserted that the non-public school was selective and therefore undemocratic. Any religious division of our people was, Mr. Adler wrote:

> . . . un-Christian and un-democratic. The most devisive force in society is religion—and here you are, a member of a body that has in its charge the most democratic institution this or any other country knows, pleading to divert public money to institutions whose fundamental tenet is division.

The function of the State Board of Education was to urge adequate financing of the public schools; yet Mr. Smith, charged Mr. Adler, was seeking to divert public school money to non-public schools. Mr. Adler wrote that no sane person would restrict one's right to send his child to the school of his choice. However, if the non-public schools found their burden too great, the remedy available to them was to increase their tuition or to reduce the number of their students. He also charged that "most of these non-public schools now return to the public school those with whom they can do nothing." The oath of a State Board member, like that of a member of a local board of education, he said, was to work in the interest of the public schools.

In his reply Mr. Smith rejected the contention that a State Board of Education member had no relationship to the non-public schools. The function of the State Board was to attend to the educational interests of the state, and this required recognition of the substantial service of independent schools to education in Connecticut. This function also required the Board to examine the appropriate measures to be taken by the state or communities "to provide aid in limited spheres to the large number of Connecticut children now attending those [independent] schools." Mr. Smith challenged the assertion that religion was a divisive force. Division was a word coined by those "who would like to suppress private and parochial schools and establish a single standardized lock-step system of state schools which all children would be compelled to attend." Divisiveness and disunity would arise only if the "enemies of religion foment it."

Mr. Smith said he was not urging the diversion of money needed for public schools to non-public schools. He had for many years advocated increased appropriations for the public schools. His interest was in limited aid for Connecticut children attending private and parochial schools. The partnership of the private and public schools, Mr. Smith said, "should be reflected in the fiscal policies of our state and local governments." In conclusion, he declared he was quite aware of his public responsibilities and Mr. Adler's attempt to define them was "gratuitous and entirely inaccurate." [31] *

Mr. Adler amplified his views on the question of public services

---

* The *Transcript* prefaced the letters with the statement that they were "made public today." Mr. Adler wrote to Mr. Smith privately and did not intend his letter for publication. The *Transcript* did not ask Mr. Adler's permission before publishing his letter. (Interview with Sigmund Adler.)

for non-public schools in a speech at the meeting of the Connecticut Conference of Congregational Christian Churches on October 3, 1956, in Torrington. He argued there that a government of free people must provide education for all of its people; that it is the right of every citizen to send his children to the school of his choice if the school meets the standards of the society in which it exists; and that parents who make this choice should pay all necessary expenses for that non-public school education. Every public dollar used for private schools, he said, meant less money for public schools. Public support for non-public schools, he declared, was not sought by the private (nonsectarian) school but by the Catholic school. The one great aim of the Catholic Church in the establishment of its schools, he stated, was the propagation of its own doctrines. Those who opposed public funds for parochial schools were subjected to name-calling attacks and appeals by Catholic newspapers that such opponents be boycotted. If public support were to be granted to religious schools it would come about because the Protestant churches defaulted in their responsibility to oppose such support. He charged that "the Catholic church cannot by its very structure be democratic, therefore, wherever it is in power it cannot permit democracy."

Mr. Adler recommended:

1. Urge your church members to serve on boards of Education.
2. Urge your children to become teachers in our public schools.
3. Quit fault-finding and make your criticisms constructive, for with every unsupported criticism you are playing directly into the hands of the public schools' foes.[32]

Mr. Adler's speech, like Mr. Smith's, received little space in Connecticut's papers. Editors, apparently, wanted to avoid handling this issue.

The presentation of Mr. Smith's views in the *Catholic Transcript* gave the appearance of an endorsement by the Hartford Archdiocese. The presentation of Mr. Adler's views at the Connecticut Conference of Congregational Christian Churches seemed to identify that body with his opposition to public services for non-public school pupils. The public expressions of most Protestants (with only a few exceptions) tended, like Mr. Adler's, to be in opposition to services. Conversely, all of the public expressions of Catholics (with one exception) were in support of services, although not necessarily in the terms adopted by Mr. Smith.

The statements of Mr. Smith and Mr. Adler, were, of course, personal views and not the official position of the Catholic or Protestant churches. In a strict sense there probably could not be an official church position on a matter that was political, not religious. This opening salvo, however, pitted Protestant against Catholic. This division on religious lines was to be intensified as the controversy grew.

The Neutrality of Public Education Groups

Public education groups did little as organizations to affect the course of the debate on public services to non-public school pupils. Their internal differences were so strong that the groups could neither support nor oppose proposals for such services.

Since the responsibility for school bus service in Connecticut was always placed on the school board, members of the Connecticut Association of Boards of Education had good reason for special interest in proposals for extending such service to non-public school pupils. A discussion of services for non-public school pupils was placed on the agenda for the Association's annual meeting on September 29, 1956, in Northford. This was but one of a list of topics, and not all of the discussion groups at the meeting considered the subject of services. The few groups which did discuss this subject were, except for a few voices, opposed to providing such services. The public school board, it was said, was concerned only with the public schools. One group adopted a resolution stating that the cost of such services should not be charged against the public school budget and such services should be administered by some public agency other than the board of education.[33] In contrast, the president of the association, Harold Murphy of Portland, speaking as an individual, was later to make a public statement in favor of services.[34]

As public attention to this subject increased, some officials of the school board association discussed whether their organization should take any action on this issue. They agreed that feeling within the association was too strong and too divided to attempt to set a policy. The Connecticut Association of Boards of Education, therefore, took no position on the proposals for public services to non-public school pupils.[35]

The Connecticut Education Association, a professional organization of about 15,000 teachers and school administrators, took an active interest in almost all educational measures before the General Assembly. On the most controversial issue of the 1957 legislative session, the auxiliary services proposal, the Association took no stand.

The Parent-Teachers Association of Connecticut also paid close attention to legislation affecting education. The legislative representative of the Association on one occasion spoke out in opposition to auxiliary services for parochial school pupils. Protests from local affiliates resulted in an announcement by the state executive committee that the Association took no position on the issue.[36]

The Connecticut Citizens for the Public Schools faced a problem similar to that of other public education groups. Their leadership and membership was divided on the issue of auxiliary services. The officers did not try to seek a policy decision for the organization. One of the vice-presidents, Mrs. Ralph C. Lasbury, felt strongly that the organization should not behave as though the issue did not exist. She decided to devote one of the organization's weekly radio discussion programs to the question of public services for non-public school pupils.

Mrs. Lasbury, Republican and Protestant, was active in various civic and educational activities in Connecticut. She was the wife of a successful tobacco grower, and her children had attended both public and (non-parochial) private schools. Her opposition to public services for parochial schools had developed in part because of experiences in her own town, South Windsor. A released-time religious education program had been a very disturbing factor in the school program. Her daughter, who did not take part in the program, reported that the pupils who stayed in school just whiled away the time with nonsense. The teacher gave them no work. For a while, at the insistence of the local priest, the Catholic children were taken out of public school classes at ten o'clock Wednesday mornings for their religious education. After a number of protests to the members of the school board, the time was changed to two o'clock Wednesday afternoon.

Mrs. Lasbury felt that the extension of public bus service to non-public schools would cut into the support of public schools. Health services, however, might well be provided to all pupils by the health department. Her town would not be able to operate a public high school economically if half of the children were drawn off to a parochial school, she thought. It just didn't make sense for a small town to have two schools. Further, the children of the town would be divided along religious lines since their activities would center around the different schools.[37]

The whole issue, Mrs. Lasbury believed, was not receiving adequate public debate. The subject was complex and explosive, and people seemed to avoid talking of it. She decided a calm public discussion of both sides of the question would be useful. She scheduled this discussion for the radio program on December 2, 1956. To speak in favor of services she invited the Reverend Joseph V. King, Superintendent of Schools for the Catholic Diocese of Norwich, and John Daly, member of the Hartford Board of Education. Speaking in opposition were Leo Parskey, Deputy Mayor of Hartford and City Council member, and Gaylord Paine, member of the South Windsor Board of Education. The program was moderated by Robert Hoskins, member of the Windsor school board and former president of the Connecticut Association of Boards of Education.

There were no new arguments presented in this discussion. The major arguments were presented effectively, without heat or bitterness. It was shown that the topic could be debated without vituperation.

The question, Father King said, was not whether towns could appropriate funds to support activities of schools, but rather whether services would be extended equally to all school children. Mr. Paine said public funds could not properly be expended directly or indirectly to aid private or parochial schools. Public funds could not be spent for services to private school pupils as pupils. Mr. Daly replied that for many years health services, instructional services, and group testing had been made available to pupils in the Hartford parochial schools. Mr. Parskey agreed with Mr. Paine. A definition of services was needed. He was most definitely opposed to aid to private schools.

As the discussion proceeded it soon became apparent that there was no opposition to health services at public expense for all children regardless of the school they attended. The differences of opinion on bus service were not resolved. Father King contended that, since the state compelled a child to attend school and recognized his right to attend any school that fulfilled state requirements, the child's parents had a right to share some of the tax money which they paid to protect the child on his way to a parochial school. It was a deprivation to say that a child had the right to attend a non-public school and then, by refusing him transportation service, to make the exercise of that right so burdensome or so onerous as to be unattainable. Mr. Paine asked what limit could be put on this definition of service to the child. Could this logic not be extended to include books, teachers, and all other educational services? Mr. Parskey said that a child on a school bus was a pupil and, therefore, school bus service must be regarded as an educational service. He had children in private schools and didn't expect them to be carried at public expense.

Mr. Hoskins interjected to ask if Father King thought that the acceptance of the principle of bus service for parochial school children would lead to requests for additional services. Father King replied that direct support for parochial schools would never be asked for. What we are asking for, said Father King, is service for children. To provide services to public school children and deny them to parochial school children was to discriminate against parents exercising a legal right and acting in accordance with their religious convictions. Mr. Daly added that it was proper that health and welfare services should be extended to all school children. Certainly no request should be expected or granted for public assistance with salaries or direct support of non-public schools.[38]

The discussion ended with the group divided on the question of bus service for parochial school children. The program provided information about the issue and illustrated again the difficulty of voluntary groups in public education. The Connecticut Citizens for Public Schools as an organization could present both sides of the issue, but it could not draw a conclusion. It could not reach a policy decision. On the question of public services for non-public school pupils, the organization took no stand.

A NEW COMMISSIONER OF EDUCATION

While the debate about public services for parochial school pupils was beginning, a parallel conflict developed over the choice of a new commissioner of education. This conflict did not involve public services for parochial school pupils, but it had the appearance of a Protestant-Catholic division. At the March, 1956, meeting of the State Board of Education, Dr. F. E. Engleman submitted his resignation (effective in September) to accept a position as executive secretary of the American Association of School Administrators. The State Board of Education immediately undertook a search for his successor.[39]

The religious division on the Board was implied in a speculative news story in the *West Hartford News* on May 17, 1956. The story predicted a four-to-four split in the Board over a choice between Deputy Commissioner of Education William H. Flaharty and William J. Sanders, Springfield (Massachusetts) Superintendent of Schools. The news story further guessed that the tie would be broken in favor of Dr. Flaharty by the Board Chairman, Mrs. Dorothy S. Hutton. The story commented that this would be another defeat for Board member Richard Joyce Smith, whose "recent controversial proposal that public funds be allocated for private school books, tuition and health services, raised eyebrows and hackles of educators and lay people throughout the state." Returning to conjecture, the story said: "Mr. Smith's camp is said also to favor the selection of Dr. Raymond Fay, present Director of Administrative Services in the State Department of Education as the new Deputy Commissioner," while the majority of five was said to be opposed to this choice. Since Mr. Smith, Dr. Sanders, and Dr. Fay were Catholics, while Mrs. Hutton, Dr. Flaharty, and "the majority" were non-Catholics, the implied religious division was clear. The story concluded, "At times the [Board] majority has felt that it was up against a determined effort to inject what they call an 'authoritarian' point of view in state educational practices." [40]

The *West Hartford News* was wrong in its prediction. At the end of May the State Board of Education chose Dr. William J. Sanders as its new secretary and Commissioner. The ballot was secret; no official vote was recorded except the unanimous one, made apparently after the choice of the majority was learned.[41]

The only other public reference, specific or indirect, to the religious affiliation of the new Commissioner of Education was contained in a resolution of the Connecticut Council of Churches. This resolution, distributed in January, 1957, included (among other statements about the church-state-school situation in Connecticut) the remark, "For the first time in recalled history the State Commissioner of Education belongs to the prominent Church which rejects the principle of Church and State separation." The Council's statement commented that the Province of Quebec had two boards of education divided on religious lines, both tax-supported. The Council asked, "Is this the median step toward which we are approaching in Connecticut?" [42]

THE STATE BOARD ASKS
FOR CLARIFICATION

The debate about public services for non-public school pupils was accelerated at the November 7, 1956, meeting of the State Board of Education. Board member Richard Joyce Smith asked that the staff of the State Department of Education make a study of Connecticut laws and report what amendments were needed to make such services legal. In support of his request, he pointed out that many Connecticut towns were providing services while other towns had refused requests. There was, he contended, great uncertainty about the meaning of the statutes.

This contention was to be repeated by Mr. Smith and others many times in the ensuing months, but little support was to be presented. Little could be presented. Five legal opinions by town counsels were on file with the State Department of Education on the question of public transportation for non-public school pupils. Four of these opinions declared such service illegal under Connecticut law. One counsel had advised that he could not "find anything illegal" about such service. The uncertainty about extending these services was caused not so much by doubt about the statutes as by differences of policy or constitutional interpretation.

In accordance with Mr. Smith's request, the State Board Chairman, Mrs. Hutton, directed the Board Secretary, Commissioner Sanders, to have such a report prepared.[43]

The week of the Board meeting an article by Mr. Smith was published in *America, The National Catholic Weekly Review*. It was the featured article, and the cover page carried the title "Aid for Our Schools." Mr. Smith treated aid and services as of the same piece in this article, which, more exactly than the cover headline, was entitled "Aid to Private and Parochial Schools." [44] * The substance of the article proved that title correct. Mr. Smith's article was a detailed argument for aid to schools and was much the same case that he had presented in April in his speech at the convention of the Connecticut Association of Independent Schools. It was based more on the principle of the public purpose of non-public schools than on the child-benefit doctrine.

* The Hartford newspapers were later to be severely criticized by the *Catholic Transcript* and some Catholic spokesmen for similar headlines. Proposals for service were described in news stories as aid for schools. The *Trancript* described the failure to make this distinction between services for children and aid for schools as distortion and prejudice.

The State of Connecticut was giving increased support to public schools and providing many special services to public school pupils, Mr. Smith wrote. In the light of such attractions it was miraculous, he thought, that non-public school enrollment was increasing. A slight increase in community services for non-public school pupils "would induce more families to shift their children from public to private schools." The demand for non-public school education, said Mr. Smith, came chiefly from Catholic families seeking "to integrate religious training with the education of their children." It was probable that a majority of Connecticut's population was Catholic, and the demand for parochial schools was bound to increase. Furthermore, other religious groups promoted parochial schools, and there was an increased interest in private school education apart from religious considerations.

He cited the *Everson*, *Cochran*, and *McCollum* cases and stated that the latter was no limitation on "community aid in non-religious spheres." He asked that the non-public school child be accorded the same treatment as the public school child in matters of health and welfare.

Mr. Smith further contended that private school tuition might also be paid out of public funds. The extent of public aid seemed "to be essentially a question of practical policy to be determined" in the community. Explaining this conclusion, he stated explicitly what was probably the strongest apprehension of the supporters of public schools. He wrote:

> If, for instance, a city in Connecticut could avoid the cost of building and operating a new school in one of its districts by contributing a relatively small amount per pupil for the extension of an existing parochial school, the community ought to be allowed that alternative as a matter of economy. Indeed, with taxes going up and the demand for more schools becoming stronger, the utilizing of private and parochial school facilities through some kind of expense-sharing arrangement seems inevitable for many towns and cities in Connecticut.

The solution apparently recommended by Mr. Smith in such a case was not expansion of the public schools but public expenditures to expand the parochial schools. This would be one way of meeting such a problem, which has not yet occurred anywhere in Connecticut, but such a novel method would strike some people and perhaps some judges as a relinquishing of public responsibility for education, as well as supporting "an establishment of religion."

Mr. Smith closed with the hope that existing laws would be clarified so there might be the development of an "integrated educational service that can best serve the particular needs of each community." ("Integrated" seems an inappropriate word here. Some might feel Mr. Smith was arguing for a more varied and more divided educational system.)

This article was reported in the *Catholic Transcript* [45] and in the *Hartford Times* [46] but, significantly, no letters to the editor on this topic were published in the daily newspapers in subsequent weeks. Privately, editors reported [47] that even though they were opposed to services for non-public school pupils, they did not intend to make any editorial comment on the issue. It was, it seemed, too hot.

One weekly newspaper, the *West Hartford News*, did comment. An editorial titled "Mr. Smith Raises His Head Again" asserted that an effort was being made "to force the State Board of Education to adopt a policy which would attempt to impose in every community expenditures of public funds for non-public schooling." Many people, "with a Yankee eye on their tax bill, would go along with Mr. Smith without a thought of the consequences." But such proposals, the editorial said, were "total abandonment of the first premise of American public education"–that public schools must be 100 per cent publicly controlled. Even partial public support of the non-public school program was an expenditure of public funds without representation and without control. To avoid such a violation of the democratic principles of our public school system, the editorial called for explicit prohibition of any public expenditures for non-public school purposes. Those who chose to take advantage of education in non-public schools, the editorial concluded, must accept the full cost of that education. [48]

In accordance with Mr. Smith's request, a proposal to amend Connecticut law to permit public services for non-public school children was presented at the December, 1956, meeting of the State

Board of Education. The proposal, drafted by the staff of the State Department of Education, suggested that the duties of local school boards could be revised to provide that they might extend to any child of compulsory school age in the town attending a local non-public school any of the safety, health, or welfare services provided to public school children. The report observed that there appeared to be no Connecticut court decisions or rulings of the office of the Attorney General stating the exact extent to which present laws permitted towns or local school boards to provide such services.

Mr. Smith spoke favorably of such an amendment and stressed the need for such a law. In opposition, Board member John Alsop of Avon said he believed the matter was not within the domain of the State Board. It was his belief that the Board's concern was with public education. Mr. Alsop proposed a resolution, which the Board adopted, that the Board Chairman, Mrs. Hutton, and the Secretary, Education Commissioner Sanders, be directed to meet with the chairmen of the General Assembly's Committees on Education to explain to them the uncertainty that existed about the meaning of present laws and to suggest that the General Assembly might consider "clarification" of the laws affecting public services to non-public schools.[49] It was to be emphasized that the State Board was not suggesting a decision one way or the other. The Board was asking for a clear statement of the meaning of the law. It was for the General Assembly to say whether the services were to be required, permitted, or prohibited.

Reports of this action of the State Board were carried in the Hartford newspapers, and in other newspapers in Connecticut via the wire services.[50] The major newspapers of the state still refrained from editorial comment and printed no letters to the editor on the subject. However, the *West Hartford News* carried an editorial entitled "Courage in the Board of Education." It stated:

> The State Board was right as rain last week in refusing to seek a change in the state laws involving the use of public funds for non-public schools. The calm head and keen mind of board member John Alsop from Hartford County prevailed over the effort of Richard

Joyce Smith to push forward his archaic idea that public funds should be used legally for broad support of services, facilities and even tuition in non-public schools.[51]

The editorial seemed extravagant in its praise. The action of the State Board might properly have been described as cautious rather than courageous. The Board did not settle the question or take a stand. It concluded that this problem was the responsibility of the legislature, not of the State Board. The board had not "refused to seek a change in the state laws" but had agreed to seek "clarification" of those laws.

The State Board was not alone in passing the issue on to the legislature. In a number of towns with Catholic schools, disputes were occurring over public services to pupils in those schools. In some of these disputes requests for services were being refused. Those who had been seeking services would not accept the local decision as final. They would seek a decision in the legislature.

V:
FOUR
LOCAL
DISPUTES

THE QUESTION of services for non-public school pupils at public expense, the office of the Connecticut Attorney General had ruled in 1952, was one to be considered locally. The report prepared by the State Department of Education in early 1956 showed that a substantial number of towns were providing such services. This report was a statement of practices and statistics; it did not include any information about the conflicts that arose in some towns over the question of providing services.

In the year preceding the 1957 legislative struggle over services for non-public school pupils, a number of towns in Connecticut were faced with the problem of beginning or continuing to provide services. The disputes over that question in four such towns are recounted in this chapter. Two of those towns were asked to begin providing transportation. One town (actually a city) had to decide whether to continue providing transportation after a school board decision that there was no legal authority to do so. One town was faced with the problem of assuming financial responsibility for the dental hygiene services provided to local parochial school pupils.

As presented here, with fictitious names for the municipalities and the participants, these case histories are intended to illuminate the nature of the conflicts about this issue and the methods used locally by proponents and opponents of services at public expense for non-public school pupils.* The populations of these municipalities were approximately 5,000, 15,000, 30,000, and 40,000. In the two smaller places the school boards found that the issue of transportation or health services was complicated by other disputes. In all four places Catholic schools were involved.

The history of these local disputes over auxiliary services shows a clear religious division, although there was also a strong tendency toward a partisan division, with Democrats inclined to favor services and Republicans inclined to oppose them. This tendency, however (like the legislative division on birth control), was produced because Catholics were largely aligned with the Democratic Party and Protestants with the Republican. In the local debates the familiar arguments were employed. The Supreme Court was quoted by each side to support its position. Attitudes toward auxiliary services often seemed to have been predetermined by the debater's attitude toward non-public schools.

All of the arguments appeared subordinate to the division, seldom publicly expressed, of Protestant against Catholic. For many, the conflict over services was but an occasion for religious partisans to exercise their strength in support of, or in opposition to, the Catholic Church.

THE PARKVILLE DISPUTE

Late in May, 1956, the Reverend Albert Daniel, pastor of the Parkville Catholic Church, wrote to the chairman of the Board of

* Much of the information presented in these case studies was obtained through personal interviews with the participants. They found it possible to talk more freely about the controversy if they could be assured that their comments would be presented anonymously. To protect that anonymity, the names of the participants and places have been changed and the figures used have been modified slightly or not given in exact terms. Similarly, sources are cited generally, e.g., Connecticut, *Register and Manual*, 1956, without a page number. The names of local newspapers are fictitious, and dates are omitted from newspaper citations. The chronology of each case study was reviewed and approved for accuracy by the participants interviewed.

Education requesting public transportation for about thirty pupils living more than one mile from the Catholic elementary school which was to be opened in September. Children living more than one mile from the Parkville public elementary schools were given such service. A few weeks later the Board chairman, the Reverend John Paul, pastor of the Parkville Congregational Church, replied to Father Daniel that the school board had voted the previous evening not to provide the requested service.[1]

Parkville is adjacent to one of the larger cities in southwest Connecticut and in 1956 had a population in excess of 30,000.[2] Its foreign-born white population was about 12 per cent.[3] More than 400 pupils, or about 12 per cent of the school-age children, were enrolled in non-puplic schools in the 1955–1956 school year.[4] These schools were not parochial schools. Some health services were provided to these pupils by the local health department. No services were provided to non-public school pupils by the board of education.[5] Like a number of other suburban towns in Connecticut, Parkville was experiencing the problems of an expanding population. Some parts of the town were almost urban in character while other areas remained sparsely settled. Pupils in these sparsely settled areas needed transportation to and from school.[6]

Parkville was a Republican town and there was a Republican majority on the school board. Five members were Republicans, four were Democrats. Four Republicans were Protestant and one was Catholic. One Democrat was Protestant and three were Catholic. Religiously, then, the board was composed of five Protestants (including the chairman, Mr. Paul) and four Catholics.[7]

The board's discussion of Father Daniel's request was begun by member David Coy, a Republican, a lawyer, and a member of Father Daniel's church. Mr. Coy stressed the Supreme Court's decision in the *Everson* case and argued that transportation was a safety service for children, not an aid to the school.[8] The chairman, Mr. Paul, argued against the request, contending that the effect of public bus service would be the promotion of religious education and therefore would be in violation of the principle of separation of church and state. He also said that public funds should be used only for public purposes and that private education should be privately supported. The non-parochial, private schools in Parkville, he pointed out, did not seek public services from the Board of Education.

Mr. Paul commented privately the following year that he had faced a public school problem connected with religion some years earlier. The local clergy at one time had discussed establishing a released-time religious education program in the Parkville public schools. The Catholic priests were in favor of such a program, but the Protestant ministers and Jewish rabbis thought the proposal was just a means of getting around the restrictions of the *McCollum* decision. The program was never begun. The school board, however, did agree to a request by the Catholic clergy to conduct religious education classes in the public schools when school was not in session. The rooms were made available on the same basis as for any other non-profit community activity. Mr. Paul didn't believe that the public school classrooms were really needed. The Catholics had rooms in their churches. It seemed to him to be merely a technique of using the public schools for religious purposes, a means of getting Catholicism into the public schools.

Mr. Paul did not think that religion should be entirely eliminated from the school activities. The Parkville schools conducted Christmas and Easter programs in the school auditoriums during assembly periods, prayers were said in the classrooms at the beginning of the school day, and grace was said at noon in the school cafeteria. There were no Jewish holidays observed in the public schools and no joint Christmas-Hanukkah programs. Mr. Paul didn't feel the minority could be allowed to dominate the majority. Some Jewish parents did object to the use of the name of Jesus in opening prayers or grace. Other than this, there had been no difficulty about religious questions in the Parkville public schools.[9]

Board of Education member Frank Martin joined Mr. Coy in support of Father Daniel's request for bus service. Mr. Martin, a Democrat, was also a member of Father Daniel's church, and he saw no violation of church-state separation in providing public transportation for Catholic school children. This was merely a health and safety service that was being sought. Catholic parents paid taxes and also paid the cost of maintaining their own schools. They were entitled to something for their tax money. Mr. Martin said later in private conversation that he had been a public school teacher, and he believed there should be religion in the public schools. In schools where he had taught there had been a variety of religious presentations at assemblies. The children of the different faiths would present a program based on the teachings of their religion. There was also joint Christmas-Hanukkah observances. At one time he had some Catholic boys in his class who wouldn't participate in the morning Bible reading and prayers. They wouldn't take their turn reading a passage from the King James Bible. Mr. Martin talked to them and persuaded them to give up their opposition. On another occasion he had an atheist boy in his class who wouldn't stand up for the morning prayer. Mr. Martin told the boy that he didn't have to pray, but he would have to stand up out of respect to the rest of the class. Mr. Martin was untroubled by, and apparently unaware of, any limitations established by the United States Supreme Court.

For a time, the three Catholic Democratic members centered their persuasion on the one Democratic Protestant member, but they were not successful.[10] When the vote was taken the four Catholic members voted for granting Father Daniel's request, the four Protestant members voted against it. The tie vote left the decision up to the chairman. Mr Paul voted "nay." Father Daniel's request was denied, five to four.[11]

Reactions to the Parkville Vote

In subsequent weeks Mr. Paul received about twenty-five letters from various parts of the country supporting or opposing his decision. Most of the letters were written, he thought, by eccentrics. Locally, he was asked by the pastor of the Parkville Episcopal Church if he was opposed to parochial schools. Mr. Paul replied that he was not opposed to parochial schools, he was "pro-public schools." He also believed that private schools should be privately supported. Some Catholics in Parkville told him they saw this request for bus service as merely an attempt to build up the new Catholic school at public expense. These Catholics, Mr. Paul thought, were also "pro-public school."

Mr. Paul later said privately that he regarded the development of this issue as a threat to the public schools. Parents with children in parochial or private schools were less inclined, he believed, to support the public schools. With the new Catholic school opening and a Jewish school to be opened soon afterward, Mr. Paul thought Parkville faced the possibility of "fragmentation." [12]

Mr. Martin later commented privately that there was no bitterness on the board about the decision. The differences of opinion were accepted without any antagonisms remaining to affect other decisions of the board. He was told by some Catholics in Parkville after the vote that they were against bus service for the Catholic school pupils.[13]

At masses two weeks after the vote, Father Daniel read the exchange of correspondence between himself and Mr. Paul. He told his parishioners he did not consider this a final answer to the parents of the parochial school students. Many other Connecticut towns were doing what the Parkville school board had been asked to do. Sooner or later the people of Parkville, he believed, would appreciate the fairness of the request. Because of the tremendous expense incurred by the parish in building the school, Father Daniel said, it was impossible to take on the additional cost of transporting the pupils. He concluded with the statement that he was willing to meet with any group of parishioners who wished to discuss the situation.[14]

Reporting the Parkville incident, *The Catholic Transcript* said that the initial enrollment of 200 pupils in the Parkville Catholic school would save the local taxpayers more than $60,000. The anticipated full enrollment of 600 would bring about an annual tax saving of more than $180,000.

Father Daniel believed that the basis of his request for bus service was the protection of the children. He thought parochial school children should receive bus service just as they received school lunch service. Instructional services and recreational services should also be made available to parochial school pupils.

Father Daniel would not seek public school textbooks for his pupils. He sought only bus service at that time. Nor did he think that he could ask for public expenditures for buildings or facilities for the parochial school. It was the policy of the Archdiocese to "go very easy." "We would not be allowed at this stage," he said in March, 1957, "to seek buildings." The more public assistance was accepted, the more public control was likely. "The source of money," he said, "is also the source of power."

Father Daniel was not seeking a released-time religious education program in Parkville even though he "knew" that the schools were at times used for the presentation of Protestantism. If the Protestants were able to get some of their teachings into the schools, he could only say, "More power to them." At least, the public school children were getting some vestiges of religion.

The Board of Education, Father Daniel thought, handled his request in a proper fashion although he disagreed with their decision. It might have been wiser, he felt, for Mr. Paul to have refrained from voting. This would have had the same practical effect as voting against the request, and it would not have appeared that a Protestant minister said "no" to a Catholic priest. Father Daniel was not going to press the issue. He had more at stake in Parkville than just bus service. He was concerned about the general standing of his parish in the community. Parkville, particularly the section where his church was located, was heavily Republican, and these people would be offended by an aggressive Catholic church. Further, many men and women in his parish were married to Protestants. The largest contribution to his building fund had come from a Jew. These were all reasons for not precipitating conflicts, Father Daniel believed, in addition to the fact that "we are Catholics and we should not forget the principles of Pauline charity we profess."

When groups of parishioners approached Father Daniel to "do something" about bus service, he advised them to wait. He did not intend to lead any campaign for bus service although he knew they might start one. It was the old-fashioned method for the priest to lead his people in such matters, but Father Daniel felt that times had changed and an educated parish looked at things differently. He advised his parishioners that the legal situation was indefinite. He hoped for a state policy that would make services to parochial school pupils a matter of local option. Such a decision, he thought, would have to be made by the legislature. It was better, he said, to wait for a decision by the General Assembly.[15]

Conclusions about Parkville

There was no great public stir in Parkville about the issue of bus service for the parochial school pupils. This was due both to Father Daniel's restraint and to the dispatch with which the school board handled the issue. There was no indulgence in personalities, and, although Father Daniel used the pulpit once to report his correspondence with the school board, there was no public pressure exerted on the board.

The Reverend Mr. Paul's deciding vote against bus service was symbolic. The division on the board was on strict religious lines. Five Protestants voted against service and four Catholics voted in favor of it. Four of the five Protestants were Republicans. Three of the four Catholics were Democrats.[16]

Aside from Mr. Coy's citation of the *Everson* case as justification for bus service, the participants in the Parkville dispute seem to have given little attention to the Supreme Court's statements about the principle of separation of church and state and about the child-benefit doctrine. Mr. Paul, in contradiction of the *Cochran* and *Everson* decisions, was opposed to bus service to parochial school students because he regarded it as an expenditure of public funds for a private purpose and as public assistance to religion. Still, ignoring the Court in the *McCollum* decision, he regarded it as proper to conduct Christian religious ceremonies or pageants during public school sessions. He was not opposed to health services for all school children if they were provided by the health department rather than by the Board of Education. For Mr. Paul the child-benefit doctrine was limited to health services, but the principle of separation of church and state did not prohibit use of the public schools to promote Christianity. The interests of the Jews or other non-Christians he dismissed with the assertion that the minority could not be allowed to dominate the majority. One corollary of that assertion might be that the majority need not respect the religious convictions of the minority.

A similar attitude was expressed by Catholic board member Martin. His concept of the relation of religion to public education seemed to be adherance of everyone to the practices of the majority. The atheist must stand with the religionist. The Catholic boy must join the Protestants in reading the King James Bible. It is not surprising that Mr. Martin found in public bus service for parochial school children no conflict with his ideas of the relation of church and state.

Father Daniel, too, seemed to place little or no limitation on the relation of church and state. His immediate aims were restricted to bus service for his pupils, but this was tactical and not a restriction of principle. He was moving slowly for the sake of better community relations, but he placed apparently no limitation on the kinds of public aid that might be given to religious institutions. Nor did he object to the introduction of religion into the classroom. Father Daniel accepted neither the restrictions of the *McCollum* decision nor the definition of separation presented in the *Everson* case.

Bus service was denied to the Parkville Catholic school pupils by five Protestants voting against four Catholics, but Father Daniel looked hopefully for action by the General Assembly.

THE SCHOOL BUS DISPUTE
IN DIAMOND CITY

Diamond City is in the center of Connecticut and in 1956 had a population of more than 40,000.[17] It is an industrial city whose principal manufactures are fine metalwork and jewelry.[18] There is a substantial foreign-born population composed principally of Italians, Poles, and French.[19] These groups had established national Roman Catholic churches and parochial schools,[20] which about 25 per cent of the Diamond City school children were attending in 1956.[21] The people of Diamond City have most frequently voted Democratic in national and state elections, Republican in local elections. In 1953 there was a sweeping victory for the local Democratic Party, which elected a mayor and a large majority on the City Council. These officials were still in office in 1956.[22]

The school board was composed of four Democrats and one member who described himself as an Independent Democrat. The Independent Democrat, John Bernard, was the only Protestant member. One member, Monroe Green, was a Jew. The other three were Catholic.[23]

At the regular meeting of the Diamond City Board of Education in May, 1956, the chairman of the board, Patrick McDowell, asked for the report of the committee which had been studying school transportation. The committee, John Bernard and Mrs. Sally Norris, submitted a report which called on the Diamond City Council to make a special appropriation to provide transportation for private school pupils. The report, which was adopted by the Board, said that the school budget was prepared in accordance with the Board's stated policy of providing transportation to eligible students to the nearest public school. It had been the practice for many years for school bus drivers voluntarily to pick up some of the most distant non-public school students and carry them to the public school nearest the non-public school of their choice. The statement pointed out that this unwritten policy was followed even though state law did not permit public school funds to be used for the transportation of children to a pri-

vate school. With an increasing number of public school students requiring bus service, it would be impossible to continue this unwritten
policy after the school year ending June, 1956. The school board expressed its sympathy for the parents of non-public school children
who faced the problem of getting their children to such schools but
declared that it had neither the responsibility nor the authority to
solve the problem. It was suggested that the City Council might
handle the matter by making a special appropriation for bus service
for non-public school children. The City Council could make such
an appropriation; the Board could not.

The school board adopted this statement of policy unanimously.
A few residents of Diamond City who had read in the newspaper
that this problem was to be discussed were in the audience. One
resident rose, after the Board's action, to state that many parochial
school children would be transferred to the public schools. It was
now his intention, he said, to transfer his children, and he would urge
other Catholic parents to do the same, because, he said, "we pay
taxes." The chairman of the Board commented that arrangements
would have to be made for all pupils attending public schools. The
law was clear that the school board had no responsibility or authority
for the transportation of children to private schools.

A woman rose to say that she spoke for parents of parochial school
pupils. This action of the school board, she said, would mean that
"we have no bus service at all. We pay for parochial schools and for
Sisters." She did not see why the school board could not help parents
of parochial school pupils since those parents helped the Board by
paying for their own schools and their own teachers. Another member of the audience asked if the Board could not explain to the City
Council if more funds were needed for this bus service.

The audience did not seem to understand that the Board of
Education was questioning its own authority to provide bus service
to parochial school pupils. The Board had concluded that it could not
on its own authority spend public school funds for any but public
school pupils.[24]

The action of the school board was headlined on the front page of the local newspapers the next day. For the rest of the week, however, there was no published comment about that action. There were no "reaction" stories from public figures, no editorial comment, and no letters to the editor. The Board had acted on a Monday night. There was no public response beyond the comments at the Board meeting until the following Sunday.

The Reaction of the Catholic Clergy

A direct appeal to the Catholics of Diamond City for political action was made by the Catholic clergy on the Sunday following the school board decision to end bus service for parochial school pupils. A protest read at all services in the nine Catholic churches said it was the clergy's duty to object to ending of "services to non-public schools." These services were "inherent rights of the children, not privileges." The Supreme Court had ruled bus service was constitutional, and the White House Conference on Education had recommended that such service be given. To deny this service would be discrimination, the statement contended. Noting the social, spiritual, and financial contributions made by the parochial schools, the statement estimated that their value to the state was more than seventy-five million dollars.

Catholic lay groups were urged to know and to protect the rights of children. It was time, the statement declared, to unite forces against any attempt to lessen the dignity of Catholic school pupils. The support and encouragement of the Catholic clergy was pledged to any orderly activity to secure legitimate services. Catholics were called upon to support both church and civic representatives in their conscientious efforts "to supply proper educational facilities" to the children of Diamond City.

In an explanation of the purposes of the statement, Monsignor Thomas Bradley said in a newspaper statement [25] that it was intended to:

1. Express the rights of all children to restricted transportation to all non-profit private or parochial schools and the duty of citizens to establish and protect this right.

2. Urge groups to await an orderly solution to any difficulties expressed by a sympathetic Board of Education.
3. Enlist the interest and prayers of the people to assist administrators of all schools in their conscientious efforts to supply proper educational facilities to the children of Diamond City.

Monsignor Bradley said he was sure everyone would work calmly for a city of ideal relations among the various groups. He praised the school board for calling attention to problems which might upset "the generous precedents of the city as regards reasonable transportation and welfare of children no matter what their race or creed."

The tone of these statements to the Diamond City Catholics was determined but restrained. A different tone was expressed by Father Brendon Baker in a sermon delivered as "An Answer to the Decision of the Board of Education." Father Baker's sermon was not solely for the guidance of his parishioners. A copy of it was sent to the office of the *Diamond City Star*, the daily newspaper.

Father Baker declared that Diamond City was a battlefield where the "Catholic Church and the various institutions of learning under her control are being attacked." The attack was being made in a manner "so effectively used by the arch-enemy of the free world—the Communists—and that is by a cold war." Father Baker quoted the Gospel of Saint Luke:

> They will lay their hand on you, and persecute you, delivering you up to the synagogues and into prisons, dragging you before kings and governors, for my name's sake.

Still quoting Christ, he said, "And you shall be betrayed by your parents and brethren, and kinsmen and friends." These stinging and prophetic words had been fulfilled in the past week, he charged. The seeds of persecution were being sown by the members of the school board. "Persecution" was too mild a word, said Father Baker; this action was segregation, denying parochial school children the same transportation benefits enjoyed by public school children. The school board evidently regarded public school children as more worthy of protection from highway hazards than parochial school children.

"They have manifested ignorance of the Constitution of the United States which clearly states that 'All men are created equal' [sic]."

The sum involved, said Father Baker, was a mere pittance, less than $2500 in a total transportation budget of more than $50,000. This revealed the Board's parsimony and its disregard of the fact that parents of parochial school pupils were taxpayers. The Board members must have been motivated by something other than monetary considerations, he asserted. They declared themselves sympathetic, but they had displayed no sympathy. Their real motivation was not compassion but persecution. The prophecy of betrayal also had been fulfilled at that meeting because members of the Board "who are our brethren," instead of defending Catholic institutions and Catholic children, "failed us." Why were they so afraid, he asked, to stand up for true principles?

The case would be reopened, Father Baker proclaimed, and it was his earnest desire that the laity would prove "more militant than those who misrepresent us on the Board." He concluded:

> You may be assured that the Catholic clergy of Diamond City will not leave a stone unturned until a reversal of this decision has been made. We shall be your leaders and we expect that you will unflinchingly follow our leadership.[26]

When Catholic Democrat Patrick McDowell, school board chairman, heard of the sermon, he flinched. A reporter for the *Diamond City Star* telephoned to get his reaction. Mr. McDowell had no comment. He later explained that he did not want to get into a public debate with Father Baker. If the priest wanted to debate a political question, McDowell thought, he should come into the political arena and not climb up into the pulpit. He had no right to use his position as a priest to hurl a diatribe at the members of the Board of Education. Further, Father Baker completely misunderstood the Board's action. The Board had not opposed bus service for parochial school pupils. It had simply declared that it did not have the legal authority to appropriate money from its budget for such service.

Mr. McDowell was deeply disturbed by Father Baker's sermon.

He discussed it with his own pastor and came to the conclusion that he should make no public reply.[27] Other officials of various faiths were offended by Father Baker's action, but no public objection was made.[28] No one could bring himself to criticize a clergyman publicly.

Comment of Public Officials and the Press

Following the action of the Catholic clergy, Mayor Anthony Carmello, Democrat and Catholic, announced that there was no question in his mind that the city had a moral obligation to give bus service to parochial school pupils. He asked the city's legal adviser to study the question and to prepare an opinion on the legality of such service.[29]

City Councilman Joseph Alza, Catholic and Democrat, announced he would present a resolution to the Council directing the school board to give non-profit private school pupils the same bus service given public school pupils.[30] Since the City Council had no legal authority to control such action by the school board, Alza's resolution seemed merely a device to stir up public feelings and so influence the Board to reverse itself.

Seeking an authoritative statement on the legality of the contended service, the *Diamond City Star* questioned the State Department of Education. The Department replied that the state Attorney General had ruled that local school boards should address such questions to their town counsel.[31] In the issue carrying this story, the *Star* asked editorially that the possible bitter controversy about this issue not be allowed to develop. A long-standing practice, the editorial stated, should be allowed to continue. The small cost could be met by a special appropriation separate from the school budget. The tax relief provided by the parochial schools and the dual burden for public and parochial schools borne by Catholic parents should not be forgotten. The editorial suggested that the Alza resolution be redrawn to substitute "parochial schools" for the words "non-profit, private schools." The editorial said it was conceivable that sometime a non-profit private school might be started in Diamond City. The editorial writer, like many another proponent of services for parochial school pupils, was concerned not only about the need of the child but about the nature of the school as well. The editorial concluded that there was no need for hasty action since the Board of Education would not take up the question again until September.[32]

The other newspaper in Diamond City, *The Chronicle*, observed editorially that the state authorities had "tossed the hot potato back into local laps." There was need for a legal opinion, and no action should be taken by the City Council, the editorial said, until legal advice was obtained. The editorial expressed grave doubts that the Council had any legal authority to give instructions to the school board as called for in the resolution of Councilman Alza. Doubt was also expressed that the jurisdiction of the Board of Education extended beyond public schools and public school pupils. The health, safety, and welfare service to all school children in Diamond City might better be handled by some other agency than the Board of Education, the editorial declared. The school board could direct a child to attend a particular public school, but, the editorial noted, a parochial school child could elect to attend any of the six parochial schools anywhere in town. Was the Board of Education obliged to give bus service to the parochial school of the pupil's choice? Some definition was needed, too, of the words, "non-profit, private school pupils." The editorial concluded that the "hot potato" should not be seized without the proper tools and good sense.[33]

Both newspapers showed appreciation of the heated nature of the issue and the legal difficulties. Neither editorial mentioned the principle of the separation of church and state. Both editorials were favorably disposed toward continuing bus service to parochial school pupils, and both asked for dispassionate discussion of the problem.

A Protestant Response

The Sunday following Father Baker's attack on the Board of Education, a sermon on the school bus issue was delivered by the Reverend Walter Esty, minister of the Diamond City Congregational

Church. Mr. Esty called on everyone to consider the problem objectively and to display respect for the opinions of others. There was nothing to be gained, he said, by losing one's temper or by acrimonious statements. It was his purpose to present some facts so that "as citizens and as Protestant Christians we may be better able" to discuss the problem with friends and neighbors and make judgments.

The Roman Church, Mr. Esty said, considered the education of the child incomplete without the element of religious faith. The complete education of the child was accomplished by the home, the church, and the parochial school working in close harmony. The public school could not enjoy that close relationship, nor could it teach *sectarian* beliefs. Yet it was the task of education as a whole "to transmit and develop the nation's entire cultural heritage, including not only the arts, sciences and skills, but the concepts of religion as well." Our system of government was based, Mr. Esty said, on religious principles. The task of education was to prepare children for democratic citizenship. If they were not taught the religious principles on which our democracy rested, were they prepared to be responsible citizens? The public schools, following the principle of separation of church and state, had held that it was the duty of the home and of the church to teach those religious principles. Mr. Esty stated that the Roman Catholic Church did not endorse the principle of separation of church and state. (In later comment Mr. Esty expressed his own belief in that principle but contradicted himself by calling for religion in the public schools.) The Roman Catholic Church could adjust to situations (as in America) where it was not the established state church. However, problems did arise as to the meaning and intent of the principle of church-state separation. The Roman Catholic bishops of the United States in 1952, Mr. Esty said, had announced that they were content to seek only auxiliary aid "from funds provided by public money for the support of parochial schools and only as may be permitted under Supreme Court decisions." *

* Mr. Esty did not give the full import of the bishop's statement. In their 1952 statement the bishops contended that the First Amendment did not prohibit the federal government "from encouraging and even aiding religion, so long

The use of public funds for direct or indirect support of private and parochial schools was more than a sectarian concern, Mr. Esty said. It was more than a legal or constitutional concern. It affected the cultural pattern of the community. It was always a tragedy, he said, when the cultural development of children became segmented and divided.

The problem of bus service, Mr. Esty stated, was one to be solved locally, and the first proper step was to secure the legal opinion of the City Attorney. Meanwhile, he suggested ten specific responsibilities for all citizens:

1. To realize that training of our youth in the moral and ethical values of religion was a major educational problem of our times.
2. To remember that the principle of separation of church and state in education was a nationwide problem to be worked out on the state and local level.
3. To remember that the outcome of this legal question rested with the Supreme Court of the United States.*
4. The Protestant who did not believe in private or parochial schools for himself must respect the right of others to have such schools if they so chose.
5. Intelligent determination must be made of the distinction between legitimate assistance to citizens' welfare and support of sectarian interests. School lunches and medical and health care were generally given to both public and parochial schools. Issues in question were bus service, textbooks, supplies, and other indirect aid.†

---

as no particular form of religion should be established by the state." The bishops also contended that recognition should be given to the importance of religion in public education. They were contending for more than auxiliary services. They declared that the state had the duty of helping the parent provide religious instruction and training for the child. This position, of course, had been rejected by the Supreme Court in the *Everson, McCollum,* and *Zorach* cases. (See above Chapter II.) It was also questioned by the Reverend John Courtney Murray, S.J., and others. See above, pp. 23–26.

* Mr. Esty ignored the apparent contradiction between his second and third points. Is the interpretation of the principle of separation of church and state to be made by the Supreme Court, or by each state, or by each community? Was he recommending that predominantly Protestant communities should adhere to one interpretation and predominantly Catholic communities to another? Is not the religious freedom of a citizen of the United States the same under the Constitution regardless of where he lives in the country?

† Obviously, Mr. Esty was not accepting the *Cochran* and *Everson* decisions as having settled the question of school books or transportation.

6. We must not stoop to bigotry or close the door on sanity and cooperation.

7. We must be cooperative, but we must not be coerced or persuaded to compromise the principle of separation of church and state.

8. We must fully support our public schools, as they are the foundation of our democratic institutions.

9. We must work to supplement and improve the religious aspects of the public schools.

10. Some plan of released-time religious education for public school children should be instituted consistent with legal decisions.*

Mr. Esty concluded that all of these responsibilities and problems constituted a challenge to the Protestant churches and Protestant homes to maintain a democratic way of life "in which diversity contributes not division but dynamic strength, where the deepest differences are respected because they have been considered together and are understood."

Mr. Esty began his list of responsibilities with the assertion that the religious training of our youth was one of our major educational problems. It is noteworthy that his list did not include any recommendation that this problem might receive greater attention of the clergy, who presumably had a primary responsibility for such matters. However, despite its omissions, evasions, and contradictions, Mr. Esty's sermon was well received. This sermon, like Father Baker's, was printed in full in the *Diamond City Star*. The Star described it as "setting forth the issues together with a plea for understanding and an objective, unemotional approach to the problem." School board chairman Patrick McDowell, one of the targets of Father Baker's sermon, thought Mr. Esty was exercising his duties as a clergyman correctly. His sermon was a model which other clergymen would do well to follow. Another board member, Monroe Green, a Democrat

---

* Mr. Esty offered no distinction between cooperation and compromise. To some people, support of public transportation for parochial school pupils would be cooperation. To others, it would be a compromise of the church-state separation principle. He seemed to be agreeing with the 1952 statement of the bishops that the public schools or some public agency should assist in the religious training of children. Of course, if Mr. Esty had limited himself to a plea for a released-time program, the *Zorach* decision offered adequate judicial support.

and a Jew, regarded this sermon as a proper expression for a minister. (Mr. Green had thought Father Baker's sermon "disgusting.") Protestant Board member John Bernard felt that Mr. Esty's sermon was "off base." Mr. Bernard did not agree with his plea to use the schools for religious purposes. He thought clergymen would do better not to discuss any political issue in the pulpit.[34]

The City Council Acts

Shortly after the Catholic clergy had protested the school board's new policy denying public bus service to parochial school pupils, Board chairman McDowell announced that he was willing to meet with the City Council to seek a solution to the problem. He was disturbed that so many seemed to misunderstand the cause of the school board's action. In asking to meet with the City Council, he said that there was no question in his mind, as a lawyer and a citizen, that pupils of local non-profit private schools were entitled to public bus service. He was also sure that the school board, which was responsible solely for the administration of the public school system, needed the assistance of the City Council in solving the transportation problem.[35]

Chairman McDowell was invited to meet with the City Council at its regular meeting one week later. That evening the gallery was jammed with spectators, including representatives of Catholic organizations, members of the school building committee, and others. Before Mr. McDowell addressed the Council, letters were read from the Catholic War Veterans and the Knights of Columbus urging equal transportation rights for qualified children whether they attended public or non-profit private schools.

Mr. McDowell explained to the City Council that bus service was first provided unofficially to parochial school pupils when there was room on buses which passed their homes. It was later found that some buses were carrying more parochial school pupils than public school pupils and that some buses were becoming overloaded. The school board had to authorize an additional bus to handle the overflow, and found that it was thus spending public school money for private school pupils. He said that the school board would be willing to administer bus service for parochial school pupils within its system, if it was found that the City Council had legal power to authorize such service.

Mayor Carmello commented that the "present mess" might have been avoided if the school board had consulted with the Mayor and the City Attorney. The gallery, described by the *Star* as "supercharged but under control," applauded the Mayor's comment. Both the Mayor and Mr. McDowell were Democrats. Mr. McDowell, however was not closely allied with the Mayor, and it may have been that this was reflected in their exchange that evening.

The City Council adopted a motion authorizing the Mayor to appoint a Council committee to meet with the Board of Education and the City Attorney to study "the pupil transportation problem and report its findings" to the Council not later than the July meeting. Councilman Alza then presented his resolution directing the city to give to pupils of local non-profit private schools the same bus service provided to public school pupils. The resolution was referred to the new Study Committee on School Bus Service. Immediately following the meeting the Mayor anounced the appointment of four Council members: two Democrats, one Catholic and one Protestant; and two Republicans, one Catholic and one Protestant. The Mayor would serve as chairman.[36]

The only public expression of direct opposition to bus service for parochial school pupils appeared in letters to the Diamond City newspapers in the days following the City Council meeting. These letters of opposition objected that the liberty guaranteed by the First Amendment could not be used to sectarian advantage without jeopardizing brotherhood; non-Catholic taxpayers should not be taxed to support Catholic education; sectarian pressure should not govern the decisions of civic leaders; our nation was founded on the complete separation of church and state; public money should not be used for private purposes; and granting this privilege would open the door for other demands later.

In refutation, letters in support of transportation argued that Catholic taxpayers were supporting public schools and getting "only crumbs"; parochial school children should have the same protection on heavily traveled roads as was given to public school pupils; minds of small children should not be divided by prejudice while they were taught to pledge allegiance to a nation with liberty and justice for all; our government was based on the principle that all men are created equal; the newspapers strongly defended freedom of the press, but treated freedom of religion as a "hot potato"; and those who pleaded for cool heads at the same time made a "federal case" out of the problem by delving into Supreme Court rulings in similar cases.[37]

The Diamond City newspapers were careful to give approximately equal display to letters on both sides of the school bus issue. The newspapers made it clear, however, that their own editorial position was in favor of continuing bus service for parochial school pupils. It was also observed that the school board's decision was a "bombshell to Roman Catholic circles," which had become accustomed to the public bus service. The editor of the *Star* said there was some sentiment on the City Council to give the school board chairman "a severe going over," but it was agreed to try to avoid an emotional controversy.[38]

Monsignor Bradley was also concerned about the heat the controversy had generated. He invited Mayor Carmello, Chairman McDowell, and the Catholic clergy of Diamond City to a meeting. Gerald Masters, Superintendent of Schools, was not Catholic and so was not invited. The whole school bus problem in Diamond City and in the state was discussed, but Monsignor Bradley's real purpose was to make clear to the other priests the manner in which he thought the local controversy should be handled. There would be no more heated political sermons.[39]

Another "bombshell" was exploded at the end of June when the City Attorney presented his legal opinion to the Mayor. After careful study of the state laws and the city charter, Mr. Kelly advised the Mayor that he found no authority in either the charter or the statutes which would permit the school board or any agency of the city to spend public funds for transportation for non-public school pupils.[40] Since Mr. Kelly was a Catholic and was sending his children to Catholic schools, his legal opinion could hardly be suspected of being influenced by any prejudice against parochial schools. However, it was Mayor Carmello's impression that Mr. Kelly was so intent on "trying to stand up straight that he fell over backwards." The Mayor had no doubt that the City Council had authority to provide for the health and safety of the children.

Mayor Carmello had sent his children to both parochial and public schools and believed in both systems. He saw no compromise of the principle of separation of church and state in providing health and safety services for parochial school children. He thought a parochial school child could receive almost any kind of special service given to public school pupils provided the service was under the control of some public agency. He did not think that school books or buildings could be provided to non-public schools at public expense. The Mayor was not opposed to some religion in the public schools. Opening prayers and Christmas and Easter pageants seemed proper activities to him. Nor would he object to similar observances of Jewish holidays. He was not greatly concerned about a consistent line of separation of church and state.

The Mayor had instituted the practice of inviting a local clergyman to offer a prayer at the opening of each meeting of the City Council. A list of the local clergy was prepared, and they were invited in rotation. This practice presented him a special problem at the meeting where the Council was to receive the report of its Study Committee. The clergyman scheduled for that evening was the Reverend Brendon Baker. The Mayor had read Father Baker's sermon in the newspaper, and he was not pleased by it. He thought, putting it mildly, the sermon was "unnecessary." He considered for a while telephoning Father Baker to suggest it might be more advisable to invite another clergyman to offer the prayer that evening, but he could think of no diplomatic way of making this suggestion. Recalling Monsignor Bradley's meeting, the Mayor decided to do nothing and hoped that Father Baker would exercise discretion at the Council meeting.[41]

The Mayor's hope was not fulfilled. Father Baker's prayer was directed more at the Council than at his Deity. He asked the Holy Ghost to enlighten the councilmen to make an equitable decision. Children of the city would be helped or injured by their verdict, and he asked that they be made to understand that all children should enjoy the same benefits. He also asked that any spirit of intolerance among them be dissolved so that in a spirit of magnanimity, representing the people of Diamond City, they might consider their problem without bias and reach a decision that would unify rather than divide the city.[42] Father Baker left little doubt in which direction, in his opinion, divine justice lay.

The report of the Study Committee on School Bus Service was presented to the Council, which was once again meeting before a large audience in the gallery. The Study Committee ignored the opinion of the City Attorney that there was no legal authority to provide public bus service to non-public school children. It was the opinion of the Mayor and school board chairman McDowell that the city charter gave the Council authority to protect the health and safety of the children of the city. The Mayor pointed out that the opinion of the City Attorney was merely advisory. The Study Committee accepted these views in preparing its report to the Council. The Committee acknowledged that the Council had no authority over public school funds once they had appropriated those funds for the use of the school board. Since the board had requested an expression of opinion from the Council, it was recommended that the school bus service in effect during the past several years be continued. The Study Committee recommended that for health, safety, and welfare reasons, all school children from kindergarten age to sixteen should be transported. The Attorney General had ruled that school bus service was a local problem, and the city charter permitted bus service for all school children for health and safety reasons.

Councilman Alza described the report as a "stopgap" compromise and predicted that the school board would not accept its proposal to continue service. He reminded the Council, "We are not talking about schools, we are talking about children." He declared the city charter gave the Council power to provide bus service for all school children. However, he proposed that a charter amendment should be prepared for submission to the next session of the General Assembly to remove any doubt that might exist because of the decisions of the school board and the City Attorney. The Mayor stated his agreement with these remarks. The City Council then voted unanimously to accept the report of the Study Committee urging the school board to continue bus service to parochial school pupils.

Councilman Alza then presented a resolution instructing the City Attorney to prepare a bill on transportation of all children of public and non-profit private schools for submission to the 1957 General Assembly. His motion was adopted, and the City Council adjourned. The question was now before the Board of Education again.[43]

The Views of Three School Board Members

The Diamond City Board of Education had been unanimous in adopting the new transportation policy which would terminate bus service for non-public school pupils. The board members were not agreed, however, on the general question of the relation of public education and religion.

Board chairman McDowell had attended public schools, but he was sending his children to local Catholic schools. He did not regard such schools as divisive because a good Catholic should be a good citizen. He thought that parochial school pupils should properly receive health services and transportation. He was not sure that public funds should be used to provide books, buildings, or instructional services. This, he thought, was going pretty far. Catholic schools didn't want the same public supervision given public schools and therefore shouldn't receive the same services. The principle of separation of church and state was not a real objection for him. Religion had a place in the public school curriculum, McDowell believed, and he favored prayers in the classroom and released-time religious education programs. He thought that the school board had tried to cooperate with any reasonable requests from Jewish parents or groups. Saturdays were no longer used to make up school days lost because of extreme bad weather. This policy had been adopted because of protests by rabbis. One year the Board had denied a request, however, to postpone opening of school because opening day fell on Yom Kippur.[44]

The views of Protestant member John Bernard were in sharp contrast to those of Mr. McDowell. Mr. Bernard was a firm believer in strict application of the principle of separation of church and state in the field of education. He regarded any public service to a parochial school pupil as a service to the school and a use of public funds for religious purposes. He thought clergymen ought to leave the public schools and public funds alone. There should be no religious practices of any kind in public schools. Mr. Bernard was even opposed to granting religious groups the privilege of renting meeting room during times when school was not in session. This was permitted non-religious community groups, but he felt religious groups should not conduct their activities in public buildings.

Mr. Bernard was also opposed to private schools of any kind. He thought all the children ought to be given an opportunity to learn how to live together. The public school did this. Children were, he felt, divided and categorized soon enough by other social activities and influences. He sent his own children to the public schools and thought that all school board members should do so. Mr. Bernard knew that his ideas were contrary to those of most other people in Diamond City. Most people in local public office did not have the independent position he was fortunate to hold. He was advertising manager of a large jewelry manufacturer, and neither he nor his company were subject to local economic pressures. His company's market was national and international. If he were working for a retailer in the city he would, Mr. Bernard believed, be subjected to economic pressure. Some years earlier he had been attacked in a sermon by a priest. (He was never sure why the priest was critical of him.) Following the sermon five Catholics came to him and apologized for the priest's remarks. A number of Catholics wrote to the bishop in protest, and the priest was transferred.

The practice of giving bus rides to parochial school pupils had been initiated by Mr. Bernard unofficially some years earlier when he was chairman of the Board of Education. He had suggested to the bus contractor that the drivers ought to pick up the parochial school children along their routes when there was room in the buses. The practice grew over the years until the buses were becoming overcrowded and difficulties began to arise. In one instance two Catholic Sisters rode the bus in the morning and organized the seating arrangements so that the public school children sat in the back and the parochial school children, who got off first, sat in the front. Within two days parents of public school children had protested to Board members and the Sisters no longer were permitted to ride the bus. Shortly after that, however, the school board authorized another bus to reduce overcrowding.[45]

School board member Monroe Green disagreed with the legal opinion of the City Attorney. Mr. Green was a lawyer and a partner in a watchmaking company. He sent his own children to the public schools but felt that non-public school pupils were permitted bus service under the *Everson* case and the police powers of the city. The Supreme Court had defined transportation as a health and safety service for children. Surely, any city under its police powers had the right to protect the health and safety of its children. Mr. Green thought the Supreme Court had gone pretty far in the development of the child-benefit theory, but he would go along with the Court's decisions. He didn't think the child-benefit theory could be extended to justify every kind of service to non-public school pupils or to justify facilities or buildings for non-public schools at public expense.

The Supreme Court had provided a rather tenuous definition of the principle of separation of church and state, Mr. Green thought. He was not sure that all religious activities should be removed from the public schools. Opening prayers might be permissible, but he did not approve of anything much beyond that. The crucifixion story and other strictly denominational doctrines should not be presented, he felt. A released-time program might be a better way to provide for the religious education of public school children. Mr. Green's review of Connecticut's laws had convinced him that there was no statutory authority for a board of education to spend public funds for transportation of non-public school pupils.[46]

The views of these three board members, Catholic, Protestant, and Jew, were marked by distinct differences.

The School Board Reverses Itself

The week after the action of the City Council the Board of Education met. One member, a Catholic Democrat, was absent because of illness. The meeting was opened by Chairman McDowell's report on his meeting with the City Council and their decision. Mr. McDowell said that the Council felt it had the power to appropriate money for bus service for non-public school pupils. The Council had intended, and it was now specifically authorizing, use of the transportation funds for such service. Since the City Council desired the Board of Education to administer bus service to non-public school pupils, Mr. McDowell recommended that the school board do so.

Several people in the audience asked to speak after Mr. McDowell presented his recommendation to the school board. Those who spoke were about evenly divided in support and in opposition. One who spoke in support of bus service was Monsignor Thomas Bradley. In urging the continuation of bus service for parochial school pupils, Monsignor Bradley pointed out that if those schools were closed the city would face a chaotic situation. "Of course," he said, "we would not descend to that." But he asked the Board to follow the rule of reason. There was no need to create a furore when there was no public opposition to continuing bus service. If transportation were not continued, numerous difficulties might arise. Many parents might decide to transfer their children to public schools. The Board would not be prepared to provide for those additional pupils nor know how many additional teachers to employ.

Monsignor Bradley advised in conclusion that under the present circumstances "at least temporarily, you will settle this matter not contrary to the rights of the children." [47]

The Board members who had been offended by the sermon of Father Baker did not regard as objectionable the appearance or statement of Monsignor Bradley. He appeared as any other citizen might appear at a Board meeting on an issue that concerned him.[48] When Monsignor Bradley concluded, Mr. Bernard observed that it might be advisable for school bus service to be handled by some other public agency. Perhaps the Board of Public Safety could handle bus service, and the Board of Education might then have some time to devote to educational matters.

Mrs. Elsie Jones rose to object to the remarks made about the school board by the Mayor at the Council meeting. The Mayor told Mr. McDowell the trouble might have been avoided if the Board of Education had consulted with him and the City Attorney. Yet when the City Attorney gave an opinion contrary to the Mayor's wishes, the Mayor turned his back on that opinion. Mrs. Jones did not feel that this was intellectually honest. Now, she asked, why is the Board of Education taking orders from the City Council?

Mr. McDowell replied that the Board was not taking orders. But he felt the proposal was a necessary compromise, a reasonable course that could be administered.

Mr. Green declared that the City Council had taken no action which changed the situation. The Mayor and the City Council had criticized the school board and then had reached the same conclusion as the school board. Mr. Green pointed out that the City Council had appropriated no funds for bus service for the parochial school pupils. He saw no reason for the school board to reverse the decision it had reached earlier.

Mrs. Sally Norris moved adoption of the recommendation of the chairman. Mr. Bernard seconded the motion. He expressed doubt that it was the right action and suggested that a one-year limit be placed on the action. Mrs. Norris accepted the amendment.[49]

At this point Superintendent of Schools Gerald Masters spoke in favor of the recommendation. Until this time he had not taken any action to influence the Board's decision. He didn't tell the Board so, but he felt unduly burdened by the entire responsibility of school transportation. He would have been very pleased if it were placed with some other agency of the city. Nor did he report to the Board that he had experienced some difficulty with the Sister-Principals of the schools each year when he requested new lists of pupils eligible for bus tickets. Frequently lists were forthcoming only after persistent requests. On several occasions it had been discovered that bus tickets were being given to parochial school pupils who were not eligible.[50] Superintendent Masters assured the Board that the system could be administered for the next year according to the same policy that had been followed in the past.

Mr. Green objected that the Board was reversing its action when no reason had been presented for such reversal. Mr Bernard commented that it was purely an expedient due to the short length of time. There were many angles to the problem, and this was the best thing the Board could do until a better solution could be found.

Chairman McDowell asked for the vote. Mrs. Norris and Mr. Bernard voted "Yes." Mr. Green voted "No." Since the fifth board member was absent, the recommendation was adopted, two to one. The school board would continue to provide bus service to parochial school pupils until after the 1957 General Assembly had decided whether it would act on the problem.[51]

Conclusions about Diamond City

The dispute in Diamond City about bus service was as much a conflict between the school board and the City Council as a difference over the service itself. The vigorous action of the clergy, however, gave the dispute more the appearance of a religious division. The original statement of the Board of Education was not in opposition to bus service for non-public school children but suggested that a further appropriation was needed for the specific purpose of transporting non-public school pupils. This announcement

evoked the call for political action by Catholic groups with the
encouragement and support of the clergy. There was no objection
expressed by public officials to the statement read at all masses about
bus service. There was general resentment by Catholics and others
over the sermon by Father Baker, but there was no public criticism
of his statements.

The school board's action was taken on a Monday night. Five
days elapsed before the Catholic clergy announced their opposition
in the churches. The day following the clergy's statements the Mayor
and Councilman Alza made their announcements. These announcements were followed by actions of the Catholic War Veterans and
the Knights of Columbus to influence the City Council to act in
support of bus service for parochial school pupils. Clearly the appeal
of the clergy for Catholic political action won a response.

The sermon of Mr. Esty was actually a statement of policy and
philosophy similar to that of other Protestant statements elsewhere
on the issue of auxiliary services and the principle of church-state
separation. He appealed for improvement of the religious aspects of
the public schools. Still, he expressed misgivings about indirect aid
to private and sectarian schools. Mr. Esty could not seem to decide
whether he wanted separation or cooperation of church and state.
Nevertheless, his sermon was accepted as a plea for understanding
and good will. Following Father Baker's sermon, such a plea was
welcome. However, it did not move any public official to make any
public statement echoing Mr. Esty's remarks, nor did it inspire any
Protestant groups to political activity.

Mr. Bernard was the only person among the civic and religious
leaders in Diamond City who wanted strict separation of church
and state. His interpretation of the principle permitted no modifications for any public service to parochial school pupils nor any religious practices at all in the public school classroom. Despite these
views, he had been moved to institute the unofficial practice of
giving bus rides to parochial school pupils when there was room on
the bus. He was also moved to vote as a matter of expediency for
reversal of the Board's decision to end such service. The Mayor,

Mr. Green, and Mr. McDowell all thought that some religious practices in the public school were not a violation of the principle of separation of church and state. Monsignor Bradley placed some emphasis on the need of the child, although he described transportation not as a health or safety service but as an "educational facility."

None of the Diamond City participants was deeply impressed by the nice distinctions made by the Supreme Court. Nor did the absence of statutory authority, as the City Attorney advised, reverse the policy conclusions of those in favor of transporting Catholic school pupils. No one actively opposed bus service for parochial school pupils in Diamond City. The school board, placed in the position of seeming to be opposed to such service, and under pressure from the Catholic clergy, the City Council, and public opinion, felt impelled to withdraw the question about its own authority and agreed to continue its "unofficial" policy. There may have been some question about the law, but there was little question about the policy desired by most of the people of Diamond City. That policy would be continued. The City Council and the school board looked for clarification of the law by the next session of the state legislature.

THE HIGH HILLS DISPUTE

The *High Hills News* in October, 1956, carried a full-page advertisement by the High Hills Town Planning Committee calling for town planning to avoid the danger of becoming "a suburb" and a target for shrewd operators and land speculators. High Hills was adjacent to one of the largest cities in western Connecticut, and the growth of that city was being felt in the demand for home sites in High Hills. The town was also a real part of "exurbia." [52] In talking to residents, a visitor in 1956 was given the impression that the "townies" were outnumbered by the newcomers—the New York City commuters and the overflow population of the adjacent city.

High Hills' economic activity includes agriculture, manufacturing, and industrial research. In 1950 High Hills had a population of a little more than 4000, but by 1956 it had increased by 30 per cent to a total of more than 5000. High Hills' foreign-born white population constituted about 15 per cent of its 1950 total.[53] The town is sparsely populated, with many miles of unpaved roads twisting over the hills that give the settlement its name. One major highway runs through the town. Outside of the central area there are no sidewalks. These road conditions were frequently mentioned in pleas for school bus service for children who were attending the High Hills Catholic School.

The school population of High Hills in 1950 was a little below 800. These children were all in the public schools. There were no local non-public schools. In 1956 the public school population had increased to almost 1200, and there were about 150 pupils in the Catholic elementary school which had opened two years earlier.[54]

High Hills had consistently cast the majority of its votes for Republican candidates, and in 1956 the Board of Education was composed of six Republicans and three Democrats. One Democratic member of the Board was a Catholic, as was one Republican member. The other seven members were Protestants.[55]

In August, 1954, one month before the High Hills Catholic School was to open, the pastor of the High Hills Catholic Church, the Reverend Everett Davey, sent a written request to the Board of Education for a released-time religious education program and for bus service for pupils of the Catholic school. The Board sought an opinion from the town counsel, Ralph Saber. Mr. Saber advised that there was no legal authority for the school board to provide transportation for non-public school pupils. The Board decided unanimously at its August meeting, with all members present and voting, to deny both of Father Davey's requests.

Following this decision there was an exchange of letters between Father Davey and Mr. Saber. This exchange suggested to Father Davey that there was some ambiguity in the interpretation of the law given by the town counsel. Because of this possible ambiguity, Father Davey thought the school board should receive another opinion from the town counsel. The school board thereupon sought such a second opinion. This second opinion confirmed the first one given the previous month.[56]

At the September meeting the school board heard from a committee consisting of Father Davey and about eight lay citizens. Most of the laymen were representatives of parish organizations, but one was a Protestant and a former chairman of the High Hills School Board. After listening to appeals for the extension of bus service to the Catholic school pupils, the Board again denied the request.

This second vote, however, was not unanimous. One Catholic Democratic member asked that her vote be recorded in favor of the request. This was Mrs. Margaret Sharkey, who soon afterward left the board at the expiration of her term.[57] The Board voted unanimously to ask for a ruling by the Attorney General of the state. The answer to this inquiry came in December, 1954, from the State Commissioner of Education. This reply quoted the opinion of the Attorney General given in 1952, that the question was properly addressed not to the state authorities but to the town counsel.

School Board Chairman Charles Ford, in a letter to Father Davey informing him of the Board's vote to reaffirm its decision, wrote that he shared with Father Davey "the view that there is no room in our town for bitterness and misunderstanding, and that we must always keep in mind the welfare of our children." [58]

Father Davey did not accept the 1954 decision as final, and two years later he decided to try again. He was to be advanced in October, 1956 to a larger parish, and he wanted to make one more try for bus service before he left High Hills.[59] In a sermon early in August he told his parishioners of their responsibility to work for bus service. He also criticized in strong terms the failure of Catholic members of the school board to vote in favor of his request for this service. One such member, Mr. Harold Chain, was attending this service, and he was very disturbed by Father Davey's remarks about him. At times during the sermon he wanted to walk out of church, but he restrained himself. Father Davey had no right to use the pulpit, Mr. Chain felt, to criticize his actions as a public official.[60]

Another parishioner who felt similarly was Superintendent of

Schools John Gavin. Dr. Gavin was offended by the impropriety of Father Davey's criticism. He sympathized with the board members who had to suffer such criticism while attending church with their families.[61]

Father Davey was intent on securing public bus service for his pupils and was not concerned about other health and welfare services. He believed that dental and physical examinations and even facilities and buildings for non-religious activities might properly be provided to non-public school pupils at public expense. However, he did not apply for school lunch or school milk service, although his school was eligible to receive these services directly from the state. He discussed this with the mothers of his pupils, and they agreed it was no problem for the children to bring their lunches.

It was the pastor's responsibility, Father Davey believed, to seek services for the pupils, and it was best to work directly with the Board of Education. He did not try to work with the political party organizations, even though both the Democratic and Republican Town Chairmen were Catholics. On one occasion he was asked by telephone if he would like the town Democratic caucus to put bus service for Catholic school pupils in the Democratic platform. He said he did not want that; he did not wish this to be a partisan issue. He was offended when a Protestant minister spoke from the pulpit and in a church newsletter against Catholics running for town office. He was disappointed, too, when Mrs. Carey, a member of his church, failed in the Republican Town Caucus to win the nomination for a place on the Board of Education.

Father Davey made no effort to secure the support of any groups other than those affiliated with his church. In 1954 one Protestant, the former school board chairman, had supported his request for bus service. Father Davey was sure there were many other Protestants in town who would also favor his request, but he did not seek their support. He was well aware of the opposition of the Protestant ministers, and he made no effort to persuade them to his point of view.[62]

In the late summer of 1956 he discussed the problem of bus

service with Dr. Wallace Doan, a member of his parish and a long-time resident of High Hills. Dr. Doan, although a Democrat, had been named by the school board (with a Republican majority) to head a committee to study the teachers' salary schedule. He was proud that his committee had been influential in securing a higher pay scale for the public school teachers. Dr. Doan felt strongly that the school board should once more be requested to extend bus service to the pupils at High Hills Catholic School. He and Father Davey agreed that it might make a better impression if the request were made by Dr. Doan rather than the priest.[63] Accordingly, Dr. Doan wrote a letter to the Board chairman asking permission to present his request at the September meeting.

Dr. Doan appeared at that meeting alone and presented a written statement to the Board. His request for bus service was based on two points; one, the financial hardship which the parish was under, an obligation of $200,000 as a result of the construction of the High Hills Catholic School; two, and most important, the transportation was needed to protect the health and safety of the children.[64]

The Board delayed its decision on Dr. Doan's request until its October meeting and sought an opinion from the new town counsel, James Dempsey, who had succeeded to the post when Mr. Saber was elected Judge of Probate for High Hills in 1954. Mr. Saber a Republican and a Protestant, had been elected Probate Judge over Mr. Dempsey, a Democrat and a Catholic, by a margin of little more than a hundred votes.[65] Mr. Dempsey advised the school board that he could not find anything illegal in the school board providing bus services to non-public school children.[66]

Between the September and October meetings of the school board a number of letters were sent to its members. Letters also appeared in the columns of the *High Hills News* and in papers of nearby cities. The governing board of the local Christian Science church sent a resolution expressing its belief in the principle of the separation of church and state, and asserting that school segregation by religion was as undemocratic and un-American as segregation by race or color. The school board was urged to refuse to appropriate public funds for aid or subsidy to non-public schools. Another letter to the Board stated that this request for bus service was a prelude to requests for books, tuition reimbursement, and other support. It was pointed out that there were more than twenty-five children in town attending private day schools in other towns who would be entitled to services equivalent to those given the pupils in the High Hills Catholic School. Other letters to the Board stated that public funds should be used only for pupils in public schools or else the board would be obliged to provide equal services to pupils at all other schools, private schools, church Sunday schools, and day nurseries. One writer, "in the interest of compromise," suggested that all school children be transported to the public schools and the school of their choice could then arrange to carry the children to the non-public school.[67]

All of the letters addressed to the Board expressed opposition to the request for bus service for non-public school children. Letters appearing in newspapers were divided. Those opposing such services contained arguments and sentiments similar to those in letters addressed to the school board. Letters favoring such services argued that refusal of bus service was religious discrimination against Catholic children. One letter proposed a system of parochial schools for each faith. Under this system children would be carried to the parochial school of their choice by buses paid for out of public funds. Children in all schools, both public and non-public, would receive low-cost or free lunches as well as medical and dental services, subsidized by public funds.

The tone of some of the letters revealed strong emotions felt by the authors. Some of the phrases and terms used included "coward" and "small, opinionated, prejudiced minority," and one charged an "attempt to eliminate God from public education." The High Hills story was reported in many of the newspapers in Connecticut and in New York City. The question of services to non-public school pupils was gaining the attention of people outside of the town of High Hills.

The school board met in October to consider the opinion of town counsel Dempsey and the petition of Dr. Doan before an audience of about twenty-five people.[68] (The board meetings were open to the public as a general rule, but there was seldom an audience.) Dr. Doan was present but Father Davey was not. Father Davey had been willing to appear at the hearing, but it was agreed he would come only if Dr. Doan thought it was necessary. It was also agreed that delegations from the local Knights of Columbus or church organizations would not appear at the hearing unless Dr. Doan called for them. Dr. Doan would have telephoned to secure this attendant support if there had been a large opposition group present at the meeting. It was preferable, he believed, to avoid the mass-meeting or town-meeting kind of debate. In that atmosphere it was likely some irresponsible statements and wild charges might be made which later would not easily be forgotten.

Dr. Doan's immediate and primary concern was with securing bus service. He believed that other services properly might be extended, but he did not include textbooks among those services. A choice of books for a parochial school, he thought, should not be made by a local school board. Something should be done about health services for the parochial school children, Dr. Doan believed. The Catholic school pupils were receiving nurse service from the Sister-Principal. She was a nurse, but that same Sister would not always be principal. Dr. Doan felt that the services of the Public Health Nurses Association given to the public school pupils might be extended to the parochial school pupils.

Dr. Doan was careful to confer with Father Davey about his activities. He and Father Davey also conferred with James Dempsey, the town counsel, as to how best to advance the petition for bus service. It was Dr. Doan's intent to make his approach one that would not cause irreparable divisions between the school board and those seeking the bus service. In one informal conference with the school board chairman, Charles Ford, Dr. Doan prefaced his discussion with the observation that he and Mr. Ford had been friends for twenty-five years and he did not want anything said or done that would disrupt that friendship. Dr. Doan, like Father Davey, was concerned that the parents of the Catholic school pupils were not active enough in the effort to secure public bus service. There was, it seemed to him, substantial lethargy.[69]

Dr. Doan was the only one to speak in favor of his petition for bus service for pupils of High Hills Catholic School. Several others in the audience urged that the petition be rejected. The Board agreed to go into executive session and adjourned to another room. A little later ministers of several local Protestant churches arrived. One of the ministers knocked on the door of the room where the Board was in executive session and asked to address the members. His request was refused. He was persistent but the Board was adamant. This request and even the appearance of the ministers was generally resented by all of the Board members. This was not a question which concerned the ministers. The Board recognized Father Davey's legitimate interest in bus service for pupils of his school, but they saw no need for a Protestant-Catholic conflict about it.

All nine members of the Board attended the executive session, as did Superintendent Gavin and town counsel Dempsey. At the beginning of the discussion the chairman called on Dr. Gavin for comment. Dr. Gavin felt he should make no attempt to influence the decision. He put himself in the position of the professional agent of the Board employed to carry out its policies. He said that if such bus service was not permitted by law, the Board obviously must follow the law. If bus service was permitted, the Board had to decide as a question of policy whether to grant the request. Beyond this observation, Dr. Gavin felt he could make no comment.

The debate was vigorous but not out of control. It continued for more than two hours.[70] When the time came for voting, Board member William Manners moved that the vote be by secret ballot. He did not want chairman Charles Ford to be placed in the position of having to cast the deciding negative vote if the Board should divide four to four. Ford was a Republican; Manners was a Democrat, but he did not regard this question as a party issue. He thought Mr. Ford and the Board would suffer if it were left for the chairman to decide the question.[71]

Meanwhile the audience waited patiently and few people left. When the Board returned, Chairman Ford announced the vote as six to three against the request. The Board then adjourned. The negative decision was accepted quietly by the audience.

To those who expressed discouragement, Dr. Doan pointed out that the first Board vote had been nine to nothing, the second eight to one, and this latest vote was six to three. In time they would succeed with their petition.[72] He told chairman Ford he intended to continue to work for bus service, but this did not dismay Mr. Ford. Differences existed, and Mr. Ford felt most people respected each other's right to differ.

Charles Ford was Republican, Protestant, and editor of the *High Hills News*. He regarded bus service as an assistance to the school. Public bus service for parochial school pupils, therefore, was a use of public funds for a religious purpose. He rejected the assertion that the Catholic school saved the town tax money. The school board had provided educational opportunities for all of the children of the town before Father Davey had set up his school. The Board was always willing to provide public education for all of the children of the town. The Catholic school provided a special kind of education which Catholic parents held necessary for their children. Therefore they should assume full responsibility for the operation of the school. Mr. Ford regretted that the Catholic Church found it necessary to set up a separate school system. Whatever unity we had achieved in this country he attributed to the unifying effect of the public schools. Since the High Hills Catholic School had been opened, he had sensed certain strains developing in town.

Mr. Ford's definition of separation of church and state did not preclude health services at public expense for parochial school pupils. Instruction and other services might also be extended if the services were under the control and direction of the Board of Education. He opposed released time for religious education because it was disruptive to the school program and placed an extra burden on the teacher. Mr. Ford thought public schools should not be theological. He knew that most people wanted opening prayers and some other religious observances in the classroom, but he would prefer such practices to be excluded. If they were included, he thought they should be in keeping with the character of the community.

In the weeks following the Board's refusal of Dr. Doan's petition Mr. Ford did not feel that the dissension in town had become intense. Some measure of the attitude of the town would be discovered when the new school building budget was presented. He had asked two Catholics if there would be some reluctance among Catholics to support the school building program because of the denial of bus service. They told him that was not their attitude. They would give all the support they could to the building program. Mr. Ford concluded that the differences about bus service, while very real, had not caused a resentment which carried over to other areas.[73]

Another member of the school board, Dr. Anthony Pinza, was concerned about the growing division in the town. He felt that serious antagonisms were developing between Catholics and Protestants. He was Republican and Episcopalian (although he had been reared as a Catholic) and one of the minority of three who had voted for Dr. Doan's petition. For Dr. Pinza, the opinion of the town counsel had been all-important. Since it was legal, Dr. Pinza felt it could not be questioned that such service was also desirable. The parochial school pupils faced the same hazards and inconveniences on their way to and from school as the public school pupils.

Dr. Pinza wanted to see all of the children in town receiving the same health and welfare services. He took pride in his successful plan for providing dental health services to the public school children. The services, for pupils who could not afford them, were paid for by the voluntary nurses association in confidence, and no stigma was applied to the child who had to receive such charity.

Much of the tension in town over the issue of bus service had been created, Dr. Pinza believed, by the clergy. His own Episcopalian minister had used the pulpit to sermonize against bus service, as Father Davey had sermonized for it. Dr. Pinza had rejected his minister's attempts to influence his vote by either sermon or private conversation. Father Davey had a right to petition the Board as a citizen, but the use of the pulpit for such purposes was most improper. Dr. Pinza resented religious interference with public duties. He knew others felt this way too. Mrs. Richard Kant, the Catholic wife of a Protestant board member, was going to an out-of-town Catholic church because of Father Davey's political sermons against the school board. Dr. Pinza regretted this activity by the clergy because he felt it resulted in the question of bus service being answered on a bigoted basis. That is, the parties involved supported or opposed bus service according to whether they were favorably disposed toward the High Hills Catholic School. Mrs. Sharkey, for instance, in 1954 had voted for bus service even though the Board had been advised it was not legal. Dr. Pinza regarded her action as bigotry equal to that of those who opposed bus service because they were opposed to the existence of Catholic schools.[74]

The dissension in town was very real to school board member William Manners. He was subjected to repeated criticism for his vote against Dr. Doan's petition. On the Sunday preceding that vote, Father Davey had announced from his pulpit that at least four members of the Board would vote in favor of bus service for Catholic school children. He listed Mr. Manners along with Dr. Pinza, Mr. Chain, and Mr. Tonti. The latter two were Catholics.[75]

Father Davey had reason to believe that Mr. Manners was sympathetic to the problems of the Catholic school pupils. His daughter had attended the High Hills Catholic School. Father Davey had talked with Mr. Manners a number of times and he had seemed favorably disposed toward granting bus service. Father Davey understood Mr. Manners to say in one of his conversations that if the Board were advised that such service could legally be given, he would vote for it.[76] Mr. Manners had meant that this was a question of state law and somebody in the state government should tell school boards the meaning of the law. If this were done and the service was clearly legal, Mr. Manners would then vote in favor of it. He could not vote for something of uncertain legality, and the legal opinion of the town counsel, James Dempsey, did not reassure him.

Mr. Manners accepted transportation as a service to the child that might be publicly provided. Health services and textbooks might be furnished all school children. Public asistance might also be given in the construction of non-public schools, Mr. Manners believed. He did not regard the principle of separation of church and state as an obstacle to these practices. He thought there ought to be some religion in the schools, public and non-public. The schools ought to have opening prayers and some Bible instruction. On all of these questions, Mr. Manners thought there should be a state decision. He wouldn't go along with any request for services to non-public school pupils until the state made a decision.

In the weeks following the vote Mr. Manners was called "turncoat," "yellow-back," and similar epithets. Both he and his wife received much verbal abuse in person and on the telephone. They were accused, because their young daughter went to the Catholic school for one year, of having used the nuns as baby sitters. (They had transferred her to public school because she had not done well in classes that included as many as forty-five pupils). They did not see why they should be criticized. They had paid the tuition.

Mr. Manners felt that much of the dissension in town had been intensified by the Protestant ministers and some bad-mannered Catholics. Father Davey, he thought, had a perfect right to appear before the Board about the request for bus service. It was his project. But the ministers had no business with the Board. Their appearance at the Board meeting "struck a very sour note." The following week Mr. Manners spoke to his own minister about it and asked, "Why did you stick your nose in?" [77]

Mr. Manners and other Board members noted a different attitude in Father Davey's successor, Father Leahy. Father Davey moved on to a larger parish and Father Leahy came to the High Hills Catholic Church a few weeks after the vote on Dr. Doan's petition. Father Leahy struck Mr. Manners as a pleasant, mild-mannered person. To Mr. Ford he seemed to be working to calm the parish. One of the Catholic board members, Mr. Chain, regarded Father Leahy's approach with favor. The proper role of the pastor, he believed, was to work in an indirect fashion by developing good relations for the church and for himself. The pastor should devote himself to winning support rather than to demanding action. Mr. Chain thought that Father Leahy would not, as Father Davey had, resort to using the pulpit to criticize the actions of local public officials.[78]

The Choice of a New Board Member

Protestant-Catholic differences were revealed in a different light in High Hills in the months following the vote on bus service. One of the Protestant members of the school board submitted his resignation for personal reasons. Dr. Pinza quickly anticipated that the religious affiliation of the succeeding member would be a major qualification in the minds of many people in town. As a means of postponing a decision and avoiding swift formation of battle lines on the question, and as gesture of courtesy and appreciation for the service of the resigning member, Dr. Pinza moved that the resignation not be accepted. He suggested that the member be asked to reconsider. Accordingly, the Board voted to table the resignation for one month.[79]

In ensuing weeks chairman Ford received several suggestions for the anticipated vacancy from the Republican town chairman. The resigning member was Republican, so by custom his replacement would be Republican. The member was also Protestant, but most of the names mentioned by the Town Chairman to Mr. Ford were those of Catholics.

When the Board was advised that the resigning member would not withdraw his resignation, it was accepted with regret. The Board proceeded to consider nominations for his successor. Mr. Manners nominated Ralph Prince.[80] He commented to Catholic board member Mr. Chain, "He's a good Methodist, Harry. You won't like that." Mr. Chain replied that he was not concerned about Mr. Prince's religion as long as he was a good man for the job. The Board found Mr. Prince qualified and elected him to fill the vacancy.

The interchange between Mr. Manners and Mr. Chain was brought to the knowledge of Mrs. Martha McNulty, Democratic Town Chairman. She was very irritated with Mr. Manners because of his vote against bus service, and this seemed to her further evidence of his anti-Catholicism. She had been instrumental in his election to the school board, and she felt he had betrayed her and the Democratic party. She decided to do something about it. Mrs. McNulty knew when and where Mr. Manners had lunch every day. She waited inside the entrance of the restaurant until she saw him coming and then went out and stopped him on the street. She criticized his actions and statements on the Board and accused him of hating Catholics.[81] Mr. Manners denied the charge and argued with her. As the exchange grew more heated and Mrs. McNulty again accused him of hating Catholics, Mr. Manners later recalled replying, "I'll tell you this, Mrs. McNulty. I hate your type of Catholic and your type of Protestant." [82] According to Mrs. McNulty, he said, "I hate you dirty Catholics."

In later weeks Mr. Manners was distressed to hear that Mrs. McNulty was telling people in town that he had said he hated "the dirty Catholics." [83] Both he and Mrs. Manners suffered many snubs and were also engaged in many arguments about the question of bus service for the Catholic school pupils. Twice as many people spoke to him who were opposed as were in favor of bus service. Two Catholics spoke to him privately of their opposition, but no Catholic made any public statements against the request for transportation.

Mr. Manners wanted to run for re-election to the school board, but he thought Mrs. McNulty would oppose his nomination.[84] She talked to a number of people active in local Democratic politics and felt confident enough to say, "We'll murder him in the caucus." She intended to see that Mr. Manners never ran for office again.[85]

Mr. Manners was sure that Mrs. McNulty would try to have nominated as many Catholics as possible. He knew he would have opposition, but there were some Protestants on the Democratic town committee who would support him. He was sure that the next town election would be fought more on religious than on party lines.[86]

Mrs. Manners was upset by the debates that were occurring on street corners and over the telephone. It seemed to her that the whole town was astir. She thought it was principally generated by a few excited Catholics. She knew the same type of Protestant who would fight for what he wanted and wouldn't give an inch. But she had never lived in a town before (Mrs. Manners had moved to High Hills five years earlier) where the Catholics were so determined. "They seem," she said, "so grim and so solid."

Mr. and Mrs. Manners agreed with school board chairman Charles Ford that the extent of the division in the town would be indicated by the vote on the new school building program.[87]

The Building Program and the School Budget

When Superintendent Gavin began his duties in High Hills, he immediately set about preparing a report for the school board on the need for more classrooms. His estimates of the expected growth in school population led him to recommend an addition to the existing elementary school and the construction of second elementary school in the south end of the town. The Board of Education accepted his recommendations, which were submitted to the town in a two-part referendum. The first part called for the appropriation of $300,000 for the school addition; the second part called for the appropriation of $15,000 to buy the site for the new school.

These recommendations initiated a debate that was related in part to the differences over school bus service for the Catholic school pupils. The opposition to the proposed addition was presented by some Catholics who argued that the cost per classroom and the cost per student were much higher than equivalent figures for the High Hills Catholic School. The opposition to the proposed new school in the south end of town was more complicated. Residents of the north section objected to the southern location. Arguments were also presented against the decentralization of the school system. It was contended that it would be less expensive to keep the school system centralized.[88]

Dr. Doan thought that opposition to the proposed expansion came chiefly from residents of the northern section of town and residents without children who saw the school expansion as the major cause of rising local taxes. He knew there were a few Catholics resentful of the denial of bus service, but he felt that their opposition to the expansion of the public school system was not substantial.[89]

In contrast, Mr. Ford and Mr. Manners thought that bus service was the real basis of the opposition. Mrs. McNulty told Mr. Ford that if the school board would give bus service to the Catholic school pupils, "we'd go along with your school building program." She also told him the bus service question was not ended and she was going to "get Manners." [90] Another Catholic woman told Mr. Ford that Catholics would oppose the school building program because of the board's vote against bus service.[91] Mr. Manners was approached by Catholics on two occasions and was told that if "you gave us buses you wouldn't be having this trouble".[92]

Mr. Ford noted that the principal opponent of the proposed expansion was one of the town's leading Catholics. His criticisms were vigorous and insistent. He described the school board as "a bunch of wild-eyed theorists and spendthrifts." Mr. Ford heard that Father Leahy had spoken to this critic and had tried to calm him down. Father Leahy was concerned that the opposition would appear to be coming from the Catholic Church.[93] Both Mr. Ford and Mr. Manners thought that much of the opposition came from parents of Catholic school pupils who saw that public school decentralization would cut down on the need for buses and reduce the chance of public bus service for Catholic school pupils.

The school board respected their superintendent, Dr. Gavin, and appreciated his difficult position. The Board did not know he was Catholic at the time he was appointed, although the application form did include the question, "Do you attend a church?" Dr. Gavin had written in reply, "Yes, but I believe firmly in the separation of church and state." The Board members had been unanimous in the selection of Dr. Gavin, and they were satisfied in their choice. He soon demonstrated that he could perform his job with a high degree of professional skill. They were gratified that he did not try to influence the decision on the request for bus service. They approved of his survey and recommendations of the town's school needs. Mr. Manners said that Dr. Gavin had great ambitions for the school system and wanted considerable expansion but that he was a realist and he would take what he could get.[94]

Dr. Gavin was keenly aware of the Protestant-Catholic division in town. It did not affect his recommendation for the building program, but he was apprehensive about the choice of a new principal he had to hire. Ten of the fifteen new teachers he had hired were Catholic. (Most of those who applied were Catholic.) Most of the applications he was receiving for the position of principal appeared to come from Catholics. He wanted to hire people on the basis of their qualifications, but he knew that if most of them were Catholic some townspeople would put a different interpretation on his decisions. He discussed this frankly with his board chairman, Mr. Ford. Mr. Ford said he thought it would be better to avoid having a school system that was entirely Catholic but Dr. Gavin couldn't hire people he didn't want. He advised that Dr. Gavin "wait and see." [95]

The town meeting discussion of the school building proposals prior to the referendum was lively and sometimes bitter. There was yelling and booing, and a number of strong statements were made. The objections appeared to come chiefly from Catholics who argued that the Catholic school was built for much less. Some Catholics rose, however, to argue that the public school services outnumbered those of the parochial school. For some, the town meeting argument served as a release, and they could leave after the meeting joking with their opponents. Some left carrying their antagonisms with them.[96]

The referendum on the building program, held shortly after the town meeting, was close. The proposed $300,000 addition to the elementary school was approved by a margin of a hundred votes. The proposed $15,000 appropriation for site purchase for the new school was defeated by about the same margin.

A short time afterward the school board submitted its operating budget for the next year to the Town Board of Finance. It called for an increase of $100,000 over the previous year. Mr. Ford was concerned that the Board might cut the proposed school budget. He knew there were three Catholics on the seven-member Board, and he wasn't sure how they felt. The Board of Finance approved the budget unanimously without any cuts. The budget was submitted to a town meeting and approved without opposition.[97]

It was not clear that the action on the school budget meant that the antagonisms generated by the school bus dispute were abating. Dr. Gavin thought there was reason to believe they were. Dr. Doan thought that some of the hard feeling remained, but Father Leahy was working slowly and quietly to reduce the rancor and to develop good will for the High Hills Catholic church. Mrs. McNulty felt differently: she had been out of town during the weeks when the school budget was under consideration. "That budget" would not have had such an easy time before the Board of Finance or in town meeting if she had been around. They wouldn't have such an easy time of it next year.

"They're so stupid," she said:

> If they'd go along with us on bus service they wouldn't have any trouble with their building program or their budget. There are a lot of big taxpayers in town who don't have any children going to school and who don't like all of the expenditure of tax money on new schools. But the trouble was that new superintendent. What a salesman! He put the whole thing over on the town.[98]

Clearly, the debate about school bus service for High Hills Catholic School pupils was not ended.

Conclusions About High Hills

The dispute in High Hills involved religious and political leaders who apparently contributed to its intensity. It was initiated by a request of Father Davey in 1954 for bus service and released time for religious education. Immediate opposition was offered by the Protestant churches in town. The religious nature of the division was emphasized by later developments: sermons by Father Davey and by Protestant ministers, the choice of the new board member, the statements of Mrs. McNulty and others, and the vote of the school board.

The opposition on the Board of Education came chiefly from Protestant Republicans. Four of the six votes of the majority were cast by Protestant Republicans. Two were cast by Protestant Democrats. Of the three votes cast in favor of bus service for the pupils of High Hills Catholic School, one was cast by a Catholic Democrat, Mr. Chain; the second by a Catholic Republican; and the third by a Protestant Republican, Dr. Pinza.[99]

The statements of Mr. Ford and Dr. Pinza suggest that the refusal was in part based not only on opposition to services but on opposition to parochial schools. Statements were made about the principle of separation of church and state, but the Board held religious considerations important enough to put a question about church attendance on the applications for the position of superintendent. In the opinion of the school board chairman, most of the people of the town wanted some religion in the schools. Father Davey wanted a released-time religious education program, but the Board unanimously refused that request.

The first reason for bus service put forth by Dr. Doan was the financial need of the parish. His second reason was protection of the pupils. These two reasons seemed clear acknowledgment that bus service was an aid to both the religious school and the pupil. Such an acknowledgment was agreement with the principal contention of opponents that public bus service to parochial school pupils was public support of religion. Other proponents of bus service specifically invoked the Supreme Court's decision in the *Everson* case and the child-benefit doctrine. The doctrine was set forth in the advisory opinion of town counsel Dempsey, wherein he declared there was nothing in the Connecticut statutes which prohibited bus service for parochial school children.

No public objection was made to lawyer Dempsey's unusual assumption that the school board could do anything the law did not specifically prohibit. The basis of the school board's decision was not statutory but constitutional. Disregarding the *Everson* decision, the Board found bus service an aid to the school, and therefore public aid to religion. However, majority and minority members thought it would be best if some state authority made a clear decision. The school board was an agent of the state and of the law. The state should say what the law meant.

There seemed to be general agreement among the Board members that the differences on the request for bus service did not affect their decisions in other areas. There was no question of the commitment of Catholics on the Board to the public schools. In the minds of the Board members there was no question of Dr. Gavin's devotion to his work. He was thought to have acted with great propriety and professional skill in a difficult period. The atmosphere of the town during the dispute, however, made Dr. Gavin acutely aware that some Protestants might measure his actions as those of a Catholic, and therefore suspect.

The behavior of certain Catholics in High Hills gave rise to some suspicion that they would oppose development of the public schools in order to win bus service for parochial school pupils. This conflict between religious groups was heightened by the Protestant ministers and by Father Davey, whose actions increased religious tensions. The replacement of Father Davey by Father Leahy relieved some of the strain. Father Leahy, it was generally agreed, was working to re-establish good will.

In the spring of 1957 there was much to be done to re-establish good will in High Hills. Mrs. McNulty was still planning to "get Manners." Dr. Gavin had to select a new principal, and most of the candidates appeared to be Catholic. The school board had to re-consider the location of the proposed new elementary school and prepare another recommendation to submit to the town. Dr. Doan planned to continue the campaign for school bus service for the parochial school pupils.

The 1957 General Assembly might provide an answer to the problem that was dividing the town.

HEALTH SERVICES IN CASTLETON

At its meeting in November, 1956, the Castleton Board of Education agreed to accept financial responsibility for the dental hygiene program in the local parochial schools. The vote was four to three. Previously the cost of this program had been met by the city of Hudson, the population center of the town of Castleton. The dental program was administered by the Castleton school board. As the cost of the dental program had increased, the Hudson City Council had decided to impose the cost of the dental program on the Town of Castleton or on the Castleton Board of Education. This could be justified, since the parochial schools' population included children from both the City of Hudson and the Town of Castleton. This action of the Hudson City Council was part of a growing dissension between the city and the town over the division of financial responsibility for municipal services.[100]

Castleton is a suburb of the city of Hartford, with a variety of manufacturing plants as well as substantial agricultural activity.[101] At the beginning of the 1956–1957 school year more than 20 per cent of the town's school population was enrolled in the two Catholic schools in Hudson.[102] In 1950 Castleton had a population of about 10,000, but by 1956 that figure had increased to 15,000. The population of the city of Hudson had also increased, from about 8,000 in 1950 to about 12,000 in 1956. The 1950 census classified about 12 per cent of the Castleton population as foreign-born white.[103]

Politically, Castleton is a Republican town, although it has elected some local Democratic candidates. The city of Hudson generally votes Democratic, although in November, 1956, the Mayor of Hudson was a Republican. He was Protestant, but his wife and children were Catholic. The City Council had a Democratic majority of seven to five Republicans. In recent years Castleton has divided its votes in local elections almost evenly between Republican and Democratic candidates.[104]

The Castleton school board in November, 1956, was composed of six Republicans and three Democrats. Five of the six Republicans were Protestants and one was a Catholic. Two of the three Democratic members were Catholics and the third was a Jew.[105]

The parochial school dental program was not the first problem involving religious groups presented to the Castleton Board of Education. A few years earlier the Protestant Ministers Association had asked the Board to consider the establishment of a released-time program of religious education. The Association could not devise a satisfactory method of administering the released-time program, so a formal request was never presented to the Board.[106] However, some time later the Board was formally requested by the Gideon Bible Association to permit the distribution of Bibles and biblical literature in the classrooms. The Board was assured there would be no proselytizing. There would merely be an announcement that the material was available to any child who wished to pick it up. The Board debated this request vigorously before denying it by a vote of five to four.[107]

In 1955 the Board debated a request by a group of Jehovah's Witnesses for evening use of a public school auditorium to present a religious motion picture. The Witnesses were given permission to use the hall on the same basis as any other community group engaged in a non-profit activity. Two Board members voted in opposition.[108]

The Views of the Participants

The November action of the Castleton Board of Education was questioned at the December meeting by Board member Horton Churchill. He contended that the Board could not legally assume financial responsibility for a dental program in a non-public school.[109]

Mr. Churchill felt strongly about the principle of separation of church and state. He was chairman of the school board at the time the request of the Gideons was denied by a five-to-four vote. As chairman, he broke a four-to-four tie by voting against the request. Later he could recall ruefully the headline on the news story about that meeting: "Churchill Votes Against Bible."

A Republican and a Protestant, Mr. Churchill did not interpret the principle of separation of church and state to mean that all religious practices should be excluded from the public schools. He sent his own children to the public schools and thought it would be permissible and appropriate to have Bible readings, without comment, presented in the classroom. He believed that our civil government recognized God, but he also felt that religion should not be imposed on people. He found it difficult to be consistent in this area. He wanted no interference with individual beliefs, but he felt we could not totally ignore the existence of God.

Mr. Churchill would have opposed a released-time religious education program if that request had ever been formally presented to the Board. He had been instrumental in having the question "Are you an atheist?" removed from the application form for new teachers. It was his conviction that the religious belief of a schoolteacher was no business of the Board of Education. This conviction was perhaps inconsistent, he recognized, with his belief that our schools should include Bible readings and should give acknowledgment to the existence of God.

Mr. Churchill opposed the school board's acceptance of responsibility for the dental program in the parochial schools and intended to seek a decision that would relieve the school board of that duty.[110]

Another member opposed to the dental program for the parochial schools was Mr. George Lord Speaker, III. Mr. Speaker lived in Speakerville on the outskirts of Castleton. His large white residence was next door to the Speakerville Congregational Church and across the street from the Speaker Mills. Like Mr. Churchill, Mr. Speaker was Republican and Protestant. He held strong religious convictions and felt the public schools had divorced themselves too completely from religion. He felt that we should remember that "we are a Christian nation, or we are supposed to be."

Mr. Speaker supported the request of the Gideons to distribute Bibles and Bible literature in the schools, and he would have favored a released-time religious education program if the Board had voted on such a request. The released-time program and distribution of Bibles were not infringements of any constitutional rights. Religion was not being forced on anyone, he contended. He had no objections to Catholics distributing their Bible if they wished to. Of course Jews might object, but all minorities were free to exercise their religion. We had to remember, he insisted, that they are *minorities* and this is supposed to be a *Christian* country.

Mr. Speaker based his opposition to the request of the Jehovah's Witnesses on civil grounds, not religious. He felt that use of a public school auditorium should not be granted to a group which refused to salute the flag or bear arms in defense of the nation. His suggestion that the film the Witnesses proposed to present be reviewed for any subversive material was not accepted by the school board. If the Witnesses had requested permission to distribute their material in the classrooms, Mr. Speaker would have opposed the request because *The Watchtower* and other publications of the Witnesses were influenced by men but "the Bible is God's word."

Strict application of the law and adherence to the school board's responsibility, Mr. Speaker believed, would not permit the board to provide dental service to non-public school children. Further, parochial schools were performing a private and religious purpose, and public authorities could not properly provide any assistance to that purpose. He recognized that there would be a substantial increase in the town's financial burden if the parochial schools should be closed. Mr. Speaker was very conscious of this burden, having served for many years on the school building committee. However, those schools were engaged in a private, religious function, and Mr. Speaker voted against granting to them services paid for out of public funds.[111]

Aaron Booker, a Democrat and the only Jew on the Castleton school board, did not regard the doctrine of separation of church and state as a divine principle. He thought its application depended on circumstances.

Mr. Booker was active in local Democratic politics and had held office in the Hudson city government before his service on the school board. He had also been an officer of the Castleton Parent-Teacher Association. He had worked for the public schools, but he believed in parochial schools. He would have sent his own children to a religious school if there had been a good Jewish one in the city of Hudson. Instead, they went to the Hudson public schools. Mr. Booker did not regard the public school as a superior training ground for democracy.

A parochial school, if it did the job it was supposed to, should produce good citizens, he believed. He favored the Canadian system which provided for public support of parochial schools of the principal denominations. Under our present system of public education, Mr. Booker believed there should be no religious activity of any kind in the public schools. He voted against the distribution of the Bibles, and he would have opposed a request for a released-time religious education program. He was opposed to prayers, psalms, Christmas carols, and any celebration of religious holidays in the public schools. It was Mr. Booker's belief that the dental program for the parochial schools was not properly before the school board. The Board of Education was responsible only for the public schools.[112]

Perhaps the most vocal of the three Catholics on the Castleton Board of Education was Dennis Doherty, a lawyer active in Democratic politics. Mr. Doherty, a lifetime resident of the city of Hudson, led the opposition to cuts in the school board budget made by the Board of Finance. In a year-long fight the town budget was three times forced to a referendum, and each time the townspeople supported the Board of Education by rejecting the budget submitted by the finance board. Eventually, the finance board members resigned and a new Board of Finance voted the school budget recommended by the Board of Education. Mr. Doherty received a good deal of the credit for the victory in this unprecedented struggle. His efforts on behalf of public education included working within the Democratic Party to get a platform commitment to increased state support for schools.

Mr. Doherty sent his own children to the Hudson public schools although he lived near one of the Catholic schools in town. His decision was based largely on the fact that the classes in the Catholic school were so large. There had been no change and no expansion in the Catholic school in twenty years although the size of the congregation had increased. The pastor was not inclined to make changes, nor had he been active in seeking public services for the Catholic school children. He, like the Protestant ministers, took no part in the debate about dental services.

As a lawyer and a member of the American Civil Liberties Union, Mr. Doherty had devoted thought and study to the question of separation of church and state. He found it hard to draw a clear, unwavering line. He voted against distribution of Bibles in the classrooms, and he would have voted against a request for a released-time religious education program if one had been made. He argued vigorously, however, for the right of the Jehovah's Witnesses to use the school auditorium. He cited the Supreme Court's defense of their right to refuse to salute the flag and to refuse to bear arms. "A democracy," he told the Board, "is tested by its granting of rights to minorities."

Mr. Doherty's views ran very close to those expressed by Justice Black's minority opinion in the *Zorach* case. He could not agree with Justice Douglas' majority opinion which gave approval to New York's released-time religious education program.

Mr. Doherty respected the sincerity of the convictions of board member Horton Churchill, who interpreted the principle of separation of church and state more severely than he did. However, he questioned the sincerity of George Lord Speaker, III, who felt church-state separation would be violated by cleaning the teeth of parochial school children but saw nothing wrong with distributing Bibles in the public schools. Mr. Doherty found it hard to view this as anything but bigotry. To him the cleaning of teeth of any school child was a health service, not an educational service, and a permissible expenditure of public funds. When Board member Churchill moved the rescinding of the Board's vote to support the parochial school dental program, Mr. Doherty voted against the motion.[113]

The views of Mr. Doherty were shared to a considerable degree by another Catholic school board member, Warren Sales. Mr. Sales was a native of Hudson and lived in the second floor of a two-family house in that city. He worked as a truck driver during the day and was attending college at night in preparation for a career of teaching. He was also active in local Democratic politics. Mr. Sales sent his own children to the Hudson public schools. He made this decision reluctantly after a month's trial of sending them to the Hudson

Catholic school nearby. He believed the religious atmosphere was extremely important in a child's education. However, the classes at the Catholic school averaged about fifty pupils per room, and this was just too much.

Like Mr. Doherty, Mr. Sales voted against the distribution of Gideon Bibles and in favor of the Jehovah's Witnesses' request to use the school auditorium. He supported this request as he would that of any responsible community group which adhered to the regulations of the Board about after-hours use of the schools. He opposed the request of the Gideons because he felt the public schools should not be used in any way to favor one religion or to favor religion generally. He would not have voted for a released-time religious education program for that reason. He thought it inadvisable to separate public school children on a religious basis.

In general, Mr. Sales believed that public services and facilities should be under public control. For this reason he voted in favor of the dental program for parochial school children. He would also favor other special services at public expense to parochial school children if the services were under public control. He did not agree, however, with any proposal that public funds be appropriated for the construction of buildings or facilities at parochial schools. Such buildings or facilities could not then be under public control.[114]

The third Catholic on the Castleton school board was Mrs. Ruth Fast and, unlike Mr. Doherty and Mr. Sales, she was Republican. Mrs. Fast was a native of New York and had moved to Castleton after her marriage. She lived in a modest frame house on the edge of town with her three children, all of whom attended public schools. She felt the distance to Hudson was too great to send the children to the Catholic schools there.

Mrs. Fast opposed the request of the Gideons on the grounds that the Gideon Bible was a sectarian book and the public schools should offer only the truth that everyone can accept. She was not opposed to some religion in the classroom but thought that such ceremonies as Easter pageants should be avoided since they could promote antagonism between Christians and Jews. Joint religious festivals such as Christmas and Hanukkah, she felt, should be dependent on the feeling of the community. She would have supported a request for a released-time religious education program. Mrs. Fast opposed the request of the Jehovah's Witnesses because she believed a school was dedicated to training the mind and heart of a child. A school should develop loyalty and integrity. If it were shown that a group could flaunt its disregard for loyalty and patriotism in a school building, the school would be failing in its job.

Mrs. Fast believed that the dental program and other health services, including transportation, could properly be provided at public expense to parochial school children. (She was not certain, however, that such services could also be provided to private non-parochial schools.) [115]

On the motion before the Castleton Board of Education in December, 1956, Mrs. Fast voted with her two Catholic and Democratic colleagues against the motion to withdraw Board support of the dental program for parochial school pupils. Voting to adopt the motion to rescind were four Republican and Protestant Board members.

The rules of the Board required a two-thirds majority to rescind a Board action. The four-to-three majority was insufficient to rescind, but the Board agreed to a request to seek legal advice on the question from the town counsel.[116]

In January, 1957, the Board received advice from the town counsel of Castleton that in his opinion the Connecticut statutes authorized the Board of Education to provide health services to public school pupils only. Board member Dennis Doherty then moved to rescind the Board's November decision to pay for dental services to parochial school pupils and to inquire of the Castleton Board of Selectmen about the use of town funds to provide such services. The motion was adopted unanimously.[117]

Conclusions About Castleton

The questions relating to religious groups faced by the Castleton Board of Education were answered by the Board without any outside influence. All of the members quoted above agreed that neither the political leaders nor the religious leaders made any effort to influence the Board's decisions about the Jehovah's Witnesses' request, the Gideon Bibles, or the dental program. Further, they all reported that they had been subjected to no public pressure or even approached by anyone who attempted to influence them outside of the Board meeting.

The members also reported that the Board's procedure was never improper. Fair treatment was accorded to all concerned in dealing with these issues. There was no indication that these disputes generated any continuing antagonisms that carried over into other fields.

There was general agreement that these issues were not partisan questions. The Board members did not regard their votes on these issues as cast on party lines, but an analysis of the voting reveals that the support for the Gideons' request and opposition to the dental program for parochial school pupils was provided by Protestant and Republican board members. More specifically, in December, 1956, when Horton Churchill moved to rescind the Board's action to support the dental program for the parochial schools, the four votes in favor were cast by Protestant Republicans. The three votes opposed were cast by two Catholic Democrats and one Catholic Republican. Aaron Booker, the Jewish Democrat, did not vote.

In November, 1956, on Mr. Doherty's motion for the school board to accept financial responsibility for the dental program, two Catholic Democrats and one Catholic Republican voted for, and three Protestant Republicans voted against the motion. The chairman, a Protestant Republican, broke the tie by voting for the motion.

The previous year another chairman, also a Protestant Republican, had broken a four-four tie on the request of the Gideons to distribute Bibles in the classrooms. The four opposition votes were cast by the two Catholic Democrats, the Catholic Republican, and the Jewish Democrat. The four votes in favor of the distribution of Bibles were all cast by Protestant Republicans.

Only one Protestant Republican, Horton Churchill, thought that the principle of separation of church and state should be invoked against both parochial school public services and Protestant Bibles in the public schools. The Catholic Republican, Mrs. Fast, while she opposed the Gideon Bible distribution and favored the dental services for parochial school pupils, differed from her Catholic Democratic fellow members in favoring the establishment of a released-time religious education program if one should have been proposed. Three Protestant Republicans found it possible to vote against the parochial school dental program after they had voted the year before in favor of distributing Protestant Bibles in the public schools.

The request of the Jehovah's Witnesses to use the school auditorium was regarded by a majority of the board as presenting no challenge to the principle of church-state separation. Even the minority of two claimed their objections were based on civil and not religious grounds.

In supporting the dental program for parochial school pupils, as was done at the meeting in November, 1956, the Castleton Board of Education was applying the logic of the Supreme Court in the *Cochran* case and the *Everson* case to health services. The justification was the child-benefit theory; the dental service was an aid to the children not to the school. The rescinding of this action at the January meeting did not reflect an abandonment of the principle but rather an acknowledgment of a lack of statutory authority. The Board, although believing in the value of the program, would not do anything illegal.

In opposing the distribution of Gideon Bibles to the pupils in the public schools the Castleton school board may be said to have acted in consonance with the Supreme Court's decision in the *McCollum* case. It was not clear, however, that the majority of the Board would have accepted the Court's opinion without qualification. Some members of the Castleton school board appeared to be voting against denominationalism, not against religion in the public schools. Only one member, Mr. Booker, a Jew and a Democrat, expressed himself as opposed to all religious activity in the public schools. Still, he favored public support of parochial schools of all denominations. Mr. Doherty's adherence to Justice Black's minority opinion in the

Zorach case suggested a clear opposition to the use of public funds to aid religion. However, Mr. Doherty also found it possible to support the dental program as a service to children and not to the parochial school.

The Castleton school board was able to decide these questions with little or no lasting bitterness and with no apparent community disturbance. All of the members agreed that the questions were better handled without the entrance of the local political or religious leaders. Neither was there any question of the Catholic Board members' commitment to the public schools. Indeed, all of the members quoted above had given ample demonstration of their devotion to public education by their work on the Board and with school organizations.

Of course the mild nature of the debate may have been due to the fact that it was largely a statutory and bookkeeping decision. Even when the Board rescinded its vote to support the dental program for parochial school pupils, there was expectation that the Selectmen would continue the program. Further, dental service was not the daily necessity that bus service could be for a family living some distance from school. Nor was it nearly as expensive to have a child's teeth cleaned once a year as it was to transport him twice a day.

The Castleton Board of Education had a series of difficult questions concerning religious groups, but the members felt they had handled those questions well. Still, since there appeared to be some question about the legality of public services to parochial school pupils, the Board members agreed that a clear decision by the state legislature would be desirable.

CONCLUSIONS ABOUT THE LOCAL DISPUTES

The need for a state law on auxiliary services was virtually the only point on which there was general agreement among the participants in the four case studies presented here.

In three instances, legal opinions were sought, but only in Castleton was the school board guided by the legal opinion it received. The Castleton school board first agreed to accept responsibility for providing dental service to parochial school pupils, then reversed itself on advice of counsel. In High Hills, the town counsel, contradicting the opinion of his predecessor, said he could not "find anything illegal" in public service for parochial school pupils. The school board still said "No." In Diamond City the City Attorney found no authority in the state law nor in the city charter for the City Council or the school board to transport parochial school pupils. Nevertheless the school board, under pressure from the public and the City Council, followed the Council's request to continue transporting parochial school pupils. The Parkville school board denied the request for transportation without seeking legal advice.

Local board of education members could reach a policy decision on the issue of auxiliary services without the benefit of legal advice, and sometimes indeed in spite of it.

The arguments used in the local disputes were the familiar ones. The principal justifications for auxiliary services were the child-benefit theory, the public purpose of parochial schools, and the tax savings they made possible. Only in Castleton was the case for auxiliary services based exclusively on the child-benefit principle. This might have been due to the fact that health services are more readily accepted as a service to the pupil, not to the school.

In all three disputes about bus service, proponents of that service mentioned the tax savings effected by parochial schools. They saw public transportation as both a service to the child and an aid to the religious school.

In the *Everson* case the Supreme Court majority relied on the child-benefit theory. Assistance to religious education was regarded as incidental and not cause for invalidating the law authorizing public transportation of non-profit private school pupils. In three of the four disputes reported above the assistance rendered the parochial school was presented as the major reason, or one of the major reasons, for requesting transportation. The service to pupils was employed as a supplementary argument. Those who sought transportation cited the

Everson case but were apparently unaware that their line of argument contradicted the basis of that decision.

Those who argued against services for parochial school pupils did not accept the interpretation made in the *Everson* case. For the opponents of auxiliary services, transportation was generally held to be a service to the parochial school, therefore public assistance to religious education. This was held to be a violation of the principle of separation of church and state. School board members in High Hills and Diamond City held private convictions against the existence of parochial schools. Such misgivings about parochial schools might have been the unexpressed basis of other opposition to public services for pupils of those schools.

In all four places the separation of church and state was presented as an argument against services. The definition of the separation principle varied. Only Mr. Bernard in Diamond City interpreted the principle so strictly as to prohibit not only public services to parochial school pupils, but also all religious activities in the public schools. The separation principle as used by other opponents of auxiliary services was not meant to prohibit religious practices in public school classrooms. Prayers, Bible reading, and religious pageants were frequently regarded as permissible and desirable public school activities by opponents of public services to parochial school pupils. The Reverend Mr. Esty in Diamond City and the Reverend Mr. Paul in Parkville both favored religion in the public schools. It might have been expected that clergymen would be favorably disposed to government assistance to the purposes of their profession. It was surprising that, while holding such views, they should still profess belief in the principle of church-state separation. They did not accept the repeated declarations of the Supreme Court that government "may not aid one religion, aid all religions or prefer one religion over another."

The familiar argument that bus service was an "opening wedge" was heard in these local disputes. There was some justification for such an assertion. Some Protestants as well as Catholics stated privately that they would support requests for some additional public services to non-public school pupils. Private statements, however, were often qualified. And they did not always coincide with public actions. When it came to a vote on auxiliary services, school board members "voted their religion." Catholics voted for services. Protestants, with two exceptions, voted against services. On the key ballots in these four local disputes, all eleven votes of Catholic board members were cast for services. Two Protestants also voted for services. Fifteen Protestants and one Jew voted against services.

If the votes of Mr. Bernard, a Protestant, and Mr. Green, a Jew, are discounted because of their expressed qualifications, there remain fifteen Protestants opposed to services and only one Protestant, Dr. Pinza, in favor. (Of course the members of the Castleton school board, Protestants and Catholics, reversed the board's action unanimously when they were advised that they had no legal authority to provide dental service to non-public school pupils.) Thus, with only one exception based on conviction—Dr. Pinza in High Hills—Protestants voted against services and Catholics voted in favor of them.

The school board members did not divide with any consistency along party lines. Generally, Republicans voted against services and Democrats voted for them. The Republicans divided three to one (twelve to four) against services. The Democratic members divided better than two to one (nine to four) in favor of services. This division, however, is a measure of the religious composition of the boards by party. Catholics in these places tended to be Democrats, Protestants tended to be Republicans. In these four local disputes, boards divided not on party lines but according to religious affiliation.

The effect of these disputes on the atmosphere of a community is difficult to determine with exactitude. In two places, Castleton and Parkville, there was apparently little community strife. The questions were handled by the school boards. There was no pressure exerted by political or religious leaders on the Castleton school board. In Parkville the political leaders did not attempt to influence the school board. They seem to have had no opportunity to do so since the board decided the question promptly. Religious leaders, Father Daniel and the Reverend Mr. Paul, were involved, but both behaved with restraint. This was in contrast to the behavior of the clergy in

Religion and Auxiliary Services

The religious affiliations of local school board members who voted for, and against, the extension of auxiliary services to pupils in non-public, non-profit schools.

	High Hills	Parkville	Diamond City	Castleton	Total
For services					
Protestant	1	0	1	0	2
Catholic	2	4	2	3	11
Jewish	0	0	0	0	0
Against services					
Protestant	6	5	0	4	1
Catholic	0	0	0	0	15
Jewish	0	0	1	0	0

Political Party and Auxiliary Services

The political party affiliations of local school board members who voted for, and against, the extension of auxiliary services to pupils in non-public, non-profit schools.

	High Hills	Parkville	Diamond City	Castleton	Total
For services					
Republican	2	1	0	1	4
Democrat	1	3	3	2	9
Against services					
Republican	4	4	0	4	12
Democrat	2	1	1	0	4

Diamond City and High Hills. In those two places the use of religious office for stimulating public opinion on a political issue stirred resentment as well as support. In those communities political leaders were also involved. In Diamond City, Mayor Carmello and Councilman Alza, both Catholic Democrats, played leading roles. In High Hills Mrs. McNulty, a Catholic Democrat, undertook a political campaign for transportation. If it cannot be said definitively that these political leaders were responding to a call for political action by the Catholic clergy, it can be observed that they did not act until after the clergymen made their appeal. It can also be observed that in these two places, High Hills and Diamond City, where the clergy were politically active, community feeling ran far higher than in Castleton, where the clergy took no part, and in Parkville, where the role of the clergy was limited. Further, differences over bus service became so great in High Hills that the development of the public school system was affected. Some Catholics expressed intentions of opposing the school building program in retaliation for the school board's refusal of bus service for parochial school pupils. This convinced some Protestants that "the Catholics were against the public schools," despite the expansion program planned and promoted by Superintendent Gavin, a Catholic, and despite the activity of other Catholics in town in support of the program.

For assistance in the resolution of their differences over public services for parochial school pupils, many people in High Hills, in Diamond City, in Parkville, and in Castleton looked to the 1957 session of the Connecticut General Assembly. They believed that a clear statement of policy was badly needed and that the representatives of the people ought to provide it.

VI:

THE

LEGISLATIVE

STRUGGLE

THE SWEEPING victory of President Eisenhower in 1956 was accompanied in Connecticut by the election of overwhelming Republican majorities in both houses of the state legislature. In the 1957 session there were in the Senate 31 Republicans and only 5 Democrats; in the House of Representatives there were 249 Republicans and only 30 Democrats.[1]

To some observers these large Republican majorities suggested a direct relation to the future of what were regarded as denominational bills. The improved chance for repeal of the birth control law was explained as "not because the voting has been a party matter, but because more Protestants than Catholics have usually been nominated and elected by the Republicans, and *vice versa*." [2] This same reasoning might have led to the conclusion that a proposal favoring public services for parochial school pupils would have little chance in the 1957 General Assembly.

Despite this apparent difficulty, Catholic parents in towns where there had been a conflict wanted the auxiliary services problem settled on the state level. Some of them spoke to their pastors. Eventually, these views were presented to Archbishop Henry J. O'Brien. The Archbishop knew that some bills, not entirely satisfactory, were being introduced. He felt that there was strong feeling among Connecticut Catholics in favor of legislative action on this issue, and he reacted accordingly. He consulted, among others, Joseph Cooney, attorney for the Archdiocese, and Monsignor Robert W. Doyle, superintendent of schools for the Archdiocese. He asked them to prepare a bill. The bill they drafted proposed simply and broadly:

> Any town which provides any municipal services for the children of the town attending public schools may provide similar services to any child of said town attending a private school not conducted for profit in said town.

This bill was later criticized for the broad term "municipal services." In Monsignor Doyle's mind this term meant medical, dental, and nursing services as furnished to public school pupils. The exclusion of profit schools was made in anticipation of the objections of opponents. Those who drafted the bill were trying to avoid from the beginning the contention of opponents that such services would aid expensive private schools.[3]

Senator Benjamin Kopacz, Republican and Catholic of Meriden, had announced in his campaign that he would work in the legislature for a bill providing public services for private school pupils. Accordingly, he introduced bills which would amend the Meriden City Charter to permit such services. When Senator Kopacz was asked by John Hurley if he would sponsor a bill permitting such services to be given by any town, he readily agreed.[4]

Mr. Hurley was to be a persistent proponent of what later came to be known as the school bus bill. He conducted a public relations service in Hartford and was Hartford agent for United States Senator William Purtell. Both Senator Purtell and Mr. Hurley were Republican and Catholic. Mr. Hurley had played a leading part in the surprisingly successful campaign for Congress by Republican Edwin May in Hartford County in 1956. It was the first time in many years that a Republican congressman had been elected from that county. To Mr. Hurley it was essential for the future of the Republican Party in Connecticut that the school bus law bill be passed by the 1957 General Assembly. The Republicans had overwhelming control of both houses. They could not evade the responsibility if the bill were defeated. What chance would Republican candidates for Governor or Congress have in 1958 if this bill were defeated, he asked.[5]

Some opponents of services for parochial school pupils anticipated the issue arising in the 1957 legislature. Sigmund Adler had been startled by the speech of Richard Joyce Smith in April, 1956, to the convention of independent schools. He had written his objections to Mr. Smith.[6] He also brought the matter to the attention of the executive committee of the Connecticut Council of Churches. He telephoned the Reverend Dr. Loyd Worley, minister of Hartford's First Methodist Church. At a meeting of the executive committee it was agreed that the responsibility for developing a campaign of opposition to the drive for services would be placed with the Committee on Civic and Moral Relationships headed by Dr. Worley.[7]

Dr. Worley was experienced in legislative matters. He had campaigned unsuccessfully in earlier sessions of the General Assembly for repeal of the birth control prohibition law and he had opposed, also unsuccessfully, the so-called "Raffles Bill" in the 1955 legislature. This law permitted municipalities to allow non-profit or charitable organizations to conduct lotteries. Many Protestant leaders had worked vigorously against the bill. Dr. Worley with others had sought to persuade Governor Abraham Ribicoff to veto the measure. They were unsuccessful. The Governor's attitude, it seemed to Dr. Worley, was that "the Catholics wanted it and they had the votes."

In preparing his campaign of opposition to the 1957 school bus bill, Dr. Worley sought the assistance of the national office of Protestants and Other Americans United for Separation of Church and State. They provided him with information, pamphlets, and other material to distribute to legislators and Connecticut residents.[8]

The bill prepared by attorney Cooney and Monsignor Doyle was transmitted to Senator Kopacz by Mr. Hurley.[9] When Senator Kopacz introduced the bill on January 24, it was designated Senate Bill 872 and was referred to the Committee on Cities and Boroughs.[10] Mr. Hurley discussed the bill with Republican State Chairman

Clarence Baldwin, a Protestant, and stressed its importance to the future of the Republican Party. Passage of the bill, he believed, would be very important in the 1958 campaigns of Senator Purtell, Congressman May, and the Republican candidate for Governor. Connecticut, he said, was 62 per cent Catholic.* How could a Republican candidate hope to win if this bill were defeated? [11]

When State Chairman Baldwin first heard about the bill early in the legislative session, he made up his mind almost immediately that he would support it. He regarded it as providing for safety services for children. All children should be protected on the road to and from school, he believed. Some towns had been doing it in Connecticut for twenty-five years. Those who asserted constitutional objections were pretty late in doing so, he thought. A long precedent had been established. Furthermore, if it were unconstitutional, a lawsuit could settle the question. He assured Mr. Hurley that he would favor the bill. [12]

Mr. Hurley suggested that Archbishop O'Brien would be interested in hearing Mr. Baldwin's view and asked if he would go to see the Archbishop. Mr. Baldwin agreed, and Mr. Hurley arranged the appointment for an evening in the middle of January. [13] The meeting was brief, lasting only about half an hour. Mr. Baldwin expressed his view of the bill as a measure to protect children. He told the Archbishop the measure would have his support and he believed the bill could be passed. One of the priests present asked Mr. Baldwin what he thought the role of the Catholic clergy should be. Mr. Baldwin replied that the best thing they could do would be to stay

* The description of Connecticut as 62 per cent Catholic has been based on the percentage of Connecticut children born in 1956, of whom 62 per cent were reported to be Catholic. See below, p. 219. A survey by the National Council of Churches may also be the source. The first news report of this survey stated that Connecticut's population was divided 62 per cent Catholic, 32 per cent Protestant, and 6 per cent Jewish (Hartford Times, April 6, 1957). A later story explained that these percentages were of church membership (Hartford Times, April 20, 1957). Almost half of Connecticut's population claimed no church membership. Thus the percentages given should be reduced by almost half. But these are mercurial statistics and recall Henry S. Commager's observation that churches use membership statistics in ways that would send a corporation executive to jail. (The American Mind [New Haven: Yale University Press, 1954], p. 166).

out of it. If the bill could be presented as a proposal for protection of children and not as a proposal of the Catholic Church, it would have a better chance of passage.[14]

The issue was recognized as a difficult one when it was brought up early in the session at a Republican legislative policy meeting in the office of the Lieutenant Governor. Present at such meetings on measures to be brought before the General Assembly were the leaders in the House and Senate, Republican State Chairman Baldwin, and some Republican county leaders. When the Kopacz bill came up for discussion before the meeting, everyone "looked sort of unhappy" and agreed this was a "tough one," but there was general support for the bill.[15] Senate president pro tempore Theodore Ryan said that he was in favor of the bill.

A Catholic Republican, Senator Ryan had experienced some opposition in his own county within the Republican Party because of his support of the birth control law. He was irritated by charges that he represented not the voters of Litchfield County but the policies of Rome. He felt he had grown accustomed to this kind of opposition, but he was annoyed by suggestions that his political activity was determined by his religious affiliation.[16]

After Senator Ryan expressed his support, Lieutenant Governor Charles Jewett, a Protestant, said he had some reservations about the bill. There were no other expressions of opposition, and it seemed agreed that the leadership would support the bill. There was little discussion of the merits of the proposal, and there was no mention of the relation of this bill to Catholic votes for Republican candidates. It was agreed there would be no public statements about the bill by the leadership until the public hearing on the measure. One of the leaders explained later, "We agreed to wait until the storm broke and then we'd see how hard it was raining." [17]

THE EARLY MANEUVERING

Five bills dealing with public services for non-public school pupils were introduced in the 1957 General Assembly.[18]

Three of these were sponsored in the Senate by Senator Benjamin Kopacz of Meriden. Two of his bills were local, amending the charter of the city of Meriden. One, Senate Bill 898, would make it permissive for the City Council to transport non-public elementary school children. Another, Senate Bill 900, would make it mandatory for the school board to provide the same bus service to pupils in non-profit private schools as was given public school pupils. The third, Senate Bill 872, would affect all towns with non-profit private schools. This was the bill which had been prepared by attorney Cooney and Monsignor Doyle and transmitted to Senator Kopacz by John Hurley.

Two bills dealing with auxiliary services were introduced in the House of Representatives. One of these, House Bill 870, introduced by Representative Louis J. Padula, Republican of Norwalk, was a companion bill to Senator Kopacz's S.B. 872. The other, House Bill 880, was introduced by Representatives David J. Dickson, Jr., and Benito Muzio, both of Stafford and both Democrats. This bill would make it mandatory for towns to provide transportation for parochial school pupils. (This was the only bill specifying parochial schools.) The Dickson-Muzio bill also called for partial state reimbursement to certain towns for transporting parochial school pupils as was done for public school pupils.

The Dickson-Muzio bill and the two bills amending Meriden's charter were referred to the House and Senate Education Committees. But Senator Kopacz's bill affecting all towns with non-profit private schools, and its companion in the House, the Padula bill, were referred to the Senate and House Committees on Cities and Boroughs. Senator Albert Snyder of Bloomfield, chairman of the Senate Committee on Cities and Boroughs, and Mr. Padula, who was himself chairman of the House Committee on Cities and Boroughs, were more favorably disposed toward the auxiliary services proposals than the chairmen of the House and Senate Education Committees.

Both Representative Edwin O. Smith, House Education chairman, and Senator Philip Bauer, Senate Education chairman, were strongly opposed to public services for parochial school pupils. Mr. Smith felt that these proposals would serve as a prelude to requests for additional aid for parochial schools. He knew that the local-option feature would appeal to many members of the House, but there had been some objections about improper delegations of state authority to the towns. He regretted that the issue of auxiliary services was being raised. He thought the dispute might be bitter. He was intent, however, on handling the proposals in the Education Committee. Both he and Senator Bauer were agreed that the Kopacz and Padula bills in Cities and Boroughs should be transferred to the Education Committees. Senator Bauer spoke to Lieutenant Governor Jewett, presiding officer of the Senate, about the Kopacz bill, S.B. 872, while Mr. Smith spoke to House majority leader Frederick Pope about the Padula bill, H.B. 870.[19]

Mr. Pope had made up his mind to support the proposal for public services to non-public school pupils on a local-option basis. He had been given much information about the issue by Richard Joyce Smith. They were both lawyers and residents of the town of Fairfield and knew each other personally. Mr. Pope spent some time studying the issue, convinced himself that the proposal was constitutional, and concluded that the law ought to state clearly that such practices were permissible. Mr. Pope, a Protestant, regarded himself as more favorably disposed to public than to private schools. Parochial schools, however, were not private in the usual sense. Most of the pupils were children of parents of average or less than average means. Mr. Pope didn't regard this issue as one to be treated "politically," but he saw the measure as one that would benefit the families in the lower income brackets. He thought it was important for the Republican Party to rid itself of the label of the "rich man's party." Although he favored the proposal for services, Mr. Pope was aware that the intense division about it among House members could cause much bad feeling and hurt the Republican Party in Connecticut. He wanted the bill handled with the utmost propriety. Therefore, when E. O. Smith asked about the transfer of the Padula bill from Cities and Boroughs to the Education Committee, he readily agreed. He did not want to give any appearance of parliamentary manipulation.[20]

Speaker Nelson Brown of Groton shared Mr. Pope's views on the committee reference of the Padula bill. As Speaker, he had made the decisions about referral of bills to the various committees. He realized it would be bad legislative procedure to have the Education Committee and the Cities and Boroughs Committee consider them simultaneously, especially when, in all probability, they would have conflicting reports. Supporters of the proposal for auxiliary services were opposed to moving the bill from Cities and Boroughs. They pressed their views on Speaker Brown. Mr. Hurley, particularly, told Mr. Brown that if he let the bill go to the Education Committee it would be dead. Mr. Brown replied that it was his function as Speaker to see that bills were properly referred; the Padula bill belonged in the Education Committee with the other bills concerning services for non-public schools.[21] Mr. Pope spoke to Mr. Padula about transferring his bill to the Education Committee, and he readily agreed.

Lieutenant Governor Jewett, who shared Senator Bauer's opposition to the Kopacz bill, agreed that it belonged in Education rather than in Cities and Boroughs.[22] On February 20, 1957, Senate Bill 872 was transferred to Education, and the following day the Padula bill, H.B. 870, was also transferred.[23] With these transfers accomplished, the Education Committee the following week set a public hearing on the various auxiliary services bills for March 12.[24] Anticipating a large attendance, the Education chairmen arranged for the hearing to be held in the Hall of the House of Representatives. In the weeks preceding the hearing, the proponents and opponents of the proposals busied themselves with organizing support for their positions.

In the early weeks of the session, the Reverend Loyd Worley devoted himself to writing many non-Catholic legislators urging defeat of auxiliary services bills. He arranged for distribution of materials supplied by Protestants and Other Americans United. Every legislator was sent a copy of a pamphlet "The Bus Wedge," by Paul Blanshard.

The Blanshard pamphlet declared that transportation for all Catholic schools would mean thirty-five million dollars annually taken from public funds and given to the Catholic Church. The demand for public bus money was described as part of a world-wide policy for general support of Catholic schools by public money. He warned:

> Every concession to a bus demand is used as a precedent for those larger concessions which constitute the whole Catholic program. The truth of these assertions can be seen by a glance at the picture in Catholic countries.

He quoted the 1948 statement of the Catholic bishops to contend they favored federal money for "support of all the major activities of all sectarian schools." He quoted the April, 1955, issue of the *Catholic World*, which stated editorially that the main question in federal aid to education was: "Is the Federal Government planning to offer any help toward the building of non-public schools?" The editorial contended, "in the matter of erecting new school buildings, it's obvious that American children are entitled to the benefits of public welfare legislation regardless of race, creed or color." Mr. Blanshard concluded:

> Yes, the Catholic demand for school bus money is only an entering wedge driven into the heart of the wall of separation between church and state by a powerful, worldwide organization which stands wherever possible for state religion and some union of church and state.[25]

In addition to distributing such material, Dr. Worley wrote, telephoned, and spoke personally with fellow Protestant clergymen and other Connecticut citizens urging them to use their influence against the bills that were to be given a public hearing on March 12.[26] He also suggested they attend the hearing and testify in opposition to the measures.[27]

Monsignor Robert Doyle and the staff of the office of the Diocesan Superintendent of Schools in Hartford were busy mimeographing and distributing material supporting proposals for services to non-public school pupils. Information about the *Everson* decision, the practices in many Connecticut towns, and the report of the Committee for the White House Conference on Education in 1955 were sent to legislators and other Connecticut citizens. Catholics, particularly those in towns with parochial schools, were urged to see their legislators and seek their support.[28]

Notice of the March 12 hearing was sent from the headquarters of the Hartford Archdiocese to all Catholic clergymen. They were advised that no priests or nuns should attend the hearing. Parish members attending were to be advised to register in favor of the proposals but to leave the speaking to those who were organizing the presentation of supporting testimony.[29]

John Hurley prepared for the public hearing by speaking to legislators and urging them to attend and speak in favor of the Kopacz bill, Senate Bill 872. He had worked out the parliamentary strategy he wanted to use. He would get the sponsors of the various measures to withdraw their bills and give their support to Senator Kopacz's bill. When the bill came out of the Joint Education Committee with an unfavorable report, it would be reported to the Senate. Mr. Hurley was certain the Senate would override the unfavorable report and pass the bill. This would put the issue up to the House with special intensity. The House members would be in a difficult position to vote against a bill that had already won Senate approval. The sponsors of other measures agreed to his suggestion.[30]

Mr. Hurley drafted a statement supporting public services for non-public school pupils. He showed the document to State Chairman Baldwin and told him that it would be helpful if a leading Protestant Republican legislator made such a statement just prior to the public hearing. Chairman Baldwin, after looking over the paper, remarked that he knew the assistant Senate majority leader, Benjamin Barringer of New Milford, agreed with the viewpoint expressed there. He said he would ask Senator Barringer if he would be willing to make such a public statement.

Senator Barringer was willing and eager.[31] Accordingly, it was announced in the newspapers on March 7 that Republican Senate leader Benjamin Barringer favored permissive legislation for towns to decide whether to provide bus service and health services to non-profit private school pupils as well as to public school pupils. He was quoted as saying it was "only reasonable that a child attending a school in his own town should not have to travel on foot on a high-way without sidewalks and be in peril of death and injury." [32]

This announcement struck both Lieutenant Governor Charles Jewett and House majority leader Frederick Pope as a violation of the agreement of the leaders to refrain from comment until the public hearing. Both protested to Mr. Baldwin, who acknowledged that he had arranged for Senator Barringer to issue the statement.[33] The public effect Mr. Hurley had achieved foreshadowed, and per-haps gave impetus to, the supporting testimony by legislators at the public hearing.

THE PUBLIC HEARING

The Hall of the House of Representatives was crowded on the morning of March 12, 1957.[34] There was an air of expectancy that was not usual for public hearings. Senate Education chairman Philip Bauer opened the hearing by first, according to custom, calling upon legislative sponsors of the bills under consideration that day. Mr. Padula and Mr. Dickson rose to announce they were withdrawing their bills in favor of a substitute for Senate Bill 872 sponsored by Senator Kopacz.

The substitute bill had been prepared and three hundred copies mimeographed by attorney Joseph Cooney, counsel to the Catholic Archdiocese of Hartford.[35] Originally S.B. 872 had defined the serv-ices to be provided as "any municipal services." [36] This broad de-scription was modified in the substitute bill to read "any of the health or safety services, including transportation." [37] In fact there was no such bill as "substitute for S.B. 872." The last date for in-troducing bills had passed without this substitute having been introduced. Committees might still raise bills, but this was not a committee bill. However, it was discussed at the hearing as though it were a bill actually under consideration by the Education Committee. The fact that there was no such bill as "substitute S.B. 872" was to cause parliamentary complications later.[38]

Perhaps the most striking feature of the public hearing occurred in the opening minutes when a succession of Republican and Democratic legislators spoke in favor of public services for non-public school pupils.[39] Among those giving supporting testimony were Senate president pro tempore Theodore Ryan, assistant Senate majority leader Barringer, Senate minority leader Arthur Healey, and several others. The senators were followed by House majority leader Pope and more than twenty other House members.

After the senators and representatives had testified (only two representatives, both Republicans, Jack Turner and Ruth Jones, testified in opposition), the chairman opened the hearing to testimony by the public.

Senator Bauer, obviously determined to keep the hearing calm and orderly, announced that the time would be divided, in twenty-minute segments, between the supporters and opponents of the bill. The first twenty minutes would be given to the bill's proponents.

Richard Joyce Smith and Sigmund Adler were seated in the front row on either side of the center aisle. These antagonists had stated their views firmly in their exchange of letters published in the *Transcript*. They met now in the legislative chamber in the manner of opposing floor leaders.

The Proponents

The chairman recognized Richard Joyce Smith, member of the State Board of Education, as the first speaker in support of the proposal. Mr. Smith deferred to and introduced William H. Mortensen, former Republican mayor of Hartford, former state senator, and a Protestant.

Mr. Mortensen said he could speak in support of the principle embodied in the proposed bill out of his experience in public office.

He had supported certain public services in Hartford for children in non-public schools. Those included medical, nursing, and instructional services. The Hartford Board of Education administered intelligence and achievement tests for eighth-grade students of non-public schools. This helped to reduce the number of potentially unqualified students who might be admitted to public high schools.

In deciding whether to provide such services, Mr. Mortensen said, local authorities need ask themselves only two questions: What are the things that operate for the support of a church or creed or private interest? And what are the things that operate for the health, welfare, and safety of children? (Mr. Mortensen had defined the problem and gave the impression that he thought he had solved it.)

It would cost Hartford $2,750,000 annually to provide public school education for the 7400 pupils in the parochial schools, Mr. Mortensen said. The people of Hartford were grateful to be spared this cost. His line of argument suggested that the health and welfare services were extended in gratitude for the public service rendered by the parochial schools. Mr. Mortensen concluded with the comment that this legislation would give towns a sound legal basis for supplying health and welfare services "to all their school children." He ignored the exclusion of pupils of profit schools.

Mr. Mortensen was followed by Richard Joyce Smith, who quoted from the study of public and non-public schools made by the State Department of Education.[40] The study, he said, showed the problem was a growing one. Services for non-public school pupils was not antagonistic to the public school system. He could not support any proposal that would hurt our public schools, he said. But children should not be penalized because their parents send them to non-public schools.

The Committee for the White House Conference on Education, Mr. Smith declared, had recommended that all school children receive basic health and safety services, regardless of whether they were enrolled in public or non-public schools.[41] This report, he noted, had been signed by his Fairfield County neighbor Roy Larsen, publisher of *Time*, a man well known for his support of public schools;

by Dr. Samuel Brownell, former president of New Haven State Teachers College and former United States Commissioner of Education; and by Dr. F. E. Engleman, Connecticut's "distinguished former Commissioner of Education and now executive secretary of the American Association of School Administrators." * No proposals supported by these Connecticut men could be interpreted as harmful to the public schools, said Mr. Smith.

Anticipating criticism for arguments he had presented elsewhere, Mr. Smith stated that he did not withdraw anything he had said previously on this subject, for he had never proposed anything contrary to the Constitution. To counter the "opening wedge" argument, he said:

> There is no evidence whatsoever that any private or parochial school in this state is seeking or ever expects to receive direct support from publc funds. This bill should be considered on its merits. The legislature will retain the power to curb abuses. The courts will be available to enjoin unauthorized services, and each town will have its own veto under this enabling act.

Mr. Smith concluded that health and safety services for non-public school pupils were clearly constitutional and it was absurd to hold that free dental examination constituted support of a child's religion.

A third supporting speaker, William Hard of New Canaan, a *Reader's Digest* editor, opened his remarks by stating that a school bus should be supported by town funds, not by school funds. He then offered four propositions:

> 1. A school bus was not a vehicle of education. The protection it gave to some school children should be given to all school children. Paraphrasing the Supreme Court of Mississippi, Mr. Hard said the state should ignore the child's creed but not his need.[42]

* Hearing Mr. Smith's complimentary reference to former Commissioner Engleman, *Hartford Times* education editor Evans Clinchy murmured, "Cut the crap, Dick, you hated his guts." It is probable that the Education Committee members were familiar with the frequent contentions between Mr. Smith and Dr. Engleman. The compliment, hardly more than the usual parliamentary courtesy, also reflected Mr. Smith's awareness of the tactical advantage of having "distinguished" authorities to quote in support of his position.

2. A private school meeting public educational standards was fulfilling a public purpose, and a school bus to that school was aiding that public purpose.

3. A school bus was totally neutral in any controversy between state and church. Highways, police, and fire protection were all public services but were never interpreted as promotion of religion if provided for churchgoers or parochial school pupils. These were services, services to people or to children, not to religion.

4. Bus service and similar problems should be left to localities for solution.

Mr. Hard asked for home rule "in matters susceptible to home rule." He concluded:

> We Catholics are deeply indebted to America. In this overwhelmingly Protestant country, we are wholly free to practice our faith in our own way without molestation; and we are also free to establish and maintain our own Catholic schools. We should exhibit gratitude and not acrimony; we should not invoke State compulsion upon our Protestant neighbors in local matters on which there may be differences of honest opinion. All we should ask—and all I here ask—is a clear law on the basis of which we can proceed to argue with our neighbors—and perhaps persuade them.

A second non-Catholic to express support was Mr. Ogden Miller, headmaster of the Gunnery, a private school in Washington, Connecticut. The Connecticut Association of Independent Schools, Mr. Miller said, had not taken any stand on this proposal, but he wished to register his own support for clarification of the law regarding public services for non-public school pupils.

The next supporting speaker, Mr. Pierce Gerety, said that as a town counsel for ten years he had listened annually to arguments about public school transportation. When parents were appealing for transportation of their children to public schools, their arguments were always based on the need and safety of the child. Hazards to children exist regardless of the school, Mr. Gerety said, and the guiding question should be, "Does the child need a ride to protect himself?" Money spent on buses was not money spent on education, Mr. Gerety contended. (This same contention would later be made by opponents who would argue that this proposal weakened support of public schools.)

The Opposition

Chairman Philip Bauer announced at the conclusion of Mr. Gerety's remarks that the first twenty minutes had expired. He called now for testimony in opposition.

The first and principal speaker opposing the bill was Sigmund Adler, Rocky Hill school board member. He submitted to the Education Committee some letters he had received from Montreal, Canada, describing the dual system of publicly supported parochial schools. Mr. Adler said he defended the right of every citizen to send his children to the school of his choice, but there were other considerations to keep in mind. Parents who chose non-public schools for their children should be willing to pay all the expenses involved. If non-public schools sought public assistance, they should be ready to accept appropriate public control. Money spent in the interest of non-public schools, Mr. Adler said, meant less money for the public schools. Transportation and health services for parochial schools was a contribution of public funds to religion. He stated:

> Some want help to buy books. Some want help for instruction in art, manual training, home economics. Some want transportation and some a combination of all or some. Some want public money for the erection of additions to their existing schools, and, since Mr. [Richard Joyce] Smith has spoken, may I interpolate that in an article which he wrote on December 10, in a magazine called *America*, he makes specific reference that it might be cheaper to add to an existing parochial school. That is public money being asked for the erection of a non-public school. Add a little here, a little there and the ultimate result is the annulment of the principle of common education for all; and if that happens, the democracy which we love will be in serious danger.

The next speaker, the Reverend Dr. Worley, announced he was testifying as chairman of the Civil Rights and Moral Affairs Committee of the Connecticut Council of Churches. He rejected the assertion that parochial schools saved tax money as "an unwanted benefit." The Council would like all children to have the benefit of a "truly American education in the one public elementary school system." The proposal, Dr. Worley said, would divide the public and foster religious segregation. It would set neighbor against neighbor and tear communities apart as Augusta, Maine, was then divided. He represented, he said, a considerable segment of Protestant thought "unalterably opposed to the diversion of tax funds to the support of private and sectarian schools."

The Reverend William Bradley of Hartford testified for the Committee on Christian Social Action of the Congregational Christian Churches of Connecticut and for the Hartford Chapter of the American Civil Liberties Union. Public support of a private school system meant the diversion of money from the public schools, he said. In the *Everson* case, which was decided by a five-to-four vote, the majority had said transportation was aid for the child. However, Mr. Bradley said, he agreed with the minority that bus service was indirect aid to the school. This amounted to public aid to religion.

Mrs. John Luther, legislative representative of the Parent-Teachers Association of Connecticut, testified that her organization believed in "public funds for public schools." There was almost an emergency situation to face, she said, "so we would like to see all funds—public funds—go to public schools." Her testimony was to provoke a side debate on the position of the P.-T.A. of Connecticut on this issue.[43]

Mrs. Ralph C. Lasbury, speaking in opposition, said she spoke only for herself and not for any organization. Mr. Richard Joyce Smith had said there had been an increase in the non-public school problem in Connecticut. Mrs. Lasbury pointed out that, although the number of pupils in non-public schools had increased, there had been no substantial increase in the percentage of all school children in non-public schools.

The *Everson* case, she maintained, had decided merely that the question of transportation for parochial school pupils was not a federal problem. This left it to the states to decide. Other states had taken a variety of actions. Perhaps, she said, we have gone too far in providing school bus service. Shouldn't we consider transportation a family responsibility instead of a public responsibility? Her five children had spent half their school years in private schools and she had provided the transportation. It was hard work, but she never thought it was a state responsibility to take her children to private schools.

The dispute about health services, Mrs. Lasbury said, could be settled by placing responsibility for all health services in the local health department and making the services available to all children. Perhaps this transportation question could be decided, she suggested, by putting it before the people of the state as a proposed constitutional amendment.

A former superintendent of schools, C. M. Larkim of Hebron, rose to declare that this was the most crucial question Connecticut had faced since the Congregational Church was disestablished in 1818. The disestablishment increased the subsequent service of that church, he said. He had an understanding of the Roman Catholic Church, its periods of great service and its periods of error. When they attempt to undermine democracy, he said, "I must rise although I know I will receive much personal abuse." This thing had been started by the brilliant Richard Joyce Smith, said Mr. Larkim. The State Board of Education was a reluctant party to the issue. The Board seemed to be afraid of Mr. Smith. His background stemmed from the Church. Mr. Larkim could understand his objectives. He didn't know about Dr. Sanders, the Commissioner of Education. Was he an educator or was he a politician? "If he is an educator," Mr. Larkim said, "I will support him to the limit, be he Jew, Gentile, or Turk."

At this point Chairman Bauer interrupted the speaker and requested that he confine himself to the issue. Mr. Larkim said he would do so. He continued by saying that he would not recommend to any young man that he interest himself in research in this field if he wanted to get anywhere in this world.* The attempt to obtain

* This writer obviously does not share Mr. Larkim's apprehensions.

these services was a disservice to the Church itself and contributed
to the Catholic-Protestant tensions that had recently been deplored
by the editor of the Catholic magazine *America*, Mr. Larkim stated.
This bill might well lead to a situation like that in New Brunswick,
Canada, where there were eight competing school systems getting
public support. Large parochial school attendance, he stated, was
accompanied by poor public school support.

Other statements of opposition that morning were made by
several Protestant ministers. The Reverend Robert Woodbury, a
Methodist, said that historically the Church of Rome has tried to
align itself with government. The Protestant Church did not seek
public funds. The parochial school should be free of government
support or control, he said. The Reverend John Wiley of New
London said the requests for service would not be limited to health,
welfare, and transportation. This group, he said, seeks benefits beyond auxiliary services. The Reverend Eugene Hough of Bristol complained about the vagueness of the bill. Neither "parochial" nor
"private" were defined in it. If the state paid for transportation, he
asked, should it not have the authority to designate the school to
be attended? If safety were the real concern, he said, the private
school could support its own buses.

John Hayworth of Hartford said that the present effort was part
of an attempt to have a state dominated by a church.

Gordon Burke of East Hartford said that his many years abroad
as a foreign service officer had taught him that the United States
was unique in placing religion apart from all public support. The
consequence of this separation was an atmosphere of friendliness
and kinship among all our people.

Methodist minister Harold Keir, executive secretary of the Connecticut Council of Churches, said that he did not know what distinction was made between service to a school and service to a child.
Pupils in some non-public schools in Connecticut were receiving at
public expense instruction in homemaking and industrial arts. Was
this a health or welfare service? If these subjects could be given, why
not instruction in other subjects, he asked. The proposal was very

vague. Why did not the supporters of this proposal specify what they meant by health and welfare services? The aims should be clearly set forth and an authoritative statement made renouncing intentions of seeking public aid or services beyond those stated. If the services were specified, each one could be debated on its merits, he said.

In effect, Mr. Keir was asking for an answer to the "wedge" argument. An authoritative statement, presumably from Archbishop O'Brien, would help to put at rest, he suggested, the apprehensions of many of those opposed to this bill because they saw transportation as the first in a series leading to broad public support of non-public school activities. No "authoritative" answer was given to Mr. Keir's question in the weeks of debate that were to follow.*

Another opponent of the measure, Richard Neuendorfer of New London, said the taxpayer properly should have control of the expenditure of his money. If this measure were adopted it would mean that the taxpayer should have control of the books, teachers, services, and curriculum of the non-public school.

More Comment on the Bill

As the hearing proceeded and others rose to speak in favor of the bill, familiar arguments were presented. The school bus was a public utility, not a religious service, one woman said. She also claimed that many parents could not afford to send their children to private or parochial schools if they had to pay the cost of transportation. She seemed unaware that this second statement might contradict her contention that transportation was not a service to religion.

The hearing was interrupted for a session of the House of Representatives at 1:00 P.M. It was resumed later in the afternoon in another chamber of the Capitol building. The audience was only a fraction of the morning attendance.

Dr. Walter Dolan of Ridgefield told the committee that this was a matter concerning the welfare of children, not church-state

---

* The Reverend Joseph V. King had answered this question three months earlier. Above, p. 94.

separation. The law was ambiguous. This bill would clarify it and permit towns to provide for the safety of all of the children. In winter many children had to walk home in the dusk of late afternoon along roads and highways with no sidewalks.

Jerome Travers, representing the Young Democrats of Meriden, said he had one child going to public school and another to parochial school. He hoped the Republican Party would not go back on its promise of greater home rule. Senator Kopacz, he said, owed his election to his stand in support of transportation for parochial school pupils. Mr. Travers contended that the average cost of educating a pupil in Meriden was $264. The parochial schools saved the city a lot of money. The taxpayers should encourage a lot of private schools. It would be cheaper than building public schools, he said. Mr. Travers seemed oblivious of the implication he had made that he was supporting a means of reducing financial support of public schools.

The sentiments of Mr. Travers were echoed in part by Colonel Charles A. Thether of Ridgefield, who noted the tax money saved by parochial schools. When he was in the Army, he said, transportation was provided for all children regardless of the school attended. Subsequently more than a dozen speakers expressed support of the proposal for services to non-public school pupils.

One voice in opposition was that of Mrs. Pauline Papp of New Haven, who said she didn't understand the complaints being made about discrimination. The public school child didn't face any such difficulty and all children could go to public school. Some of her children went to public schools and some went to private schools. She transported those who went to private schools, and she didn't expect public transportation to be provided for them.

Richard Anderson of Rockville testified that he had attended parochial school for twelve years and he wanted to state his opposition to this measure. In our country everyone had his religious freedom. In foreign countries it was rather different. Only a short while ago President Eisenhower had said he favored separation of church and state. The committee, said Mr. Anderson, should follow that principle. He closed with the ominous declaration that the spiritual power of the church would die when it laid hold of the civil power.

Senator Bauer asked for further testimony, and no one else came forward. The public hearing was declared closed.

Conclusions about the Hearing

Several significant features of the hearing may be noted. The Republican leadership of both houses went on record in support of public services for non-public school pupils on a local-option basis. Consequently, legislators who opposed this bill would be opposing the leadership in a legislature with overwhelming Republican majorities. No consideration was given to a mandatory policy that all school children in Connecticut be given health and welfare services on an equal basis. Mr. Hard borrowed from the Mississippi textbook case to argue that the state had a duty to ignore the child's creed but not his need.[44] Neither Mr. Hard nor anyone else explained why parochial school children in some towns should ride and in other towns walk. It was obvious, but unspoken, that there was no chance of passing a mandatory bill based on the principle that all school children should receive auxiliary services on an equal basis with public school children. Instead, principle was compromised without question and the expediency of "home rule" was paraded as a virtue.[45]

Testifying in support of the bill, following the legislators, were prominent Catholic laymen and two Protestants. There were no priests or nuns present. In contrast, Protestant ministers were conspicuously present and were outspoken in their opposition. Other opposition was presented by citizens noted as supporters of public education, such as Sigmund Adler and Mrs. Ralph C. Lasbury.

The arguments presented on both sides were the usual ones heard in debate over this question. The bill did not mention Catholic schools, but it was obviously supported by those interested in services for Catholic school children. The opposition frequently was directed not against the bill but against what the bill might lead to, or indeed against parochial schools.

The Reverend Harold Keir was alone among the opposition in giving any consideration to the child-benefit theory as justification for services. He based his opposition on the bill's vagueness. He asked for the services to be specified and for a renunciation of any public assistance beyond that stated.

Supporters of the bill employed arguments based chiefly on the child-benefit theory and the tax savings made possible by parochial schools. Sometimes the tax savings argument was so used as to contradict the contention that all that was being sought was service for children. Among the bill's supporters giving extended testimony at the hearing, only Richard Joyce Smith and Pierce Gerety held consistently to the child-benefit theory. They were both lawyers.

AGREEMENT AMONG THE DEMOCRATS

Shortly after the public hearing, House Democratic leader Representative Samuel Googel of New Britain held a caucus to discuss the position of the House Democrats on the bill for auxiliary services.

Mr. Googel was Jewish but was conscious of the wishes of many Catholic constituents. Some opponents in the New Britain Democratic Party had tried to prevent his renomination by circulating a charge that he had voted in favor of repeal of the birth-control prohibition law in 1955. He was able to prove, however, that this was false. Representative Googel first heard of the bill for auxiliary services from Democratic Senator Henry Cooney of Hartford. (Senator Cooney was a brother of Joseph Cooney, attorney for the Connecticut Archdiocese.) Senator Cooney, a few weeks before the public hearing, asked Mr. Googel if he would testify in support of the proposal for auxiliary services. Mr. Googel said he would. Because of a conflicting committee meeting he was unable to appear personally, but he did register with the Education Committee his support of the proposal for auxiliary services.

At the Democratic caucus it was quickly determined that the thirty Democrats in the House were almost unanimous in their support of auxiliary services. Only one member, William A. Murray, Jr., of Durham, would not agree. He "reserved" his vote. However, in the weeks following the caucus, Representative Murray was impressed with the importance of Democratic unanimity on this measure. He was persuaded to go along with the party.[46]

DISAGREEMENT IN THE P.–T. A.

The testimony of Mrs. John Luther at the public hearing resulted in many telephone inquiries and protests to the state office of the Parent-Teachers Association of Connecticut. In general the callers objected to Mrs. Luther's statement of opposition to auxiliary services since the organization had not been consulted on this issue. They complained that Mrs. Luther's comments were unauthorized. Similar protests appeared in letters published in newspapers. Mrs. Anna T. Lazorik of Hartford wrote:

> As president of the Moylan-Wilston P.–T.A., I wish to state that Mrs. Luther does not speak for me or for my unit. I favor the bill, and I know that many of our members do.
> We must keep the record straight on such matters and we must not allow our organization to be drawn into such controversies.

Mrs. Lazorik said that the P.–T.A. National Congress urged "between educators and the general public such united efforts as will secure for every child the highest advantages in physical, mental, social and spiritual education.[47]

Mrs. John Horan, president of the Mary Hooker P.–T.A., in Hartford, wrote that her group did not vote on the measure so Mrs. Luther could not be speaking for them. Other P.–T.A. units in Hartford, she said, had not been polled either.[48]

The following month the Moylan-Wilson P.–T.A. adopted a resolution calling for retraction of Mrs. Luther's statement. The resolution also asked that all P.–T.A. units be polled before state officers made policy statements.[49] A few days later the state president, Mrs.

Roy L. Cole of Stonington, wrote a letter to unit chairmen explaining that Mrs. Luther's stand was in accord with national policy. That policy had been adopted at the national convention in 1956 and had been approved by Conecticut units in November, 1955. It read:

> All funds appropriated by the federal government for support of education within the states and territories should go to publicly controlled, tax-supported schools only.[50]

This letter was not sufficient to satisfy those P.–T.A. members protesting Mrs. Luther's statement. The Board of Managers of the state organization felt obliged to act to prevent a floor debate on auxiliary services at the state convention on April 24. The evening before the convention opened the Board of Managers in a formal statement announced:

> . . . the state association has taken no position on Senate Bill 872 or on the specific subject of providing health and safety services from public funds to children in non-public schools.
> Mrs. Eleanor Luther, legislative chairman, indicated to the Board of Managers that in speaking at the legislative hearing . . . she did not intend to record the association in opposition to any specified bill but rather to express a policy which she felt applied to the situation.[51]

This statement was supplemented by a resolution requesting a study of better means of communication between state headquarters and local units. This action was sufficient to quiet protests. There was no floor debate about auxiliary services at the convention.[52]

THE BATTLE IN THE PRESS

The arguments heard in the Hall of the House of Representatives at the public hearing were repeated in the days following. The views of the proponents were presented in the columns of the *Catholic Transcript* and in full-page advertisements in the *Hartford Times* and the *Hartford Courant*. The views of those on both sides were expressed in limited degree in letters-to-the-editor columns of the Hartford papers and some others in Connecticut. Opposition was voiced in the pulpits of some Protestant churches. More than two months were to pass before the Catholic bishops of Connecticut were to speak out at a crucial point in the legislative struggle.

Two days after the hearing on March 12, the *Catholic Transcript* carried an editorial protesting the newspaper coverage of the testimony. The editorial, "The Hartford Papers Trick Their Readers," objected that these papers had reported the measure under discussion as providing for aid to private and religious schools. "By the strongest and most despicable means possible," the editorial said, "a completely wrong and prejudiced idea is planted in readers' minds." The *Transcript* also objected that supporters of the bill had been described as "representatives of Catholic churches, prominent Catholic laymen." The *Transcript* said there were "no Catholic churches represented." There were Catholic laymen but also "two widely known and universally respected Protestants, Mr. William H. Mortensen, former Mayor of Hartford, and Mr. Ogden Miller, Head of the Gunnery School." The omission of these names, the *Transcript* charged, was deliberate. After this "contemptible performance" by the Hartford papers, the *Transcript* questioned if one could believe anything in their columns.[58]

Similar sentiments were expressed in an open letter carried as a full-page advertisement in the *Hartford Sunday Courant* of March 17 and the *Hartford Times* of March 19. The letter, signed by thirty Hartford area residents, presumably Catholic, explained that the bill was a measure to provide for services to children, not to religious schools. The newspapers had misrepresented the character of the bill. The letter also said that the bill had been supported by non-Catholics as well as Catholics, and mentioned Mr. Mortensen and Mr. Miller.

The bill was also described as providing an aid to the child rather than to religion by Joseph Cooney at the first annual communion breakfast of the Holy Name Society of the Hartford Police Department on Sunday, March 26. Mr. Cooney said, "There is a small minority who claim it is an aid to the parochial school or to the church." Referring to the dispute about school bus transportation then under way in Stamford, he said that objections were being made by "certain people whose opposition we can always count on when we take a position." [54]

The criticism directed at the Hartford papers by the *Transcript* was in turn criticized by the Hartford Unitarian minister, Payson Miller, in a sermon on April 7. He knew that the *Transcript* editor regarded him as anti-Catholic, although the literature and music of Roman Catholicism were often used in Mr. Miller's church. He was opposed, Mr. Miller said, "to the dogmatic exclusiveness, authoritarianism, totalitarianism, and arrogance of the Roman Catholic Church." The *Transcript*, he said, attacked the *Hartford Courant* and *Hartford Times* for inaccurate and biased reporting when the *Transcript's* own coverage of the public hearing grossly violated the principles it tried to apply to other newspapers. The speakers at the hearing and the support manifested by the audience showed no obvious imbalance between proponents and opponents, Mr. Miller said, yet the *Transcript* presented a "loaded" report which gave sixty column inches to the bill's supporters and six inches to opponents.

Joseph Cooney was criticized by Mr. Miller for his statement to the communion breakfast that "factual, non-partisan presentation of such issues could always be found in the *Catholic Transcript*." Mr. Miller commented that "a communion breakfast seems a singularly inappropriate time to make an untruthful statement with such momentous implications." Freedom of information was endangered by the attack on the Hartford papers, Mr. Miller said. The *Transcript* had charged that the Hartford papers had given an untrue picture to "the people whose patronage they depend on." The *Transcript* editorial had concluded, "Who, after this, can believe anything in their columns?" This might easily be paraphrased, Mr. Miller pointed out, to read, "Why do you bother to read these papers any more? If you don't buy them some people are going to get hurt economically and they will have to get in line or go out of business."

The logical way to deal with such pressures was to maintain counterpressure, Mr. Miller said. Such was the purpose of the organization Protestant and Other Americans United for Separation of

Church and State. This organization was "shocked into existence," Mr. Miller said, by the declaration of the Catholic bishops of the United States in 1948 to work "patiently, persistently and perseveringly" for the destruction of the separation of church and state. The POAU, the books of Paul Blanshard, and the growing unity of spirit among American Protestants Mr. Miller described as three forces "defending equality of religion against those who seek special privilege for their own church." [55]

This sermon was mimeographed and distributed to legislators and others in Connecticut. Some interest in the report of pressure on newspapers was shown by those who read the sermon both in Connecticut and out of state. Mr. Miller received requests for additional copies.[56]

The Reverend Loyd Worley was also concerned and wrote a letter for publication in one of the Hartford newspapers. He received a reply from the editor saying that the arguments on both sides seemed unlimited and likely to get out of hand if carried on in the newspapers. "For the sake of the community as well as in our own interests," the editor wrote, "I hope to avoid such exchanges. In the long run they will do more harm than good." The editor said he was withholding the letter from publication and he hoped Dr. Worley concurred in this judgment.[57]

It was clear from the limited number of letters from readers published in the Hartford newspapers on this issue that these journals were "playing down" the dispute. The letter to Mr. Worley gave two reasons, the welfare of the community and the interest of the newspaper. The second reason suggests that the newspaper management feared economic reprisals in terms of cancellation of subscriptions or advertising.

THE INACTIVITY OF JEWISH GROUPS

The determined opposition of some Protestant spokesmen against services, and the strenuous efforts of Catholic spokesmen for services, presented a sharp contrast with the limited activity of Jewish groups in Connecticut during this debate. No Connecticut Jewish group took an official public stand on the issue. Opposition to the school bus bill was expressed by attorney Joseph Steinberg in a panel discussion on "Focus," a television program presented on WNBC–TV, the West Hartford station.[58] Although he was introduced as a representative of the Anti-Defamation League of B'nai Brith, the views he expressed were his own. His organization did not take an official stand on the Connecticut issue.

Among other objections, Mr. Steinberg posed the question of where to draw the line on health and welfare benefits for non-public school children. Would the public be asked to pay for the cost of a gymnasium or the salary of a physical education instructor? Bus service, Mr. Steinberg contended, was part of the cost of operating a school. Public transportation for non-public school pupils was equivalent to a contribution of public funds to that school.[59]

No official of any other Jewish group offered any public comment on this issue. Privately, an official of a leading Jewish civic organization reported that the executive committee had discussed the matter and concluded that it very likely would result in difficult social and economic pressures on Jews if they took an active part. They decided, therefore, to stay out of the controversy.

The silence of Jewish groups reduced the possibility of embarrassment for Governor Abraham Ribicoff. His eventual approval of the bill upon its passage by the legislature in 1957 would thus not be given in the face of strong public opposition by groups of his own religious affiliation.

THE BIRTH-CONTROL ISSUE

An attempt to repeal the Connecticut prohibition against distribution of birth-control devices was made in each session of the General Assembly. The 1957 session was no exception. The vote on the issue in the House gave some measure of Catholic strength in that body and, for some observers, seemed a measure of the prospect of the school bus bill.

The debate in the House on April 18 reflected in some degree the Catholic and Protestant division. Representative Mary Q. Fahey observed that the Church had a right and a duty to oppose what was "indecent and immoral." Proponents of repeal argued that the prohibition was widely violated, that contraceptive devices for married women whose health would be adversely affected by pregnancy was a health measure. Opponents took the view that it was a moral issue. "Legislators and doctors," said Representative Thomas Kerrigan, "had no right to tamper with God's law." * Birth control, he contended, was race suicide. Representative Charles Nash of Salisbury remarked, "The gentleman from Hartford is full of bull."

The bill was debated for less than an hour and was passed by the House, 170 to 58.[60] The 58 negative votes could be interpreted as the Catholic membership of the House. The 170 votes could be assumed to be almost entirely those of Protestant members. Although the bill passed with ease in the House, it was generally understood that it would be defeated in the Senate. Senator Edward A. Sandula of Bridgeport was quoted as saying that an off-the-record count of state senators showed the bill could not possibly pass. He said he had refused offers of some legislators who would drop their opposition to the auxiliary services bill in exchange for passage of the birth-control bill. Birth-control adherents, he said, "are schemers who are always willing to make deals to get a bill through." [61]

Senator Sandula was correct in his prediction of the Senate's action. The birth-control bill was defeated in the Senate without debate on a voice vote.[62] A majority of the Senators apparently were Catholics, and their convictions on this issue were firm. There was no need for debate. It could safely be predicted that the Senate would favor the bill for public services to non-public school pupils. The struggle would be in the House.

---

* Mr. Kerrigan was, of course, speaking of the Catholic viewpoint on moral law, not of the Connecticut statute which the proposed bill would amend. That statute, originally adopted in 1879, was once known as "the little Comstock Law." It prohibited the making or distributing of "any obscene, lewd or lascivious" publication or any article intended to be used for "preventing conception or causing unlawful abortion." This Connecticut statute closely followed the law enacted by Congress in 1873 at the urging of famed morals crusader Anthony Comstock. (*Tileston* v. *Ullman*, 129 Conn. 84.) Adopted when the state and the legislature were under predominantly Protestant influence, it was the product not of Catholic doctrine but of a persistent Puritanism.

THE LEADERSHIP TRIES TO LEAD

Early in April the Joint Committee on Education reported it had prepared a bill which would make it illegal for a board of education to spend public funds for the benefit of any but public school pupils. The joint chairmen, Senator Bauer and Representative E. O. Smith, said the bill was intended for discussion purposes so the Committee would have both sides of the highly controversial issue before it.[63] Here was strong indication of the sentiment of the Committee on Education.

This new bill was regarded very unfavorably by Speaker Nelson Brown. A bill like this, he said, could kill the Republican Party in Connecticut. He made a personal survey of each member of the Education Committee, recording his name and how he stood on this new bill. The result of his survey showed that a majority of the Committee was opposed to reporting out the bill. He showed the results to the Education Committee chairmen.[64] No attempt was made to bring out the bill restricting a school board's expenditures to public school pupils. The leadership had successfully blocked the countermove of the Education chairmen.

The Republican Party leadership made another move early in April to promote public services for non-public school pupils. Shortly after the beginning of the session, State Chairman Clarence Baldwin had telephoned Mr. Meade Alcorn about the major issues coming before the General Assembly. Mr. Alcorn, Republican National Committeeman from Connecticut, had recently accepted the post of Republican National Chairman. Among the issues Mr. Alcorn supported in that telephone conversation was the proposal for a permissive statute on public services for non-public school pupils. At Mr. Baldwin's request, Mr. Alcorn wrote him a letter stating that support. Mr. Alcorn said later that he might have written more tentatively if he had known that the letter was to be made public.[65]

In a meeting at the State Capitol, State Chairman Baldwin, informed Republican legislative and political leaders about Mr. Alcorn's letter. Word of the letter reached *Hartford Courant* reporter

Jack Zaiman, who went to Mr. Baldwin and asked about it. Mr. Baldwin showed him the relevant paragraph.[66] Jack Zaiman's story, headlined "Alcorn Backs Services to Private School Pupils," appeared on the front page of the *Hartford Courant* on April 13.

The leadership was expressing itself.

A few days later the Republican State Committee sent out a news release reporting that Senators André G. Desrosiers of Windham and Henry J. Dunleavy of Thompson favored the bill on auxiliary services.[67] It was not surprising that a senator from Windham, with 33 per cent of its school children in non-public schools, and a senator from Thompson, with 49 per cent of its school children in non-public schools, should take such a position.[68] The real news in the story seemed to be that the Republican State Committee was trying to build up sentiment for the bill.

The Republican leadership was also busy making a careful estimate of the division in the House of Representatives. The results showed the House divided, with possibly a majority of about twenty in favor of the bill. In Fairfield County, Bill Brennan's district, a slight majority of the thirty-nine House members were reported in favor of the bill, and the forty-one House Republicans from New Haven County were reported about equally divided.[69]

An estimated majority is a long way from passage of a bill, and the Republican leadership was aware that the fate of the measure was very much in doubt. The principal hurdle was the seemingly implacable opposition of House Education Chairman E. O. Smith. He told James Mutrie, a reporter for the *New Haven Register*, the week after Alcorn's letter was released, that the sentiment on the committee was opposed to the bill. If it had to be reported out at that time, it would be reported out unfavorably.[70]

There was some sentiment among supporters of the bill for pressure by the leadership to force the bill out of committee. John Hurley told State Chairman Baldwin that it ought to be brought out before the Assembly disposed of the local bills. Most representatives had one or more bills pertaining to their own towns. If these were still pending, they could be used as leverage to persuade representatives to support the Kopacz bill.[71] Neither chairman Baldwin nor House majority leader Pope wanted to employ such measures on this bill. Feeling was running high enough on this issue, they believed. They wanted the question to be decided "on its merits."

Mr. Pope asserted later that he had never tried to pressure any House member and never initiated a discussion of the issue. If someone asked him about it, he explained his position and let it go at that. He was concerned about more than this bill. He did not want the division over this one bill to endanger passage of the rest of the Republican legislative program. The Republican Party, he felt, would be judged on the full record of the General Assembly, not on only one bill, important as it was to many people.[72]

State Chairman Baldwin agreed that the Education Committee was late in bringing out the bill, but he rejected Mr. Hurley's suggestion. He would not use pressure on anyone on this issue. If you pushed people on this, he felt, you might lose them. Those who were still on the fence would resent pressure and very possibly turn against you.[73]

By the beginning of May the Joint Education Committee still had not acted on the bill. The House leadership decided to bring the question before the House Republican caucus. They hoped to settle the issue first, rather than have it pass the Senate and be killed later in the House. (The House and Senate committees considered bills jointly and reported them to the chamber in which they originated. The Kopacz bill, Senate Bill 872, would be reported to the Senate.) They may have reasoned that if the caucus favored the bill, the Education Committee would be under a special obligation to report. If the caucus strongly opposed the bill, the committee could bury it and relieve the House of the responsibility for defeating it.

On May 4 majority leader Pope announced that the bill would be brought before the caucus the following Wednesday, May 8.[74] The day before the caucus, the Education Committee acted. They spent two hours in discussion. The original Kopacz bill, S.B. 872, which carried the words "any municipal services," was defeated by a vote of nine to four. The revised bill substituted for S.B. 872, which used the words "any of the health or safety services, including transportation," was defeated by a vote of ten to seven.

In their comments about the Committee's action, co-chairmen Bauer and Smith revealed that they did not accept the child-benefit theory. Senator Bauer said it was the feeling of the Committee that public funds should not be used for private purposes. Representative Smith said the Committee also felt that public grants to private schools might lead to regulation of the schools, which they themselves did not want.[75] To chairmen Bauer and Smith this proposal meant services for schools, not for children.

Following this action, the Committee secretary, Representative Lucy Hammer, discovered that no such bill as "substitute for S.B. 872" had ever been presented. The certified copy of S.B. 872 was in the Committee's files. So were mimeographed copies entitled "substitute for S.B. 872," but these mimeographed copies had been distributed by attorney Joseph Cooney. When the office of the Legislative Commissioner confirmed that no such bill as "substitute for S.B. 872" had been introduced, Mrs. Hammer informed Chairman Smith. He told her the Committee would report out unfavorably the bill it had received, S.B. 872.[76]

THE HOUSE REPUBLICAN CAUCUS SAYS "NO"

The caucus of the Republican Representatives held in the Hall of the House on Wednesday, May 8, was devoted solely to the school bus bill.[77] The debate was lively and went on for two and one-half hours. This was the longest caucus of the session. Majority leader Pope presided.

The arguments offered on both sides were similar to those made at the public hearing. State Chairman Baldwin took the unusual step of addressing the caucus, the only time he did so during the 1957 legislative session. He told the group that the proposal provided for services to children and that there were many years of precedent set by a number of towns, and he reminded the caucus that this was permissive legislation. Each town could decide for itself. The Republican Party in Connecticut stood for home rule, and this measure was simply another application of the home-rule principle.

Near the end of the debate, Speaker Nelson Brown also spoke in support of the measure. He emphasized that the House was being asked to permit protection to be extended to all school children. In conclusion, he reminded the members of the biblical injunction, "Suffer the little children to come unto me, for of such is the kingdom of heaven." An irreverent opponent of the measure in the back of the hall murmured to his neighbor, "But must they go in a tax-supported bus?" The leadership had not persuaded everybody.

From the tenor of the debate, it was clear to majority leader Fred Pope that the caucus would not support S.B. 872 or its substitute. He proposed in their stead a hypothetical bill.

He had worked out this measure in his mind as he listened to the caucus debate. He included four provisions which he thought would meet enough objections to win majority support and still satisfy those who were working for the original bill. Pope's proposal had four features. It would:

1. Be limited to transportation.
2. Be permissive.
3. Include a provision for a local referendum.
4. Limit transportation to schools within the town.

After the majority leader described this proposed new bill, he asked for a vote.

Reporters and others, waiting outside the locked doors, watched expectantly through the windows. It was a standing vote. As the "ayes" rose, the reporters made a quick estimate while the tellers walked the aisles making the count. The "ayes" sat down and the "nays" rose. Once more the tellers took the count while the reporters hastily made their estimate. It was clear the caucus was almost evenly divided. *Hartford Courant* reporter Irving Kravsow exclaimed, "They've got it. With the Democratic votes, they've got it."

In a moment the caucus adjourned and the doorkeepers inside

the Hall opened the doors. The first reporter challenged a door-keeper, "What was the count?"

"Ninety-nine to ninety, against the bill," the doorkeeper replied.

The reporters rushed onto the rostrum to quiz Fred Pope.

Ninety-nine to 90. A total of 189 votes. Sixty Republicans had been absent. There were 30 Democratic votes which could be counted for the bill. The issue in the House was still very much in doubt. Ninety Republicans and 30 Democrats favored the bill. These 120 votes were only 20 less than a bare majority of the House membership. Among the 60 absent Republicans there well might be enough votes to pass the bill.

The next step would be for the Senate to take. But there were more than eight hundred bills to be acted on and only about three weeks left until the mandatory adjournment date of June 5.[78]

THE SENATE SAYS "YES"

On Monday, May 14, five days after the House caucus, the Senate debated the unfavorable report of the Education Committee on S.B. 872.[79] The debate was opened by Senator Theodore Ryan. He asked for rejection of the unfavorable report and adoption of an amendment which he proposed. It was a broad rewriting of the bill, substituting two sections. Section One provided that municipalities could furnish to pupils of local private schools "any of the medical, dental, nursing, and transportation services" provided to public school pupils. Private schools included only those in which a majority of the pupils were from the municipality.[80] Section One also provided that municipalities providing any or all of the specified services on the effective date of the act might continue furnishing those services until the municipality voted otherwise according to the referendum provided for in Section Two.

Section Two described the referendum procedure. Five per cent of the voters of the town could petition for a referendum, and a majority of those voting would decide the question. The two sections were designated Senate Amendment Schedule A.

The amended act met three of the four provisions in the hypothetical bill debated in the House caucus. The bill was permissive, there was a referendum provision, and the services were limited to local schools. The kinds of services were redefined. Instead of "municipal services" or "health, welfare, and safety services, including transportation," they were described as "medical, dental, nursing, and transportation." The hypothetical bill, however, had included only transportation. The description of the non-public schools was obviously a roundabout way of excluding almost all except Catholic parish schools. Senator Ryan was trying to meet some of the objections of opponents of the measure. He viewed the services as services to children, but he was also aware that one of the objections made was that a town would have to provide these services to pupils of expensive private schools. The child-benefit theory was compromised by Senator Ryan for the sake of meeting this anticipated objection, although he was still to rely on the theory in Senate debate.

Senator Ryan drafted Section One of his amendment by himself and later consulted Senator Kopacz. The latter said he was agreeable to any change that would improve the bill's chance for passage. Senator Ryan also discussed his amendments with John Hurley.[31]

After Senator Ryan had introduced his amendments and cited the child-benefit theory and the *Everson* case in their support, the presiding officer, Lieutenant Governor Charles Jewett, asked for the constitutional privilege of participating in the debate. This was unprecedented in the memory of observers of the Connecticut legislature. The Senate went into Committee of the Whole.

The room was quiet as Lieutenant Governor Jewett handed the gavel to the presiding Senator and stepped down from the chair. The Senators and the gallery audience watched him as he walked to the other end of the chamber and took his place at the microphone. There seemed to be a general awareness of the momentous nature of this action—of its crucial importance in the political career of Charles W. Jewett.

He didn't think he would change the vote of even one Senator, the Lieutenant Governor began, but he wanted to give "urgent warning" that a serious constitutional problem was posed by this bill. He thought the bill unconstitutional and "a dangerous first step in undermining the established relationship between church and state in Connecticut." Private preparatory schools and country day schools were not pressing for public services. Those mainly involved were the Roman Catholic parochial schools. Transportation was now an integral part of modern education, and this was a proposal to use public funds to subsidize religious education. It would relieve the parent or the parochial school of the burden of transportation and place it on the state. This, he said, would be the first step down "a primrose path." It was tragic that the bill had been brought up. It was tragic that it was being made a local issue to divide Connecticut towns. The bill, he concluded, was for the benefit of one religious faith rather than for the public good.

The Lieutenant Governor walked back to an empty chair near the front of the chamber.

Senator Bauer then rose to speak against the bill. His committee had received no more explosive bill than this one. Hundreds of letters had been received on both sides of the issue. It had been debated in committee, he said, with restraint. The committee had regarded the bill as unconstitutional. Bus service, he declared, was an indispensable part of the educational system. Hence, service for a religious school was aid to religion. If bus service was provided, why could not other services be given? What limit was there? Senator Bauer also argued that a referendum held on this question should not be merely local, but state-wide. If any private school children were entitled to these services, then all such children were equally entitled. A state-wide referendum was needed also to protect minority rights. Further, if services were supplied because of a favorable vote in a local referendum, tax money collected from people in all towns would help pay for those services through state grants-in-aid. Yet those who were taxed in other towns would have no voice in a local referendum.

These questions and criticisms of the procedural aspects of the amended S.B. 872 were specific challenges to the home-rule argument that was used so frequently in the debate on this proposal. Senator Bauer's challenges, specific and direct though they were, were ignored. His argument recognized the child-benefit theory of the supporters of the bill and showed the weakness of basing such a decision on the principle of home rule.

The bill's supporters made no attempt to answer him. It had been agreed in the caucus of Republican Senators that they would not reply to each other's arguments in floor debate. Each Senator would merely state his own arguments without acrimony.[82]

Assistant majority leader Barringer said he wanted to support the bill as an American citizen and not as a representative of any sect. He had read the *Everson* case and thought there was much to be said on both sides, but the question of constitutionality could be left to the courts. The Senate should decide the question on the basis of equity and the Golden Rule. A great share of the educational load was borne by those who supported parochial schools. They got little in return, he said. They did not choose to use the public schools, but they did choose to use the school buses. "I don't think you can have a double standard for children on the side of the road," he said, "and if a child is sick I don't think you should ask him his religion before giving him treatment."

Mrs. Florence Finney, Republican Senator from Greenwich, argued that public schools were planned with regard for population centers. Pupils could be assigned to the school nearest their homes. But there was no public control over the school assignment of private school pupils. She was prejudiced, she said, in favor of public schools. The cost of transportation for private schools would result in that much reduction of the support for public schools. The proclaimed tax saving was incidental to the main purpose of private schools, which were established for special reasons, not for the general interest. Mrs. Finney warned that government control followed government subsidy and that if private schools wished to avoid government interference they should not seek government funds.

At the end of the debate the Committee of the Whole rose and reported to the Senate that no decision had been reached on the unfavorable report of the Education Committee on Senate Bill 872. Senator Ryan moved rejection of the unfavorable report and adoption of the amendments he had proposed. By voice vote Senator Ryan's motion was adopted. The bill was later transmitted to the office of the Legislative Commissioner for approval of the wording of the amendment before final action on the bill by the Senate.

Shortly after the Senate's action, House majority leader Pope and Speaker Brown told Senator Ryan that the inclusion of medical, dental, and nursing services made the passage of the bill in the House very unlikely. The bill had a chance of passage if it was limited to bus service. This was one of the features of the hypothetical bill discussed in the House caucus, they reminded Senator Ryan. After some reflection Senator Ryan decided to amend the bill further and strike out all services but transportation. This revision he discussed with neither Senator Kopacz nor Mr. Hurley. The bill, he decided, would be sent to the House as Mr. Pope and Speaker Brown had advised.[83] Accordingly, when the Bill was returned to the Senate from the office of the Legislative Commissioner on May 21, Senator Ryan offered Senate Amendment Schedule B. The rules were suspended and Schedule B was adopted, deleting from the bill references to services other than transportation. The bill, with the restrictions desired by the House leaders, was then adopted by the Senate. The bill was permissive, was limited to bus service, and included provision for a local referendum. Only children attending local non-public schools were covered.[84]

The child-benefit theory was a useful basis for argumentation, but the bill as it passed the Senate was designed to avoid the various objections that were presented against the original bill. The major objection, however, was that this measure provided for public aid to religious schools. A bill covering children attending all local schools might have been consistently defended by use of the child-benefit theory. The bill as it passed the Senate, in effect, limited service almost entirely to parochial school pupils. The supporters of the bill appeared to have accepted transportation as a benefit to schools as well as to pupils. They had compromised the basis of their argument; but, as the comments of the opposition in the Senate revealed, the child-benefit theory as a justification for transportation was not accepted by opponents of the bill. To Lieutenant Governor Jewett, Senator Bauer, and Senator Finney, school bus service was an aid to the school. To them the issue was separation of church and state.

The bill had passed the Senate—but it was May 21. Less than three weeks were left before adjournment. It was very questionable whether the House would get a chance to vote on the bill.

HURLEY'S STRATEGY FAILS

The bill that passed the Senate was an amended bill, not the one that had been considered by the Joint Committee on Education. On matters of difference between the House and Senate, the committees of the General Assembly operated as committees of their separate chambers, not jointly. With the passage of an amended bill by the Senate, there suddenly arose a question crucial to the future of the measure. Should the bill be placed on the calendar of the House for action, or should it be returned to the House Committee on Education? Mr. Hurley's strategy had not anticipated this development. Clearly, a bill returned to committee this late in the session was almost certainly lost if the committee should be opposed to the measure.

House rule ten stated that bills not carrying joint committee favorable reports were to be sent back to the House committee. Rule seventeen of the joint rules of the House and Senate provided: "All bills and resolutions reported adversely shall, after one printing on the calendar and with one reading by the clerk, be rejected on motion without further action." [85]

The House leadership was intent on getting the bill before the House. They were certain that if the bill were referred to the House Committee on Education, Chairman E. O. Smith would not let it come out of committee in the few days remaining in the session. The bill had to be placed on the calendar to have any chance of passage. State Chairman Baldwin took the view that the amended bill as received from the Senate was a joint unfavorable report and should be placed on the House calendar as provided in joint rule seventeen. Unquestionably that would have been the situation if S.B. 872 had not needed revision. Majority leader Pope felt that a bill in which there was such intense interest deserved to be brought before the House for a vote.[86]

When the bill was received in the House of Representatives on May 22, the day following its passage in the Senate, Speaker Brown declared that in accordance with joint rule seventeen he was ordering the bill placed on the House calendar. He pointed out this rule provided for all bills and resolution adversely reported to be rejected on motion "after one printing on the calendar." Representative E. O. Smith rose to appeal the Speaker's ruling. In accordance with House rule ten the bill should be referred to the House Committee on Education, he said. The Committee had acted on S.B. 872 as originally presented. The House Committee had not had before it this amended bill, which had passed the Senate the day before. Indeed, it had been ordered printed by the Senate "as if favorably reported."

Mr. Pope replied that there was a contradiction between the two rules and that rule seventeen justified bringing the bill before the House for a vote.

In the debate that followed, supporters of the bill argued in defense of the Speaker's ruling. Opponents argued that rule ten required the bill to be referred to committee. There was general recognition that this procedural vote was actually a vote on the bill itself. John W. Fitzgerald of Bristol charged the House "was just ducking the issue." David J. Dickson, who had sponsored one of the bills withdrawn at the public hearing, said, "We know what will happen if this bill goes back to Mr. Republican, the gentleman from Mansfield [E. O. Smith]. It will die."

After almost an hour of debate, which sometimes was centered on the ruling and sometimes on the bill but always restrained and never vituperative, the Speaker put the appeal to a vote.

The vote was taken by roll call on the automatic vote-counting machine. Illuminated roster boards on either side of the Hall recorded whether the member had flipped the switch on the top of his desk to yea or nay. The total vote was automatically computed and recorded by lighted numbers lined across the top of the roster board. A yea vote would place the bill on the calendar. A nay vote would reverse the Speaker's ruling and send the bill back to the Education Committee.

The members voted. The lighted boards showed 103 yeas, 138 nays. The bill would go back to committee.[87]

The strategy conceived by Mr. Hurley was based on the assumption that the House would be faced with the decision of accepting or rejecting a bill passed by the Senate. That strategy had not anticipated this parliamentary twist. On May 22 the House sent the bill back to the Education Committee, where, it was generally assumed, the measure would die. If not reported out by the Committee, the bill could be brought out only by a petition signed by a majority of the House membership. Some supporters of the school bus bill announced immediately after the vote reversing the Speaker's ruling that they would seek to obtain signatures for such a petition. Their prospects seemed doubtful. There had been only 103 votes to support the Speaker, and 140 signatures were needed on the petition to bring out the bill.[88]

THE *TRANSCRIPT* SPEAKS

The apparent defeat of the school bus bill inspired a bitter editorial in the *Catholic Transcript*, charging the opponents of the measure with bigotry and promising that the issue would be corrected at the next election.

Following the public hearing on March 12 the *Transcript* had criticized the Hartford newspapers for implying that this measure was a Catholic one and a proposal to aid schools rather than pupils. Monsignor John Kennedy, *Transcript* editor, was aware that the editorial and the full-page advertisements which he had helped Catholic laymen to prepare had been regarded by some as giving an unfortunate impression of Catholic aggressiveness. He did not agree with this view. He was satisfied that the editorial and the advertisements had achieved the desired effect. Subsequently the Hartford newspapers were a lot more careful.[89]

The *Transcript* had refrained from further editorial comment on the school bus issue until the middle of May. When the date of adjournment was only three weeks away and the bill was still in committee (on May 16), the *Transcript* ran a front page editorial entitled "How Many Must Die?" The editorial decried the "dereliction of duty on the part of public authority" in the murder of a nine-year old girl seized as she walked alone to school. The little girl's murder was attributed to the failure of the school board (the girl attended a public school) to provide transportation for children living less than one and one-half miles from school. The murder was described in vivid terms ("snatched from the highway . . . strangled, and stabbed 22 times, six times through the heart. What paroxysms of dread she had to endure before dying. . . . Her small, torn body was found as darkness came down.") Then the editorial declared that the same thing could happen to any of those children who were "refused their right to safety and welfare measures merely because they exercise their right to attend an accredited school of their choice." After citing the *Pierce* case and the *Everson* case, the editorial concluded by asking, "How many of these children have to be butchered before established constitutional principle is allowed to prevail?"

In any publication but a religious newspaper the manipulation of this terrible affair for political purposes might have been regarded as unprincipled journalism. A news editor at the *Hartford Courant*, however, regarded the editorial as newsworthy and reprinted it with the caption, "From the *Catholic Transcript.*" [90] The *Courant* had consistently avoided any editorial comment on this issue. The news editor may have felt impatient with the lack of comment in the editorial columns.

In the May 23 issue the *Transcript* made brief and bitter comment about a "certain segment of the Republican Party." The editorial, entitled "Rule or Ruin?," charged bigotry to those who voted to return the school bus bill to committee. It declared:

Behind all the endless and endlessly tricky parliamentary maneuvering, behind all the pretended, always shifting objections to this, that or the other feature of the proposed legislation, behind all the sancti-monious concern for constitutionality, there has been but one reality at work.

It is an ugly one. It is bigotry.

The reversal of the Speaker's ruling was called the "latest shabby act in the months-long shabby performance." The editorial asked if this faction was the real Republican Party. Could it override the party leadership? "What is to be done in the next election?" Bus service should not be a political issue. It had been made one by a faction of the Republican Party. "A political issue," the editorial concluded, "can only be corrected at the polls. This one will be." [91]

There were a number of supporters of the school bus bill who read the editorial with despair. State Chairman Baldwin thought: "This is just the kind of thing I told them not to do." [92] Majority leader Pope felt the editorial was a great mistake.[93] Mr. Hurley thought it was a mistake also. It gave the bill's opponents ammuni-tion, and it gave the fence-sitters justification for voting against the bill.[94] Both Senator Ryan and Senator Kopacz viewed the editorial as a regrettable act. They felt the bill had a better chance if its han-dling were left to the legislators who supported it.[95]

The editorial was widely distributed and discussed among members of the legislature. There was a growing feeling of resentment. At least seven members of the House came to State Chairman Baldwin and told him the editorial had changed their minds. They would vote against the bill if it came to the floor. Mr. Baldwin couldn't be sure how many others reacted the same way, but he knew the editorial had lost votes for the bill. On Thursday, the day the editorial was pub-lished, petitions to bring the bill out of committee were being circu-lated. It looked as though the 140 signatures might be obtained. But if the bill were brought out, Chairman Baldwin doubted whether it would pass. Before the editorial he had felt certain that if the bill could be brought to the floor it would be passed with a majority of about twenty votes. Now it would be very close.[96]

Despite, or perhaps because of, the resentment engendered by the *Transcript* editorial, John Hurley, Representative George Bennett,

and seven other members of the legislature made swift progress with
their petitions to bring out the school bus bill. They were able to
obtain signatures from a number of legislators who were not in favor
of the bill. Some signed because they wanted the bill to pass, some
because they believed this important issue should be debated on the
floor, and some because they wanted the opportunity to attack the
bill publicly.[97]

The petition drive had begun Wednesday afternoon, May 22,
after the House had voted to send the bill back to committee. By
Thursday evening 132 signatures had been obtained. Before noon
Friday, Representative Bennett was able to announce that 141 signa-
tures had been obtained and a half-dozen others had been promised.
The school bus bill would be debated on the floor of the House.[98]

THE PROTESTANT OPPOSITION

Prior to the public hearing, mail received by the Committee on
Education was largely in favor of public services for non-public school
pupils. After the hearing, the opposition mail began to increase until
the end of May, when the letters being received were running eight to
one against the school bus bill.[99] A good part of this mail was probably due to the activity of Protestant ministers. Public education organizations, such as the Connecticut Citizens for the Public Schools,
the Connecticut Association of Boards of Education, and the Parent-
Teachers Associations of Connecticut, had not found it possible to
take a stand one way or the other on this issue. The testimony of
Mrs. Lasbury, Mrs. Luther, and Sigmund Adler at the public hearing
demonstrated that there was opposition to the school bus bill among
some citizens interested in public education issues. However, the organizations in which they were active took no stand on the controversial proposal. The task of organizing opposition to the bill was
undertaken chiefly by Protestant churchmen.[100]

On March 21 the Connecticut Council of Churches headquarters
mailed to its membership Legislative Bulletin Number One. The
Bulletin declared there was no time to be lost for those who were

"opposed to the use of tax money for private and parochial schools." The drive would succeed unless opposition was expressed in person, by telephone, or by letter to members of the Committee on Education and other legislators.

In subsequent weeks Protestant ministers wrote letters, telephoned legislators, and used their pulpits and church newsletters to encourage their parishioners to oppose the school bus bill. The Plainville Council of Churches sent to "every Protestant church-goer" a mimeographed letter addressed to "Friends of American Public Education." It said that the amount of mail sent to legislators for the school bus bill was coming in "with a flood and the amount 'opposed' is just a trickle." The letter continued, "Unless you think our public schools *need less money* or unless you like to be taxed for institutions out of public control, IT IS TIME TO ACT." Recipients were asked to write to the Committee on Education and to ask their friends to write opposing any "form of infringement on the separation of church and state."

The Reverend Payson Miller, Unitarian minister, mimeographed his sermon criticizing the *Catholic Transcript* and sent it to members of the General Assembly and other Connecticut citizens. He advised his congregation from the pulpit to use their influence in opposition to the school bus bill. Copies of his sermon and names of the members of the Education Committee were made available in the vestry.

Dr. Worley, in his weekly bulletin of March 24, advised his parishioners that citizens with "convictions on the issue of public tax money for the benefit of parochial and private education, including transportation, should express themselves" to the chairmen of the Education Committee. Mr. Worley attended meetings of several Protestant organizations in various towns and made speeches about this issue. He wrote letters to newspaper editors, other Protestant clergymen, and legislators. In one of his letters, Dr. Worley quoted from Richard Joyce Smith's article in *America*, "Even a slight increase in community services to the children of these schools [private and parochial] would induce more families to shift their children from public to private schools." This was the "true motive" of the current drive, Dr. Worley declared. He quoted from a letter of Stanley High, a resident of Darien and a senior editor of *Reader's Digest,* to "offset the public hearing testimony of William Hard, a resident of New Canaan and a *Reader's Digest* editor." Dr. High protested against the use of "public education funds for private and parochial purposes." This was the first step in breaking down the separation of church and state. It was a use of public funds for institutions which were wholly beyond public control. To Dr. High, this was taxation without representation. Dr. Worley concluded:

> It would appear that in some parts of the state and especially in Hartford, there is a "discussion black-out" on this important issue. I sympathize with the desire of the newspapers to eliminate ill-feeling from their columns. But it ought to be possible to debate this important issue on the level of common sense and good taste.

Dr. Worley also wrote to Republican National Chairman Meade Alcorn to protest that his public support of the school bus bill was a disservice to the Republican Party. In his reply, Mr. Alcorn, obviously irritated, said that as a Protestant he deplored the attitude of many fellow Protestants who had made this issue a matter for bitter religious controversy. To Mr. Alcorn it was simply a matter of home rule. Transporting a child to a Catholic school was not different from transporting a blind child to an institute for the blind. Mr. Alcorn thought some Protestants were doing a disservice to their faith.

Dr. Worley felt impelled to reply that this "bitter religious controversy" was not started by Protestants but accepted by many Americans of a variety of religious faiths. He also answered Mr. Alcorn's implied charge of anti-Catholicism by stating that in 1948 as a minister in Stamford he had been honored as having done the most to help interfaith good will. The chairman of the committee which honored him was Dr. George N. Shuster, an eminent Catholic layman. Dr. Worley did not regard himself as anti-Catholic.

Protestant ministers for the most part concentrated their efforts on letter writing or telephoning. They did not meet with Mr. Alcorn, Mr. Baldwin, or the legislative leaders, except in one instance. Several ministers met with Representative Rodney Eielson, one of the assistant majority leaders in the House. They may have expected Mr. Eielson to be particularly receptive to their persuasion since his late father had been a Protestant minister. In their interview one of the ministers told Mr. Eielson that his work for the school bus bill "would make your father turn over in his grave." The interview served to irritate rather than persuade Mr. Eielson.[101]

In general, the campaign of the Protestant churchmen was spasmodic and not organized. The Methodist and Congregational ministers were particularly active, but there was no apparent effort made by Baptist, Lutheran, or Presbyterian churchmen. The most vocal opponents of the bill, Dr. Worley and Mr. Miller, were both located in Hartford, where the newspapers were following a conscious policy of "playing down" the controversy. Some ministers made use of the newsletters or bulletins issued by their churches and sermonized against the bill. The Protestant clergy, however, did not have available the medium of a weekly newspaper like the *Catholic Transcript*. They did not have a public relations counselor like Mr. Hurley or a legislative representative like Mr. Cooney (although some legislators thought this was no great disadvantage). Most of all, the Protestant churchmen had no spokesman, aside from Lieutenant Governor Charles Jewett, in the Republican legislative policy-making group.

THE BISHOPS SPEAK;
THE MINISTERS REPLY

The three Catholic bishops of Connecticut, on Sunday, May 26, in a message to be read at all Catholic masses (and distributed for publication in Sunday newspapers), alerted parishioners to the forthcoming action in the House on the school bus bill and advised that they "carefully observe the action taken, especially that of your local representative." The message reviewed briefly the provisions of the bill, the clarification asked by the State Board of Education, and the ruling of the United States Supreme Court, which, they said, meant that:

. . . public welfare benefits cannot be held from a child because he exercises his American right of religious freedom by attending a school under religious auspices when that school meets standard educational requirements.[102]

The message implied that the State Board of Education had asked for "the clarification" provided in the school bus bill.* The Board, of course, had been careful to avoid stating whether the clarification should specifically prohibit, permit, or make mandatory auxiliary services to non-public school pupils. The paragraph devoted to the Supreme Court's ruling seemed to say exactly the opposite of what the Supreme Court said. There was nothing in the *Cochran* case that suggested the view presented by the bishops. In the *Everson* case the Court said that it did not "mean to intimate that a state could not provide transportation only to children attending public schools." This hardly seemed to support the interpretation offered by the bishops.[103]

The bishops' message declared that every state bordering Connecticut [New York, Massachusetts, and Rhode Island] had laws permitting such services. The proposal was not new and did not violate constitutional principles or the principle of separation of church and state. It was a measure for the protection of children. Despite the intense interest of a great number of Connecticut citizens, the legislature was almost prevented from acting on the bill and only extraordinary efforts, the message declared, had brought it before the whole legislature. The bishops concluded:

As the matter is one of fundamental American justice and of the most acute concern to so many of our Catholic parents and children,

* The statement began: "At the start of the present session of the State Legislature there was introduced a proposal to clarify any Connecticut town's right to provide, if it chooses, bus transportation and some health services to children of the town attending non-public, non-profit schools.

"The clarification had been requested by the State Board of Education. It was needed."

Read by someone not familiar with the action of the State Board of Education, these sentences might suggest that the Board had requested this proposed law.

since more than 62% of the children born in Connecticut in 1956 are Catholic, you should carefully observe the action taken, especially that of your local representative.[104]

Reaction to the bishops' message in the General Assembly was similar to that evoked by the editorial of the *Transcript* calling for correction at the polls. Senator Ryan regretted that the bishops found it neccessary to take such a step. He didn't think it helped the bill at all.[105] Senator Kopacz thought the action was unwise. He was sure that it had lost votes for the bill by alienating some members.[106] A stronger reaction was voiced by a newspaperman in the Capitol who commented, "They threaten every newspaper in the state for suggesting it's a religious question and then they make it doubly clear by using the churches to rally their support." [107]

The opponents of the bill also released public statements in the last few days before the House was to act. On the same Sunday the bishops sent their message to the churches, Representative John M. Lupton, Republican of Weston, made a public statement that the bill was wrong for what it proposed to do and for the method proposed to do it. The legislature was trying to wash its hands of the actual decision on this proposition. Such procedure was "Pontius Pilate politics at its very worst." The bill was unconstitutional, Mr. Lupton said, and should be the subject of a court decision rather than legislation. He charged that the immense pressure "being exerted by some leaders in both parties to get this bill passed is unbelievably bad political leadership." [108]

The following day the Greater Hartford Council of Churches at its spring meeting endorsed a statement opposing the school bus bill. The statement, distributed to House members and the newspapers, asked the consideration of "those legislators and citizens who are free to make independent decisions." Attention was called to Article Seven, Section One of the Connecticut Constitution, providing that no one should be compelled by law to join or support any church or religious association. The United States Supreme Court, the Council's statement said:

. . . has never approved the expenditure of public funds for parochial school buses, or ruled that the states must provide such funds. The 5 to 4 decision which was interpretative of an amendment not mentioning schools does not protect tax expenditures from the more specific prohibitions of many state constitutions and statutes.

Private school authorities were not taking part in this drive for tax funds, it was declared. "It is realistic to recognize the fact that this special privilege is being urged by one religious sect alone." Some political leaders were said to foster "home rule" on issues that would relieve them of making a decision. Home rule would simply multiply a controversy that should be settled "on the state or court level." The statement ended with the words, "We would discourage any political reprisals and express confidence in the independent good judgment of our elected representatives." [109]

It was quite clear that the Protestant ministers read the *Catholic Transcript*, but it was not clear that they had actually read the opinion of the Supreme Court in the *Everson* case. The ministers were no better authorities on constitutional law than the bishops. In the *Everson* case the Supreme Court said quite plainly that New Jersey, as part of a general program, could spend tax funds for transportation of parochial school pupils without violating the First Amendment.

If the devil can quote Scripture for his purposes, cannot clergymen quote Supreme Court opinions for theirs?

It is reasonable to infer that the "legislators and citizens free to make independent decisions" referred to by the statement were not Catholics. The ministers did not explain why Catholics were judged to be more obedient to the political wishes of their clergymen than Protestants.

At this late hour in the campaign, the Presbyterian Church made known its opposition to the school bus bill. The Connecticut Valley Presbytery expressed its adherence to the policy of its national body condemning "the continuing attempt of parochial school authorities, of whatever denomination or faith, to obtain and use public tax funds for purposes of private education." [110]

Obviously, neither the Connecticut Valley Presbytery nor the Greater Hartford Council of Churches accepted the evaluation of the *Everson* decision that transportation was a service to the child, not to the school. For these Protestants, the Catholics were seeking to destroy the separation of church and state with their demands for services to religious schools.

ATTEMPTS TO COMPROMISE

On Monday, May 27, the Republican leadership found itself coming close to a showdown on the hottest issue of the 1957 General Assembly. The leadership was fully and publicly committed to the school bus bill but was not able to command the support of a majority of the Republican members of the House of Representatives. The bill had been defeated in the Republican House caucus and had suffered another setback when the House voted to send it back to committee.

There was resentment among opponents of the bill toward their leadership for its stand. Representative Robert Cairns of Madison had told State Chairman Baldwin that the leadership was wrong in committing the party to a bill that most of the Republican members of the House opposed.[111] Representative Lucy Hammer of North Branford, clerk of the Education Committee, was offended by the leadership's action and particularly by the letter sent by National Chairman Alcorn supporting the bill. She wrote to Mr. Alcorn objecting to his intervention. She did not see why this bill should be made a party issue. Why were members not left free to vote their convictions, as on the birth-control bill, without pressure from the leadership? Before Mr. Alcorn made public commitments on legislative issues, why did he not consult with the Republicans in the legislature who had to face those issues? She did not think he was aware of how strongly opposed to this bill were the majority of Republicans.

Mr. Alcorn replied to Mrs. Hammer that he saw this permissive bill as simply another application of the principle of home rule which the Republican Party in Connecticut always upheld. He did not know how he would vote on this issue if it came up in his own town of Suffield, but he thought the town should have the right to decide for itself. Mrs. Hammer took this reply to be evidence that Mr. Alcorn really had not committed himself in favor of bus service for parochial school pupils. In support of this contention, she showed the letter to some people in the legislature. The word began to spread that Meade Alcorn was not in favor of the school bus bill. Chairman Baldwin telephoned Mr. Alcorn about this development and requested another letter reiterating his support of the bill. The second letter from Mr. Alcorn confirmed his earlier stand.[112]

The Democrats faced no dilemma, since it had been clear very early in the session that almost all, if not all, Democrats in the legislature would vote for the bill. Democratic leaders in the House and Senate had testified for the bill. The Democratic Governor, maintaining an unbroken silence on the issue, kept himself apart from the controversy. He would have to commit himself only if the legislature passed the bill. Then he would have to decide whether to approve or veto. The Republicans faced the immediate problem of what promised to be a bitter floor fight among themselves. It seemed that they had nothing to gain and much to lose.

Mrs. Ralph C. Lasbury, Republican and Protestant, was deeply concerned about this controversy and did some reading on the subject. She was impressed by the way New York State had handled the issue. She was convinced that the proposal had constitutional implications, and she made copies of the constitutional amendment New York had adopted back in 1938. This amendment prohibited all public aid, direct or indirect, to sectarian institutions, "but the legislature may provide for the transportation of children to and from any school or institution of learning." Mrs. Lasbury gave a copy of this amendment to Representative E. O. Smith as a possible compromise measure to offer the supporters of the school bus bill.[113]

Mr. Smith had copies made of the New York State amendment. He passed them out to several supporters and opponents of the school bus bill with the general comment that this might be something worth talking about. He met John Hurley in the hall outside of the Speaker's office and said that Senator Purtell ought to do something about this school bus issue. Mr. Hurley declared that the Senator didn't have anything to do with it. Mr. Smith replied that he would be affected by it, every Republican candidate would be affected by it. "It will hurt all of us." Mr. Smith showed Mr. Hurley a copy of the New York State amendment and asked why the leadership didn't try something like that. Mr. Hurley thought this was something worth talking about with State Chairman Baldwin. He and Mr. Smith went into the Speaker's office to see Mr. Baldwin. The State Chairman thought the possibility of a constitutional amendment was worth discussing, and they agreed to set up a committee of supporters and opponents of the bill to consider it.[114]

The school bus bill was reported out of the House committee unfavorably on Tuesday, May 29. Tuesday afternoon an informal committee of five opponents and five supporters of the bill met for several hours. From time to time Mr. Baldwin joined them. This group had no official status, but its recommendations would have great, perhaps decisive, influence on the action of the House.

In this committee, some of the opponents of the bill proposed that it be set aside and that the House adopt a resolution proposing a constitutional amendment similar to that of New York State. Under Connecticut procedure this resolution would have to be adopted by simple majority vote in the House of Representatives of the 1957 legislature, by a two-thirds vote in both houses of a later session of the legislature, and then approved by a majority vote in a state referendum. Following this difficult and lengthy, but not unusual, amendment procedure, the legislature would still have to adopt a law providing for transportation of non-public school pupils.

Some of the supporters of the bill made the counterproposal that the present bill be defeated, that the provisions of the constitutional amendment be adopted as law (permitting bus service but prohibiting all other aid direct or indirect to religious institutions), and that the resolution proposing a constitutional amendment similar to New York also be adopted. The effect of this counterproposal would be to legalize school bus service to non-public school pupils pending adoption of a constitutional amendment.

The opponents of the bill viewed the counterproposal as a surrender on the issue of transportation. The supporters of the bill saw the compromise offer of a constitutional amendment as no gain at all for their position. It would postpone the decision for at least four years, perhaps longer. The committee broke up after several hours, and it seemed that a compromise agreement could not be reached. The issue would go to the floor of the House for decision the next day.[115]

The next morning, Wednesday, May 29, Speaker Nelson Brown asked Education chairman E. O. Smith if any complicating motions would be presented in the debate on the bill. Mr. Smith said there would not be. The opponents intended to oppose the bill without parliamentary maneuvering.[116]

Later in the morning Mr. Padula and Mr. Bennett approached Representative E. O. Smith to tell him they had given more thought to the possibility of a compromise on a resolution for a constitutional amendment. They did not agree with the decision in the compromise committee. They thought sidetracking the bill and adopting a resolution for a constitutional amendment might be a better procedure than risking defeat of the bill. Mr. Smith suggested a caucus, and they sought out majority leader Pope. He was about to go into a meeting with the rest of the leadership, and he said he would see if they wanted to arrange a caucus. It was now past noon. The House was scheduled to meet at one o'clock. The galleries were filled with spectators who had come to watch the final decision in this long struggle.[117]

The Republican leadership saw little advantage in a compromise attempt at that time. They had begun to feel more confident of the bill's prospects since the compromise had been offered. They took this to be a sign of some loss of strength among the bill's opponents. A resolution for a constitutional amendment could still be adopted if the bill were defeated.[118] They had nothing to gain by holding a caucus. Their decision may have been affected by the knowledge that at no time had a majority of the House Republicans supported their stand on the school bus bill.

When Mr. Pope came out of the Speaker's office after the meeting, the Hall of the House was filling with members. He looked across the Hall, caught Mr. Smith's eye, and shook his head, indicating that there would be no caucus. Mr. Smith thought that a rump caucus might still be called. Those interested might be invited to go off to another room in the Capitol and hold a caucus even without the approval of the leadership. However, it was very late. The thing is rolling now, Mr. Smith thought, we might as well let it go.[119]

THE SPEAKER DECIDES

Amid all the talk that buzzed in the corridors of the State Capitol on the morning of May 29, 1957, there was general agreement that the vote that afternoon was going to be close. Neither Speaker Nelson Brown nor majority leader Pope would predict the result. Mr. Brown did say that the question would be settled either way by less than a ten-vote margin.[120] In conversation with a newsman that morning, he said, "It's going to be close, very close. It could be a tie, and I would have to break it." He shuddered and added, "I hate to think about that possibility." [121] Robert Cairns predicted that the bill would be defeated by a very close vote.[122]

Speaker Brown called the House to order at 1:15 P.M.[123] Senate Bill 872 was taken from the table. Education chairman E. O. Smith moved that the unfavorable report of his committee be accepted and the bill rejected. Mr. Pope asked that the motion be defeated as contrary to the intention of the petition signed by a majority of the members. This bill should be given full debate. Let the bill come to the floor, he said; "you can debate it and still vote against it if you are opposed to it." After a few other members commented, the motion to reject the bill was defeated by a roll-call vote, 106 to 153. As the lights flashed the result on the voting board, the gallery cheered. On request of a House member, the Speaker reprimanded the gallery.

The committee's unfavorable report had been rejected, but the House did not yet have before it the bill that had passed the Senate. Senate Bill 872 still had to be amended by House adoption of Senate Amendments Schedule A and Schedule B, which provided for local referendums and specified only transportation services.

Mr. Pope moved adoption of Senate Amendments Schedule A and B. After some discussion about parliamentary procedure, it was made clear to the House by Mr. Pope, the Speaker, and House clerk John Wassung that the bill, as it passed the Senate, would not actually be before the House until the two amendments were adopted.

Mr. Pope proceeded to explain the bill as amended by the Senate. He emphasized that it was permissive, it would allow towns to do what was being done in twenty-eight towns according to the report of the State Department of Education. Bus service, he said, was not inconsistent with the First Amendment nor with the Connecticut Constitution. He cited the *Everson* case, and noted that many other states provided this service, including nine of the largest states, and that four state courts—Maryland, Kentucky, California, and Massachusetts [sic]— had sustained the practice as not unconstitutional.[124] A spirit of tolerance and fairness was needed, Mr. Pope said; it was unfortunate that there had been so much acrimony and vindictiveness. The question was not one of religion or education, he concluded, it was a question of service for all children.

Following Mr. Pope, Representative E. O. Smith challenged the constitutionality of the bill and the wisdom of those who had permitted this issue to come before the House. "Who is responsible?" he asked, and charged, " I say frankly I feel some of the Republican leaders are responsible." The original bill was an atrocious bill that would have "opened the doors wide." The bill as amended would still provide financial benefit to a church. "If they don't have to spend money on transportation," he said, "they will spend it on something else." He declared that it was canon law that Catholic children must attend Catholic schools; these schools were established for religious purposes.

Democratic leader Samuel Googel rose to a point of order and objected that the remarks of Mr. Smith were not germane to the bill. Speaker Brown had expected that some such objection might be made during this debate, and he had made up his mind that he would uphold such a point of order. He ruled that Mr. Googel's objection was well taken. Mr. Smith sat down as required by the rules. Mr. Lupton appealed the ruling.

A debate then began over whether there should be any mention of the Catholic Church in the debate on the bill. Opponents of the bill rose to defend Mr. Smith and argue that the question of church-state relations was a vital factor. Supporters of the bill objected to remarks or innuendoes about the Catholic Church. Mr. Googel said he had the greatest respect for Mr. Smith but he thought references to the Catholic Church or Catholic schools were not germane. Mrs. Mary James rose to ask facetiously if denominational schools were excluded from this bill. Mr. Lupton said that if this point of order were upheld anyone who mentioned that there was a religious question involved would be ruled out of order. Mr. Marsters said it was essential the House explore the philosophy behind this legislation. Mr. Pope, rather consciously playing the moderator, said it was important that members limit themselves in this debate. He asked for restraint. Mrs. Marie Boutellier said she was in favor of the bill but members should be free to speak. On a voice vote, the Speaker ruled that the appeal had been sustained. A roll-call vote was asked for. The members threw their switches, the lights flashed on the boards, the clerk threw the tally switch, and numbers leaped across the top of the roster boards as the votes were computed. They totaled 153 to sustain the appeal and 106 to deny it. The Speaker was overruled and Mr. Smith could proceed.

The vote appeared to be the House members' stamp of approval on E. O. Smith. The leaders and observers wondered whether this reflected their attitude on the bill itself.

Mr. Smith continued by stating that he was trying to show that the authorities of the Church aspired for aid beyond bus service. They sought tax support for Catholic schools. He quoted from the 1948 statement of the Catholic bishops of the United States to support his statements. Winston Churchill once remarked that he had never read *Mein Kampf*, said Mr. Smith. History might have been different if he had. "We should, stop, look and listen to these statements of the Catholic Church." He hated to see the public schools undermined and children separated on religious lines. The public schools were open to all. A child in need of transportation could hop on a school bus and ride to a public school. The cost of transportation to parochial schools called for in this bill would mean that towns would need more state aid to help provide it. This was the beginning of a real threat to the public schools, and it was time that the friends of the public schools awakened.

Replying to Mr. Smith, Mrs. Boutellier said that the First Amendment was intended to prohibit only government support of a single religion but not public aid to religion generally. But this bill did not provide support for any church or religion. It was a safety service, and at her own Episcopal church on Sundays there were policemen to control traffic. Bus service would not be a subsidy for private schools since few of them provided transportation for their pupils.

Mr. Bennett argued that twenty-eight towns were then giving service and the Committee for the White House Conference on Education had recommended that local communities provide health and safety services.

Mr. Pinney said the bill should be defeated because of its faulty construction, its unconstitutionality, the unfortunate political climate created by the "tactics of some people," and the proposed misuse of public funds for private purposes. He asked the House to consider a constitutional amendment similar to the one adopted by New York. This would be a reasonable compromise. Those who wanted bus service would get something, and those who were concerned about the constitutionality of such service could be satisfied. And it would put this controversial question to the people of the state.

Representative Bernadette C. Maynard, Lisbon Republican, objected that avoidance of the issue was cowardly. The parochial schools made possible great tax savings. The legislature had voted funds for polio vaccine for everyone below twenty-one. The state provided school lunch service to non-public school pupils. Money was appropriated to the Newington Home for Crippled Children, the American School for the Deaf, and the Mystic Oral School. It seemed to Mrs. Maynard that the underlying reason for opposition to this bill was religious prejudice.

Mr. Pope said he had no objection to a constitutional amendment, but that would entail a four-year delay and he believed the question needed to be decided by this legislature.

Representative Mary Cunningham, New Canaan Republican, said that in 1818 Connecticut had thrown off the yoke of the Congregational Church. It would be a grave mistake to start giving financial aid to parochial schools. But, she said, she would be able to take a favorable decision on this bill with better grace if every member were voting his convictions. Every House member knew the terrific pressure being exerted to pass this bill.

Representative Dickson complained that it was a disgrace that this proposal caused such argument. The private schools took a great burden off the taxpayer. "It's about time we lower our heads and say a prayer and thank God we have private schools," he said.

Representative Richard Noyes, Farmington Republican, listed a series of reasons for rejecting the bill. It violated Article Seven of the Connecticut Constitution, which said no one could be compelled to support a religious organization. The safety of the child was the responsibility of the parent and the private school. How about children going to Boy Scout meetings? Would buses be provided for them? he asked. We paid taxes to maintain a universal public school system for all children, not just for our own. Those who were childless must still contribute their taxes. The home-rule provision was recognized as faulty by those who drafted the bill because it was twice amended to limit the kinds of service authorized. The legislature could not delegate all authority to the towns. Would you give towns the right to decide to coin money by local referendum? The tax savings argument was fallacious because there were many organizations doing worthy public services. Private recreation clubs reduced the cost of recreation centers for the towns. Would you give them public services? he asked. Finally, he said, the proponents pleaded for fairness, but under this bill many children in the state would be excluded by the local referendum provision.

There were many practical problems, Mr. Noyes added, that would follow upon adoption of this bill. What ground rules would be established and by whom? The public school board? Would bus service be provided for Sunday schools as well as parochial schools? What divisions would this cause in the towns? We have seen, he said, how far church groups will go. Do you, he asked the members, want this kind of atmosphere in your town? Furthermore, he concluded, the public schools need all our support.

Time after time as the debate proceeded the opponents argued that the bill provided public aid for private and religious schools. Time after time the proponents replied that this bill provided only for services to children. Then they might, by implication or specifically, contradict themselves by referring to the tax savings made possible by these schools, which were therefore deserving of this aid. Often it seemed that the proponents were pleading the cause of the schools rather than that of the children. Some opponents based their objections to the bill on opposition to parochial schools.

Representative Thomas Quinlan, Washington Republican, said that he sent his own children to Catholic schools but he was opposed to this bill. We owed our remarkable growth, he said, to freedom from government control. It was a short-sighted policy, he said, to seek public aid.

Other speakers expressed opposition to the bill and advised members to vote their own convictions, not be swayed by pressures related to their jobs or businesses, nor threats of reprisals or fear of being called "bigot."

Mrs. Hammer rose to ask some questions about the administration of the bill. Who would say who could ride, what schools would be served, and what hours the buses would run? If the proponents of the bill were concerned about children's safety, why did they exclude children attending schools out of town or profit schools?

And who was to decide whether a school was operated for profit? The bill gave no definition.

After this lengthy debate, Mr. Pope reminded the members that the bill would not be on the floor in the form it passed the Senate until the House adopted Senate Amendments Schedule A and B. One member asked what the situation would be if the House adopted one amendment without adopting the other. Speaker Brown replied, "We'd be in a mess." On a roll-call vote the Senate amendments were adopted 152 to 116. This substantial margin seemed to contradict the impression given by the vote on the Speaker's ruling. Did it mean that the majority favored the bill, or was the House merely accommodating Mr. Pope in his plea for its proper consideration?

At this point Representative Francis Barnett, Glastonbury Republican, offered an amendment to the bill which would eliminate the referendum and make it mandatory for towns to provide transportation to non-public school pupils. Everyone agreed, said Mr. Barnett, that we don't want our towns torn apart on this issue. We should decide it here, he declared. Mr. Pope and several other members expressed opposition. This attempt to treat transportation as a matter of welfare and minority rights, to require towns to serve all school children equally, was given scant consideration. Those who used the child-benefit theory in debate knew that a bill consistent with that theory would not pass. Mr. Barnett withdrew his amendment.

Another amendment was offered by Representative Harold Douglass, Greenwich Republican, to eliminate the referendum provision and to provide that the bill remain effective until a constitutional amendment was submitted to the people. This amendment from an opponent of the measure caused a stir on the floor. Mr. Pope asked for and obtained a five-minute recess.

The leaders and many of the legislators moved swiftly into the Speaker's office to discuss the Douglass amendment. Mr. Baldwin, Mr. Hurley, and Senator Ryan were there, and even John Bailey, Democratic State Chairman. The room was crowded with legislators and many others. The five-minute recess stretched out to almost an hour while the proponents and opponents worked over the possibility of compromise on the Douglass amendment. No agreement could be reached. The House reconvened, and Mr. Douglass withdrew his amendment.

Representative A. Searle Pinney, who had served on the compromise committee and who had earlier urged the house to give consideration to a constitutional amendment, chose this moment to move for suspension of the rules and consideration of his resolution for a constitutional amendment. On a voice vote the Speaker declared the motion lost. Mr. Pinney doubted the chair, and the Speaker ordered a standing vote. A two-thirds vote was needed to suspend the rules. The standing vote totaled 140 for suspension, 87 against. Mr. Pinney came within twelve votes of obtaining an opportunity to present his resolution for a constitutional amendment. If 140 members, an absolute majority of the House membership of 279, wanted this resolution presented, it is reasonable to conclude that they wanted to adopt it. It would seem to follow that once the House had adopted this resolution, the bill itself would have stood little chance of passage. The motion failed, and it became clear that the House would soon have to vote on the bill itself.

A few more members wanted to debate, and the House membership was disposed to continue as long as anyone wanted to be heard. Mr. Lupton, who had issued the public statement against "Pontius Pilate politics," asked for rejection of the bill. He said everyone should realize that "we are all equally sincere when we believe that our own faith is the one true faith." The *Everson* case impressed him because of the Supreme Court's reluctance to rule against a state law even at the verge of constitutionality. The majority argument in that case, he said, was a fine basis for ruling in the other direction. The bill before the House, he stated, did not aid freedom of religion. It respresented a threat bigger than any yet touched upon in the debate. Was it right or fair to ask a man to vote against his church or his country? That was why we had separation of church and state. The bitterness, he stated, had served to warn us of the dangers in this kind of legislation. This path would lead us to a different America, he warned.

Democratic leader Samuel Googel rose to object that this was a transportation bill, not a religious bill. Representative Charles Tomasino, New Haven Republican, said this was a bill for the safety of children. There were no ulterior motives. It was not an opening wedge. Others spoke of the need of protecting children, and one mentioned the recent killing of a little girl walking to school.

In opposition, Mr. Cairns asked why, if this was a measure to protect children, some school children were excluded. Representative Jack Turner of Bethany challenged the denial that this bill was an opening wedge. He had read the remarks of Richard Joyce Smith and gained a different impression. What kind of services did Mr. Smith propose? he asked. By Mr. Smith's definition, health and welfare services included medical, dental, nursing, and body-building services, as well as remedial reading, psychological services, standardized books, and aid in building schools. The recent editorial comments of the *Catholic Transcript* suggested for him the comment of Senator McClellan, "Those who deal in low blows detract more from themselves than those they attack."

Mr. Googel spoke again to disagree with the "prophets of doom." Towns which had given service had experienced little dissension. There was a difference between support of schools and aid to children, he said. This bill was simply a question of home rule. He reminded the members of the tax savings made possible by private schools. Those who questioned the constitutionality of the bill should pass it and let it be given a court test. He was proud to announce that all thirty Democrats in the House would vote in favor of the bill. The Democrats cheered. The Republicans were on notice now as to who would bear the responsibility if this bill were defeated. When Mr. Googel sought to speak again, Mr. Noyes, Farmington Republican, objected. A special rule permitted members to speak but once in this debate.

Mrs. Marjorie Farmer, Darien Republican, declared that tax savings could not justify violation of the member's oath to protect the Constitution of Connecticut. If a court test were desired it could be brought in any one of the twenty-eight towns that were then giving service.

Representative Allen Mopsik, Plainfield Democrat, argued in support of the bill that the people in his town knew what was best for his town. They wouldn't know what to do if the private schools closed, he said.

John E. Larson, Deep River Republican, replied that he would welcome an opportunity to pay more taxes to have some say about what was taught in those schools.

The members seemed to be losing their enthusiasm for debate. There were a few calls for the previous question. Some other members shouted protests. It seemed that some still wanted to talk. The motion for the previous question (which would end the debate and permit an immediate vote on the bill) was rejected, 136 to 98.

Only one more member wanted to speak. Rodney Eielson spoke briefly in support of the bill and asked for its passage.

The House was now ready for the vote. Almost five and one-half hours had passed since the debate began. The issue had been thoroughly discussed. Some strong remarks had been made, but the debate had been orderly. Each side had been given full opportunity to influence votes. Now the time had come for a decision. This, at last, was the crucial vote—the vote that would decide the fate of the bill.

Those who were not yet committed had reached the end of the line. All of the clamor of the preceding months, all of the letters, telephone calls, conferences, sermons, editorials, claims, charges, threats, and arguments, all of the persuasion, pressure, predictions, and pleas were now focussed on the mind of the uncommitted legislator. By judgment or impulse, by reason or emotion, he now had to decide, put his hand on his voting switch, and place himself on one side or the other.

Once more the voting machine was made ready, the members threw their switches to record their votes, the Speaker asked if all had voted, the clerk locked the machine and threw the switch to tally the vote. The members and the audience in the gallery watched in fascination as the numbers danced across the top of the voting board following the automatic computation.

The numbers stopped—and they matched. Ayes, 133; nays, 133.

A murmur of astonishment ran across the hall and gallery. The clerk reran the computer twice, and each time the total remained 133 to 133. The clerk announced the vote.

Speaker Nelson Brown declared, "The Chair votes 'Aye.' The bill is passed," and brought down his gavel. The gallery raised the roof.

Representative William O'Brien, Portland Democrat, sought the floor as exactly one-half of the members cheered. On a point of personal privilege, Mr. O'Brien praised the Speaker as a man of courage and fairness. This brought more applause.

Mr. Pinney rose to introduce his resolution calling on the Constitutional Amendments Committee to report a constitutional amendment. This was the amendment borrowed from the New York Constitution. Mr. Pope said he would join with Mr. Pinney in asking for this amendment. On a roll-call vote, the resolution was adopted, 167 to 60. There were fifty-two members not voting or absent on this vote, compared to only thirteen absent or not voting on the bill.*

Immediately after the vote on the school bus bill, Mr. Baldwin and Mr. Hurley in the Speaker's office went over the vote as automatically recorded on a roster of the House membership. They noticed that most of those absent or not voting were members known to be opposed to the bill. They sent a message to Mr. Pope and asked him to come to the Speaker's office. Mr. Baldwin told Mr.

* This amendment was to receive a more limited endorsement when the report of the Constitutional Amendments Committee was submitted to the House the following week. The resolution proposing an amendment similar to the New York provision was adopted, but the vote was 148 to 101. Thirty members were absent or not voting. Voting in opposition to the amendment resolution were some of the supporters of the school bus bill, such as Mr. Kerrigan, Mr. Bennett, and Mr. Muzio, as well as opponents of the bill such as E. O. Smith and Mrs. Hammer. (Connecticut, "House Journal," June 6, 1957.) This combined opposition of supporters and opponents of the bill did not suggest a favorable future for the amendment when it was considered in the 1959 General Assembly. It seemed unlikely that the proposed amendment would win the support of two-thirds of both houses. Much would depend, of course, on how the school bus bill worked out in practice in the two years intervening.

Pope he thought the bill ought to be sent to the Governor right away under suspension of the rules. On the next legislative day some one of the opponents might ask for reconsideration of the bill. Mr. Pope recognized the possibility, but he wondered about attempting to ask for suspension of the rules. A two-thirds vote was needed, and those opposed to the bill might easily defeat the motion. Perhaps the motion could be made later on for immediate transmittal of all bills and resolutions on which the House that day had acted without the opposition moving to obstruct transmittal of S.B. 872 to the Governor.[125]

The opposition, or E. O. Smith at least, was aware of the opportunity to continue the struggle. He was not so inclined. The issue had been fought hard all the way down the line, the bill had been brought to a vote, and the House had passed it. The decision could stand.

The action that the Republican leadership sought actually was taken by the Democratic leader, Mr. Googel, while the Republican leaders were talking it over in the Speaker's office. When Mr. Pope returned to the floor he learned from House clerk Wassung that Mr. Googel had moved for suspension of the rules and immediate transmittal of the bill to the Governor. The Governor, it seemed, had taken the unusual step of asking to have the bill sent to him.[126] *

THE REASONS WHY

In the days following the big vote, there were many who studied the battle over the school bus bill to determine why it had been voted. For some, the explanation was simply "the Catholic Church." For others, it was "the will of God." For those who reflected on the absentee members, the bill's success might have seemed accidental.

* Mr. Googel reported that he was asked to make the motion by John Bailey, Democratic State Chairman. Possibly the Governor didn't want to spend the long Memorial Day week end listening to protests and pleas for a veto from Protestant ministers. One plea for a veto was telegraphed by the Connecticut Chapter of the American Civil Liberties Union, but the Governor had already signed the bill (*Hartford Courant*, May 30, 1957).

One legislator, an opponent of the bill, had suffered a heart attack one week before the crucial vote and was in the hospital on the day of decision. Another opponent, a dairy farmer, couldn't stay for the vote; his cows had to be milked. Still another opposed to the bill had planned a long week-end vacation with his wife. When the House recessed late in the afternoon so that the leaders could discuss the proposed Douglass amendment, the couple conferred in the lobby. The wife wanted to know, "How long is this thing going on?" The legislator turned to a fellow legislator and asked, "When do you think we'll get to vote on the bill?"

"About six or seven o'clock," was the reply.

"Well," the wife exclaimed, "I'm not going to hang around here until then!"

Her husband looked unhappy, shrugged his shoulders and sighed, "All right, let's go." *

One of the opponents of the bill studied the names of those who voted for it and made an analysis: "30 Democrats, 45 Catholic Republicans, 9 Brennan's boys, 7 Lavieri's boys, 6 Carpenter's boys, 2 Brown and McKenzie, 16 town pressure, 4 early commitments, 4 Cappy Baldwin, 3 crackpots, 2 cowards." Since this analysis accounted for only 128 of the 134 votes for the bill, there were, apparently, six votes for which the analyst could find no explanation at all.

A more precise analysis of the vote reveals that one of the important factors in the eventual passage of the school bus bill was the demonstrated local popular support in its favor.

In a final vote on the bill a definite influence on a House member was the existence of a parochial school in his town. In 1957 there were fifty towns in Connecticut with Catholic schools. These towns had a total of 103 representatives in the House. Of these 103 members from Catholic school towns, 79, or more than 76 per cent, voted in favor of the school bus bill.

There were 119 towns without Catholic schools represented in

* One can only speculate how the news of the passage of the bill by one vote affected the success of the vacation.

the House by 176 members. Of these 176 members, only 56, or 31 per cent, voted for the bill. Conversely, 110 members, or 62 per cent of the 176 members from non-Catholic school towns, voted against the bill. Of the 12 members absent or abstaining, only one was from a Catholic school town.[127]

It is fair to say, then, that the interests of his constituency probably had a substantial influence on a member's vote. A town which had a Catholic school most likely had a substantial Catholic population. Many Catholic parents in that town obviously had a direct and deep interest in the fate of the school bus bill. It affected their children. Representatives responded to that interest. The proportion of Catholics was probably not as high among populations of towns without Catholic schools. In such towns the dominant sentiment, as reflected in the House vote, was against the bill but not in the same intensity as the sentiment in favor of the bill in Catholic school towns.

Undoubtedly another crucial factor in the eventual passage of the bill was the early and continuing support of the Republican leadership. While the House members were influenced by the interests of voters in their own towns, the Republican leaders were concerned with the larger constituency that would make itself felt in state-wide elections. In 1954 the Republican candidate for Governor lost by only 3115 votes, and the Republican candidate for Lieutenant Governor won by only 5452 votes in an election with a total vote of close to a million.[128] The Republican state leadership did not need to worry much about losing control of the House, but they were vulnerable in state-wide contests.

The effort of the Republican leadership was assumed by many to be motivated by a concern for "Catholic votes." A Republican legislator who voted against the school bus bill later wrote to Mr. Worley:

> I regret Mr. Brown, the Speaker, had the opportunity to cast the deciding vote but he was under orders from the so-called leadership, starting with Mr. Meade Alcorn and the purpose is to get votes next year.

"To get votes," as used here, obviously meant "Catholic votes." One Republican legislator remarked, "Some people will agree to anything for a few votes." Still another commented, "They [presumably the Republican leadership] are doing everything they can to to get Ed May re-elected."

John Hurley's enhanced standing in Republican Party circles was often attributed to his successful handling of the 1956 campaign to elect Edwin May to Congress. May's election was assumed to be the result of many Hartford County Catholics, normally Democratic voters, switching to the Republican side. One opponent of the school bus bill said that Meade Alcorn's national standing was won because of the election of a Republican congressman from traditionally Democratic Hartford County. (It would be difficult to say which contributed most significantly to the success of Ed May's campaign; a Democratic primary fight over the nomination, the political skill of Hurley and Alcorn, or the overwhelming Eisenhower victory in Connecticut.)

The attraction of Catholic votes for Republican candidates might well have been in the minds of the Republican leaders, but it was little mentioned in their discussions of the school bus bill. However, John Hurley strongly reminded the leadership of his claim that Connecticut was "62 per cent Catholic." Republican support for the school bus bill was essential, he felt, to the 1958 campaigns of Congressman May, Senator Purtell, and the Republican candidate for Governor. No one else made this argument for the bill so directly.

Winning votes is the primary concern of a political party in a democracy. It is to be expected that politicians would have this in mind when discussing political actions. Obviously they must give consideration to a measure desired by a substantial segment of voters. But when those voters are aligned not vocationally or geographically but denominationally, a political leader is disinclined to acknowledge that alignment. He can speak forthrightly about doing something for the farmers or the teachers, for the homeowner or the city dweller. It is difficult for him to say candidly that he thinks something should be done for the Catholics or the Protestants or the Jews.

The obvious reason for the passage of the school bus bill was seldom stated in objective terms. The Republican leaders and many Republican legislators responded to the interest of a substantial segment of the voters who campaigned vigorously for the bill. Catholics appeared to be solidly for the measure. Opposition to the bill was entirely Protestant, but not all Protestants were opposed. Since the Democrats were for the bill, the Republicans had little to lose by being for it also. But they had much to lose by being against it. Protestant Republican voters opposed to the bill would find little comfort in pulling the Democratic lever in the voting booth. But could the Republican Party hope to hold the Catholic voters it had won in the Eisenhower years if the school bus bill were defeated? For the Republican state leadership the weight of the political factors were all on the side of the bill. This evaluation was made early, and the leadership held to it unwaveringly.

As with almost any legislative act, the success of the school bus bill was the result of a variety of factors. Two of these were major: the influence of voters in Catholic school towns and the support of the Republican state leadership.

The school bus bill was passed by the House at 6:55 P.M., on May 29. The Governor signed it at 8:35 P.M. He made no comment on the bill.

The swift signing of the bill by the Governor seemed symbolic of the attitude of the political leaders. It was a job they wanted to have done with. The tactics of the clergy had not permitted the political leaders any joy in their struggle. The passage of the bill was not so much a moment of triumph as the end of an unpleasant task.

VII:

AFTERMATH

SHORTLY AFTER the passage of the school bus bill, majority leader Fred Pope stopped Mrs. Lucy Hammer outside the Speaker's office. He mentioned a pending local bill for her town and asked when she wanted it to come up for a vote. Mrs. Hammer replied that she was still interested in the bill and hoped it would pass. They agreed on a date for action.

Mrs. Hammer was pleased by this conversation. She knew that the majority leader was making it clear that there would be no reprisals by the leadership against those who had opposed the school bus bill. The issue was settled, and prior differences could be forgotten.[1]

Mr. Noyes, Farmington Republican, apologized to Democratic minority leader Sam Googel for raising a point of order against him in the final debate on the bill. Mr. Googel told him cordially not to worry about it. The minority leader held no resentment. He knew how easy it was to get carried away in the midst of a strenuous debate.[2]

Reconciliation was not difficult for the legislators. In the parliamentary course of the bill, no one had violated their sense of fair play. They had not inflicted severe wounds on one another. One observer, remarking on the restrained character of the House debate, called it "a supreme demonstration of the capacity of the democratic process to handle the most explosive of issues. One way of getting religious matters out of politics is to let them in and deal with them and resolve them." He suggested that the birth-control issue also "ought to be given a fair chance at being resolved in the political arena, so it can get out of that arena." [3]

The *Hartford Times*, silent at the time reprisals were called for, spoke out editorially against such a course after the bill was law. The *Times* thought it "regrettable" that threats of reprisals had ever been made, and it expressed the wish that local discussions would be as temperate as the House debate. The editorial concluded with the hope that "the preliminary pressures that have evidenced themselves within the Republican Party, from the National Chairman down, will be lacking." [4]

There was no inclination among Republican leaders to attempt reprisals. Meade Alcorn received a suggestion that action be taken against House education chairman E. O. Smith and flatly rejected it.[5] Cappy Baldwin, too, rebuffed proposals to punish Mr. Smith and others who had opposed the school bus bill. Mr. Baldwin had differed strongly with Mr. Smith on the question of bringing the bill out of committee, but he harbored no resentment against the education chairman.[6]

Both Senator Kopacz and Senator Ryan were immensely pleased with the passage of the school bus bill and were not in favor of any reprisals against those who had opposed it. Neither of them held any feeling of antagonism against Senator Bauer for his opposition. Senator Ryan was disappointed by the statement of Lieutenant Governor Jewett against the bill. He knew it was something the Lieutenant Governor felt he had to do. They lunched together the day he was to make the statement, and Mr. Jewett was visibly agitated. The tone of the statement, the sounding of a "warning," suggested to Senator Ryan something of the argument of the Blanshard pamphlet, "The Bus Wedge." The pamphlet, and that line of argument, Senator Ryan regarded as anti-Catholic. He regretted that the Lieutenant Governor, whom he liked and respected, had followed such an approach.[7]

Senator Kopacz felt differently. He was not at all offended by the Lieutenant Governor's statement. When Mr. Jewett completed his remarks to the Senate, Senator Kopacz was the first to shake his hand and to congratulate him. "I disagree with you, Chuck," Senator Kopacz said, "but that was a fine statement." A man, the Senator felt, must do what he believes in.[8]

John Hurley regarded the Jewett speech as unnecessary and politically foolish. He was not offended by it nor by the opposition of E. O. Smith. The education chairman, Mr. Hurley felt, worked for the defeat of the school bus bill as he would for any other bill he opposed. The opposition of some people, however, Mr. Hurley regarded as "vicious." He was satisfied with the bill as adopted. The dropping of health services was a necessary compromise. The essential point had been won. For Mr. Hurley the contest was closed. He certainly wanted no more of that kind of struggle.[9]

Among those who opposed the bill there was some feeling that this was not the end. They were certain that the legislature had passed a bill that violated the Connecticut Constitution. Both Representatives Smith and Cairns intended to encourage any effort that might be made to test the law in the courts. Mr. Cairns was convinced that lasting antagonisms had been caused by the struggle over the bill. Mrs. Hammer, Mr. Smith, and Mr. Cairns were all convinced that Senator Purtell, a Catholic, would find it more difficult to win re-election because of the resentment over the school bus battle. Mrs. Hammer sensed a growing uneasiness over the political influence of the Catholic Church. She "knew" that many people saw the Church's influence as pervasive.[10]

While the politicians found reconciliation an easy matter among themselves, there were those who felt that the effects of the school bus fight would color Connecticut politics for some time. Both Republican State Chairman Baldwin and Republican National Chairman Alcorn thought that Mr. Jewett's statement had reduced considerably the likelihood of his nomination for higher office. Mr. Baldwin felt that others who had played a leading part in the struggle, such as Speaker Nelson Brown and Senator Ted Ryan, would find their identification with the bill a political handicap in the future.[11]

Some part of the public would be alienated by those who had been in the forefront of this fight on one side or the other. On this issue, the politicians could forgive and forget. The clergy and the public, or some of them at least, could not.

THE FIGHT GOES ON

Protestant and Catholic rejoined the battle as soon as the school bus bill became law. The fight in Connecticut was now drawing national attention.

A vigorous protest against "mounting Roman Catholic pressure for government subsidies" for parochial schools was made by Glenn L. Archer, executive director of POAU, in a speech to the Southern Baptist Convention in Chicago the week following the adoption of the school bus bill. The Connecticut law, said Mr. Archer, was an example of such pressure. He criticized Archbishop Henry J. O'Brien for describing the bill's opponents as "bigots" and for sneering at their "sanctimonious concern for the constitutionality" of the bus bill. The Archbishop had threatened to close Hartford's Catholic schools, Mr. Archer charged, unless bus service was provided for them. There would be serious consequences, he said, if Catholic priests, as they did in Connecticut, resorted to political action to enforce their demands for subsidies.[12]

Such charges were called a "prime example of falsification" by Monsignor John S. Kennedy, editor of the *Catholic Transcript*. Mr. Archer, the Monsignor said, had quoted out of context from an editorial that the Archbishop had not seen.[13] (Monsignor Kennedy might also have observed that it would have been patently foolish for anyone to demand bus service for pupils in Hartford's parochial schools, since Hartford did not provide bus service even to public school pupils.)

Monsignor Kennedy responded with an attack of his own on opponents of the school bus bill. After first praising those who had helped to pass the bill for their "intelligent and spirited bipartisan leadership," the *Transcript* editorially denounced Education chairman E. O. Smith, the Reverend Loyd Worley, POAU, and the American Civil Liberties Union. Mr. Smith's view of Catholic schools as divisive was motivated by "an intensive drive to make education a totalitarian, governmental monopoly." The editorial conceded that while "some of the opponents undoubtedly voiced and voted their honest, if hardly objective, convictions, others betrayed nasty prejudices."

Describing the Reverend Loyd Worley as "the non-legislative leader of the opposition," the editorial warned:

> Connecticut must now perforce be acutely curious about him and causes he may have advocated, and organizations he may have been associated with in the past. The people will want to know the calibre and record of a man who would wield major influence over their legislature and the future of their children.

After this insinuating criticism of Dr. Worley for unnamed previous associations, the *Transcript* editorially attacked Protestants and Other Americans United as "a shabby clique" and "a small, but noisy band of bigots whose stock-in-trade is fomenting hatred of Catholicism and Catholics." The editorial also noted the attempt to create the "false impression" that the Parent-Teachers Associations of Connecticut opposed the school bus bill. The American Civil Liberties Union was charged with taking a stand in favor of discrimination.[14]

Dr. Worley made prompt reply. He wrote to the editor of the *Transcript* that he had received, "evidently from your office, a marked copy of your issue of June 6th containing an editorial headed 'Connecticut Awakened.'" Dr. Worley took the editorial to be "a veiled threat to expose me as some kind of dangerous subversive character. I hope this possible inference is mistaken." He laid no claim to perfection, but he tried to follow the great moral and spiritual teachers. He could give a reasonable defense of his advocacies or associations. He had in his first parish opposed the Ku Klux Klan. He had opposed school board candidates who had taken an "un-American attitude towards an elementary school teacher of the

Roman Catholic faith." And he had once been selected for a Citizens Award of the Stamford Jewish War Veterans by a committee headed by Dr. George Shuster, president of Hunter College and a distinguished Catholic layman. Dr. Worley said he had tried to place on a high level his opposition to special privilege for any one religious group. He would continue to do so.

Dr. Worley had this letter to the *Transcript* mimeographed and distributed it to his parishioners and to some of the opponents of the school bus bill. He thought it "only fair that our members should read the reply which the *Transcript* probably will not print." [15] He was correct; the letter was not printed.

In his newsletter to his congregation, the Reverend Payson Miller, Unitarian minister, defended Dr. Worley as a "good, courageous and dedicated man who has been threatened with investigation by the *Catholic Transcript*." Mr. Worley's efforts to influence legislation, Mr. Miller said, were more admirable than those of the *Transcript*.[16]

The annual New York East Conference of Methodist Churches adopted a resolution calling for "such immediate action as will test the constitutionality" of the bill. The resolution also called for the formation of organizations to fight the next step to draw support from local public school budgets. Representative E. O. Smith and other legislators were commended for their firm stand "for American principles in spite of threats of reprisals from the Roman Catholic hierarchy and state and national leaders of the Republican party." [17]

In his report as Chairman of the Civil Rights and Moral Affairs Committee of the Connecticut Council of Churches, Mr. Worley called for opposition to ecclesiastical domination of the public schools. He asked for a court test of the constitutionality of the school bus bill and suggested that plans be made to defeat the proposed constitutional amendment. He also called for local action to defeat requests for service in the towns. He sent a letter to "all Connecticut citizens who oppose special church privilege and to all non-Roman church leaders." The Connecticut Council of Churches was not equipped to provide much assistance to communities in campaigns against demands for bus service for parochial schools. The best source of factual material, he advised, was the Washington headquarters of POAU. He concluded that no matter how much "we may regret involvement in this conflict, it is being forced upon us." It would probably continue for some time "unless we are prepared to surrender at once those freedoms which our forefathers established on this continent." [18]

The editor of the *Transcript* reported on the Connecticut legislative fight in a magazine article. He recommended that Catholics discuss their differences with non-Catholics to eliminate needless acrimony. "Easy, habitual relations" were needed, he advised, to cultivate understanding and good will. But in the same article he charged that opponents of the bus bill regarded Catholics as "second class citizens." Such opponents, he said were anti-Catholic propagandists and promoters of "militant totalitarian secularism posing as Americanism." [19]

Such comments were hardly likely to promote good will or to eliminate acrimony. The Connecticut clergy did not seem inclined to change their tactics. The Protestant ministers who had been so active opposing the bus bill resolved to carry on the fight. The Reverend Loyd Worley and the Reverend Payson Miller assisted in the organization of a Hartford chapter of Protestants and Other American United.[20]

The struggle, it seemed, would go on. Now the battle would be shifted to the towns.

SOME LOCAL REACTIONS

Some of the opponents of the school bus bill had anticipated that it would cause a bitter religious fight in each of Connecticut's 169 towns. This prediction did not suggest much analysis of the law nor of the Catholic school system in the state. The provisions of the bill limited its effects to the 50 towns with parochial schools and any other towns in which a parochial school was constructed. It was not likely that the 28 towns already providing transportation for parochial school pupils would undertake a referendum to end the service. Obviously, the sentiment in those towns was in favor of transportation. Of the 22 towns not transporting local parochial school pupils, 5 did not transport public school pupils. Thus local conflicts could be expected mainly in the 17 towns that contained Catholic schools and that transported public school pupils but not Catholic school pupils. The expected area of conflict was about one-tenth that predicted by some of the bill's opponents.

It seemed most likely that the petitions for a referendum on transportation would be initiated in those towns that had a large percentage of their children in Catholic schools. It could be assumed that the Catholic school enrollment reflected a direct interest among a substantial number of parents in obtaining public transportation for their children in Catholic schools. In High Hills the Catholic school was comparatively new, and only about 12 per cent of the school children were enrolled in it. The request for bus service was denied. In Diamond City about 25 per cent of the school children were attending Catholic schools, which had long been established. The school board's move to curtail transportation for them was reversed.

Such local needs and attitudes might not be the sole influences in determining local action under the new school bus law. In Parkville Father Daniel had advised his parishioners to wait until the legislature had acted. He was conscious of the need for maintaining the good will of the community and was following the policy of the Archdiocese to "go very easy." It was possible that the Archbishop, after passage of the school bus bill, would maintain this policy or modify it only after long deliberation. Much thought might well be given to advising pastors whether they should encourage or discourage petitions for a referendum on transportation.

Plans of the opponents of the school bus bill were largely dependent upon what steps might be taken to secure transportation in a town with a Catholic school. There were two lines of action to prepare for. The New York East Methodist Conference called for local organization to develop opposition to any referendum. (Significantly, it was not suggested that a petition be brought for a referendum to end service in any of the towns which were then transporting parochial school pupils. The Conference probably assumed that such a referendum would not be successful.) Representatives Cairns and E. O. Smith looked for some move to test the bill in the courts. Bringing such a case would entail financing, a careful selection of the town in which to bring the complaint, and competent legal counsel to handle a case that might eventually be appealed to the Supreme Court of the United States.

The provisions of the school bus law affected a limited number of towns. There were comments in some of those towns which revealed unfamiliarity with the new law. In Manchester, the Reverend John F. Hannon said he hoped the town fathers were giving the matter some thought.[21] The remark suggested that Father Hannon did not appreciate that the law now placed the decision not with the "town fathers" but with the town voters. In New Britain, the Reverend Lucyan Bojnowski announced he would seek free bus service for pupils of the Sacred Heart School.[22] This was a puzzling announcement, since New Britain did not provide bus service for its public school pupils.[23] In Stamford, Martin F. Armstrong, president of the Parents Association of St. Cecilia's School, announced his candidacy for the Republican nomination for Mayor. Free bus service for parochial school pupils, he said, would be a major plank in his platform.[24] Mr. Armstrong seemed not to appreciate that the authority for this decision lay not with the mayor or his council but with the voters. There was not yet a general awareness in Connecticut of how the new law should be applied.

In Diamond City, the school board was faced with the problem of adopting an official policy to succeed its former "unofficial" policy. Formerly, parochial school pupils had been transported to the nearest public school, from which they walked to the parochial school. The school board members and others considered whether the new law meant that parochial school pupils would be given transportation directly to the Catholic school they attended. The Mayor named a committee of the City Council to study the problem. With pupils attending a Polish Catholic school, a French Catholic School, and an Italian Catholic school, instead of the nearest Catholic school, a more extensive transportation system would be required to provide service directly to each school. After discussion among political leaders and Catholic school officials, it was agreed that parochial school pupils would be transported to the nearest Catholic school, as public school pupils were transported to the nearest public school. The parent could still send his child to a more distant national Parish school, but the local public officials agreed that the city had no obligation to carry him there.*

In Parkville, Father Daniel waited. There was a law now, but he was not inclined to precipitate a contest at once. Nor did Father Leahy in High Hills encourage a petition. A referendum would mean more community strife. Mrs. McNulty, however, had her revenge. The Democratic caucus did not renominate Mr. Manners.

Nor was Mr. Manners the only local casualty. In other towns school board members failed of renomination or of re-election apparently because of the school bus issue. A leading official of the Connecticut Association of Boards of Education, a Catholic and a Democrat, expressed his concern.

* Interviews with Catholic school official and with Diamond City Superintendent of Schools, and minutes of Diamond City Council.
    The policy adopted by Diamond City can be viewed as an application of the doctrine expressed by the Catholic bishops of the United States that the state has a responsibility to encourage and assist the religious education of the child (see above, p. 17). Diamond City's obligation extends to the nearest Catholic school for the Catholic school pupil. The obligation is connected with the religious school rather than with the child or the parent. This policy contradicts the argument that the right of the parent to direct the education of his child and to choose his child's school is negated by refusal of public bus service. Perhaps for Catholic school officials the primary consideration was that the child should be assisted to get a Catholic education, but it is difficult to see why a government agency should have any authority to discriminate between accredited religious schools.
    A true application of the child-benefit principle and equal protection of the laws could have been made here. The Diamond City school board could have agreed to transport any Catholic school pupil as far as any public school pupil was transported. If the greatest distance a public school pupil was carried should be three miles, it would be "equal treatment" to give all school pupils transportation up to the same limit.

"This fight has been carried on too long," he said. "We have lost too many good school board people just because they held the wrong viewpoint on this one issue." This was, he felt, a narrow and a dangerous approach to the selection of public officials.

DIALOGUE AND DIVISION

A week or so after the school bus bill became law, Charles Benham, staff executive of the Hartford office of the National Conference of Christians and Jews, arranged a luncheon meeting for a discussion of a proposed television series on group relations. He invited the Reverend Harold Keir, Rabbi Abraham Feldman, and Father Robert McGrath. Subsequently a thirteen-week series. "New Horizons in Human Relations," was produced on the Hartford television station WHCT–TV.[25]

This television series was similar to others being promoted in other states by the NCCJ with the cooperation of network officials. Nationally and in Connecticut efforts were being made to reduce Protestant-Catholic conflict.

In pursuance of improved interfaith relations, the Hartford office of the NCCJ initiated monthly "round table" luncheons. With the cooperation of Mr. Keir, Rabbi Feldman, and Monsignor Doyle, monthly luncheons were held so that a small group of clergymen of the several faiths could meet for informal discussions. The purpose of these meetings was to provide the clergymen an opportunity to know each other better. Such knowledge would help to prevent interreligious strife.[26]

Other Connecticut citizens proceeded with the organization of the Greater Hartford chapter of "Americans United" (POAU). A notice was sent out on October 14, 1957, to "All Connecticut Citizens who oppose SPECIAL CHURCH PRIVILEGE." A meeting was to be held at Hartford's Seventh Day Adventist Church on Sunday afternoon, November 3, for organizational purposes.[27]

In the month following its organization, the new chapter was able to announce on December 30, 1957, that a public meeting would be held in Hartford on January 9, 1958, at the Central Baptist Church Auditorium. The topic of the meeting would be "Public Money and Private Schools." The featured speaker would be Paul Blanshard.[28]

News of this meeting impelled Monsignor Doyle and Monsignor Kennedy, *Transcript* editor, to request a special meeting of the "round table" group. At this meeting they reported that many Catholics had been disturbed by the announcement of the Blanshard meeting. Did this kind of activity represent the predominant attitude of Connecticut's Protestants? The ministers replied that it did not. The POAU was an independent organization. It had no official connection with any church. The priests asked if there could not be a public statement making it clear to Catholics that this meeting was not sponsored by Connecticut's Protestant churches.

The ministers were not certain that such a statement was necessary or appropriate. Would the Catholic Church, they asked, take such action in similar circumstances? Suppose a speaker like Father Coughlin should hold a public meeting in Hartford; would there be official disavowal by the Catholic Church of any connection with such a meeting?

The priests gave full assurance that there would be an official statement of disavowal in such a case.

During the discussion it became obvious to Mr. Keir that there was need for a statement and that it should probably come from the Connecticut Council of Churches. The next day he went to discuss the matter with the Council president, Dr. Russell Henry Stafford, president of the Hartford Seminary Foundation.

Dr. Stafford agreed that Mr. Keir should issue a public statement to make it clear that the Council was not connected with the POAU nor the meeting. In addition, Dr. Stafford would write a letter expressing his own views. He told Mr. Keir that he had very strong opinions on this subject.

On the day of the meeting Mr. Keir issued a statement to the Hartford newspapers explaining that the Greater Hartford chapter of POAU had no official relation with any Protestant church or council of churches. The fact that a church provided an auditorium for the presentation of views, even minority views, did not necessarily mean that the church endorsed those views. Protestants generally upheld the freedom of anyone to present his opinions publicly.

While some Protestants supported the views of Paul Blanshard about "Roman Catholic power and strategy," Mr. Keir said, there are many others who "would prefer that [Protestant-Catholic relations] be those of reconciliation, understanding, good will, and the opportunity for the two religious groups to sit down and discuss areas of tension and conflict." [29]

The Central Baptist Church Auditorium was filled with about 900 people on the evening of January 9, 1958, to hear Paul Blanshard. He presented arguments similar to those expressed in his pamphlet "The Bus Wedge." [30] Mr. Blanshard, legal counsel to the national office of POAU, announced that the national board of directors had instructed him "to say to you tonight that if you want to fight that case [against the Connecticut school bus law] clear through to the Supreme Court of the United States, we will support you morally and financially." [31]

This speech inspired another editorial in the *Transcript*, repeating charges of bigotry against opponents of the school bus bill who were involved in the meeting. A second editorial in the same issue praised a statement in the "Letters" column by Dr. Stafford. He expressed his "strong dissent from Blanshard's position on two grounds especially." To the Seminary president, Blanshard appeared to be a "secularist" who did not recognize any instance where "conscience takes precedence over civil law." Further, his statements about the Catholic Church, Dr. Stafford felt, were "biased and one-sided." Anti-Catholic feelings did not fairly represent the attitude of Connecticut Protestants.[32]

The statements by Mr. Keir and Dr. Stafford about the Blanshard meeting precipitated a conflict within the Connecticut Council of Churches that had been developing for some time.[33] The council had firmly opposed the school bus bill, but there were some members who were willing to accept the legislative decision. There were others who felt continued activity was necessary to defeat any local referendum and to support a court challenge of the law's constitutionality.

Protests were registered with the state office of the Connecticut Council of Churches by ministers and church trustees who felt that the Keir and Stafford letters were a disservice to Connecticut Protestants. It was also charged that these letters appeared to commit the Council to a stand—opposition to POAU and to Blanshard—which the membership in fact had not voted.

These differences were debated at a spirited meeting of the Board of Directors of the Council on January 28, 1958. Dr. Stafford explained that Mr. Keir's news release was intended to clarify the sponsorship of the meeting. His own letter was also "in the nature of a clarification to which he attached his personal opinion of the speaker."

The Reverend William S. Terrell, executive secretary of the Connecticut Baptist Convention, read a resolution which had been unanimously adopted on January 17 by the Convention's Board of Managers, expressing their approval of POAU and of "those responsible for bringing Mr. Blanshard to Connecticut." The Board of Managers also expressed disapproval of the Keir and Stafford statements.

Dr. Stafford and Mr. Keir were then "closely questioned as to why they acted as they did in this matter." After much discussion and after several motions were made, debated, found unsatisfactory, and withdrawn, it was finally agreed that the council would take no formal action. Dr. Stafford and Mr. Keir would write "a letter of clarification" to the Baptist Board of Managers.[34]

At no time prior to or during the battle over the school bus bill had the Board of Directors of the Connecticut Council of Churches debated the issue or voted to take a stand on it. Opposition to the bill had been expressed chiefly through the Council's Committee on Civil Rights and Moral Affairs, headed by Dr. Worley. In the

discussion of the Keir and Stafford statements there was clear indication that a substantial number of Council members did not agree
with the views presented by Dr. Worley's committee. Only now
were they making themselves heard. One consequence of the Council's contention over the Keir and Stafford statements was the establishment of an executive committee to advise the staff and to act for
the Board when some official action was needed and all the members
could not be brought together.[35]

In later weeks Dr. Worley and the Reverend Jack Grenfell,
minister of the South Park Methodist Church in Hartford, resigned
from committees of the Council. They had both been active in opposing the school bus bill. They felt that they had been let down by
the Keir and Stafford letters, and that the Council had committed a
disservice to Connecticut Protestantism. They were asked to reconsider, and upon their refusal, the resignations were accepted with
regret.

Dr. Worley expressed his sorrow that Mr. Keir did not first speak
to those who were sponsoring the Blanshard meeting. If there was
need for an explanation, it could have been made by the sponsors
and not as a "stab in the back." In a later letter, Dr. Worley expressed his disappointment that Dr. Stafford and Mr. Keir had
repudiated his committee and were working with the editor of
Transcript, who had attacked Dr. Worley as a "subversive" and a
"bigot."

The Reverend Payson Miller delivered a sermon defending the
work of Paul Blanshard and questioning the wisdom of the Keir
and Stafford statements. He did not question the integrity of the
two men; he did question their judgment. Mr. Miller expressed appreciation for Mr. Keir's "fine spirit" and his desire for reconciliation.
But he asked if reconciliation was possible so long as one church
insisted upon "special privileges from the state." The "Roman
Catholic sources" who raised the queries about the Blanshard meeting, Mr. Miller suggested, might be asked if they had ever made any
attempt to "curb the *Transcript*, which is well known as a bigoted,
anti-Protestant journal." Paul Blanshard was a religious man, Mr.

Miller concluded, and he urged Protestants not to be timid and confused.[36]

Some Protestant clergy and laymen continued their efforts in support of the local organization of POAU. From April 28 to May 1, 1958, evening public meetings were held in major cities of Connecticut—Hartford, New Haven, New London, Bridgeport, and Watertown. The speakers were Glenn Archer, executive director of POAU, and the Reverend C. Stanley Lowell, associate director. At the Hartford meeting, Dr. Archer renewed the offer of his organization to give legal support to any Connecticut group wishing to test the constitutionality of the school bus law. The meeting was attended by about 150 people and was held at the South Park Methodist Church.[37]

The *Transcript* commented on the meeting editorially, describing it as a "POAU Flop" with the "usual high pressure pitch for pelf ($3 minimum), a telltale hallmark of every POAU occasion," [38] The *Transcript* declared that the small attendance was "fresh evidence of the good sense and fair-mindedness of our Protestant neighbors. It is a tribute, also, to their ministerial leadership."

The latter comment may have been the product of the continued meetings of Protestant, Catholic, and Jewish clergy at the monthly "round table" sponsored by the NCCJ. Nothing specific seemed to be accomplished at these meetings, but some Protestant and Catholic clergymen were getting to know each other. One minister commented, "At least we are talking to each other now."

A few Connecticut Protestants and Catholics took advantage of another opportunity early in May, 1958, to discuss controversial questions of church and state in a week-long seminar. It was held in New York City and was sponsored by the Fund for the Republic.[39] This seminar, "Religion and the Free Society," although not directly a part of the Connecticut story, was to have considerable influence on Protestant-Catholic relations in the United States. This influence was difficult to assess but was obvious to all who followed interreligious affairs. The participants, approximately one hundred in number, came from all parts of the nation. The effect of that seminar, where Protestant, Catholic, and Jew debated vigorously, rationally, and responsibly, was to be felt in Connecticut as well as other states. It was a landmark in a movement, neither organized nor structured, which was to be known as "the Dialogue." *

During the week's discussion it was recognized that faith in each other's sincerity was essential for a successful dialogue. Repeated Protestant questions about the Catholic commitment to a free society suggested that this essential was lacking. One priest responded by reversing the challenge and asking Protestants to consider Catholic apprehensions about Protestantism's lack of stable principles of morality.[40]

A Catholic resident of New Haven commented that the Seminar had largely been "a critique of the Roman Catholic Church." He regarded this as most welcome. He said:

> This conference gives solemn warning that, whoever is responsible, the image of the Catholic Church which has been created in the American mind is not an image of the Church of Christ. It is largely the image of a power structure. Bricks are not made without straw and a part of this responsibility, a heavy part, rests with Catholics themselves. There is a need for a reassessment of attitude. This great uneasiness which one feels—that there is no Catholic theology of toleration apart from people like Father Murray—much more must be done in that direction.[41]

A Protestant from Connecticut responded to the priest's query about Protestant intentions:

> If Protestant dominance grows, what will the Protestants do to the Catholics?
>
> They will use the force of law and other means of social organization to promote Protestantism . . . and to impose disadvantages on Catholics; they will attempt to make the public schools Protestant

* The term "the dialogue" comes from the opening address by Father John Courtney Murray, S.J., who quoted a Dominican friar, Father Thomas Gilby, to define civilization as "men locked together in argument. From this dialogue, the community becomes a political community." Those who experienced the Connecticut conflict found special pertinence in Father Murray's comment, "Civility has fled when there is lack of reasonable conversation according to reasonable laws and men are no longer locked in argument."

schools. They will seek laws to make Catholics adhere to Protestant views on gambling and alcohol, while objecting to Catholic insistence on maintaining laws against birth control. They will frown on and will not encourage . . . the growth of Catholic schools.

These are not things that *might* happen. They are happening right now in hundreds of towns across the nation.

The Connecticut Protestant suggested that such consequences might be avoided if Catholics asked Protestants to join a Legion of *Political* Decency to guard against political means of religious proselytizing. He recommended the organization of:

> A League that would insist that the religious mission is advanced most speedily, not by coercion of laws, but by reasonable persuasion and spiritual appeal:
>
> A League that would insist that there are areas where the Church alone exercised authority and the State could neither forbid nor permit —in fact, areas where the State was not competent to act.
>
> [Priests and ministers should agree] that the command to go and teach all nations was given to the Apostles and not to Caesar's legionnaires.
>
> In short, I urge you to seek general recognition that the Church (of any faith) is working against itself when it permits legal or quasi-legal agencies to take over part of the Church's responsibilities.
>
> With such recognition, with such agreement, we could then place our faith in the free response of men's hearts to the divine message.[42]

Dr. George N. Shuster, president of Hunter College and former member of the Connecticut State Board of Education, closed the Seminar. The sponsors had feared that the conference might produce only "meaningless assent," he said. But the discussion of "Religion in a Free Society" had brought the participants to "the verge of a new era of inter-group discussion."

Another national organization was concerned about conflicts between religious groups. The National Citizens Council for Better Schools (due in part to the urging of Mrs. Ralph C. Lasbury of South Windsor) sponsored a regional conference on church and state in education. Participants came from Massachusetts, Rhode

Island, and Connecticut. At this one-day meeting in Lee, Massachusetts, there was intensive discussion of the various issues involving public and Catholic schools. The conference was not intended to provide answers to the issues. Rather it was the hope of the sponsors that there would be some agreement on ways in which such disputes might be handled to avoid deep antagonisms and severe community division. A variety of suggestions were included in the report of the conference. Perhaps the most specific suggestion was that there ought to be conferences in each state for religious, educational, and political leaders to discuss rules to follow when these issues were raised.[43]

Such issues were raised in two small Connecticut towns in the summer of 1958.[44]

In the town of Brookfield a new Catholic school, St. Joseph's, was to open in September, 1958. In July, parishioners of St. Joseph's secured the required number of voters' signatures for a referendum on the question of bus service for pupils of the new school. There was no great community stir. Those seeking bus service worked diligently to get their supporters to the polls on August 9, the day of the referendum. There were 838 ballots cast, 59 per cent of the eligible vote. The petition for bus service was approved—502 votes in favor, 305 votes opposed. This first use of the Connecticut school bus law had resulted in a somewhat surprising success for Catholic parents.

In the neighboring community of Newtown Catholic parents also circulated petitions in July for transportation for pupils of the new St. Rose's school, which was to open in September with 190 pupils. This was about 17 per cent of the school population of Newtown. Eventually, St. Rose's would enroll about 360 pupils, or about 21 per cent of the Newtown school children. The success of the Brookfield petition caused considerable stir in Newtown. Most opponents of the petition had assumed that the request would be easily defeated. Now they were not so sure. There was some increased activity to turn out the vote. The referendum was held on Saturday, August 16, just one week following the Brookfield vote. Both sides had campaigned to turn out their vote, and balloting was heavy.

The result was 1243 votes in favor, 1218 votes opposed. The petition was approved by the narrow margin of 25 votes.[45]

This second successful use of the school bus law by Catholic parents stirred some Newtown residents to more determined opposition. They held a meeting a few weeks later, on September 12, and formed an organization, Citizens for the Connecticut Constitution. They set for their purpose the recruiting of members throughout Connecticut to provide financial support of a court case against the school bus law. If necessary, they would carry their case to the Supreme Court of the United States.

THE "BALANCED" TICKETS

The school bus fight was done with, and Connecticut's state political leaders wanted no more of such struggles. There was little doubt, however, that the "Catholic" vote was one of the factors governing the decisions at the state political conventions in the summer of 1958.

In the Republican Party an active contest was being conducted for the nomination for governor. The principal candidates who emerged were John Alsop and Frederick Zeller, both Protestants. Alsop was viewed as representative of the Eisenhower wing as well as of the "Yankee Connecticut" forces. Fred Zeller, long-time occupant of the state comptroller's office, was viewed as the candidate of the "Old Guard." After a close convention contest (in which Alsop actually led at the end of the first roll call although he lacked a majority of the votes), Zeller was nominated when Bill Brennan, Fairfield County political leader, came to his support with some dramatic vote-switching. The convention then proceeded to nominate a state ticket which included five Catholics.[46]

In the Democratic Party there was a different contest, a three-man race for the nomination for United States senator. The aspirants were Thomas J. Dodd, former Hartford County congressman; Chester Bowles, former governor and former ambassador to India; and William Benton, former assistant secretary of state and former

senator. The first was Catholic, the latter two, Protestant. Governor
Ribicoff and Democratic State Chairman John Bailey had taken a
"neutral" position on the contest.

Dodd was nominated on the first ballot, as a result of what some
observers felt was an unpublicized indication by Ribicoff and Bailey
that Dodd was their choice. This selection of Dodd was, the "Connecticut Yankee" said, a sequel to the Republican convention. That
convention had been:

> . . . a defeat for the "Yankee Connecticut" forces which were also
> on the losing side of the controversial school bus bill.
> Putting it bluntly and realistically . . . the Republican convention
> repelled the die-hard Yankees, and propelled them toward Ribicoff,
> while it manufactured its own strongest appeal to Catholic Connecti-
> cut. What better Democratic strategy than to have Ribicoff receive
> the malcontent Yankee Republicans on one side of the Democratic
> ticket, and Dodd protect the party's traditional standing with the
> Catholics on the other?
> [If the Republican nominee for governor] had been Alsop, then
> the Democratic nominee for Senator would, in our opinion, have been
> Bowles, because then it would have been Catholic voters who might
> have felt doubtful about the Republican ticket, and Yankees who
> might have been attracted to it.

The "Connecticut Yankee" concluded this analysis by reporting
that at the end of the battle over the school bus bill he had disagreed
with those who said that it "would color all Connecticut politics
for some time to come." For such a thing to happen would be
"nonsensical." After the 1958 state conventions, he confessed:

> Now we are not so sure. It looks as if it helped to decide first the Re-
> publican convention, and then called the signals for Ribicoff and
> Bailey, telling them who they were neutral for.[47]

This great concern for "ticket balancing" in hopes of attracting
each religious and nationality group was made ridiculous by the
1958 election results. The immense popularity of Governor Ribicoff
and the colorless Republican campaign resulted in the greatest
Democratic victory in memory.[48] Ribicoff defeated Zeller by a plural-

ity of 246,368, sweeping into office with him the other Democrats for state office. The Democratic candidates also won in the senatorial and in all five congressional contests. The overwhelming victory gave the Democrats control of both houses of the state legislature.* It was the first time they had controlled the lower house since 1876.[49]

If the fight over the school bus bill in 1957 had any influence at all on the state election in 1958, it was buried in the overriding triumph of Governor Ribicoff. Religion was not the only influence guiding the Connecticut voter, nor did the 1958 election results suggest that it was the primary influence. The Ribicoff plurality of almost 250,000 votes was from 76,000 to 90,000 higher than the pluralities won by the other Democratic candidates on the state ticket. Ribicoff, the only Jew on the Democratic slate, ran far higher than the Catholics and Protestants running with him.[50] The Connecticut voter was not moved politically as much by considerations of religion or party as he was by a popular personality.

Governor Ribicoff, however, had not been identified with the school bus struggle except by promptly signing the bill into law. This acquiescence to the legislative decision probably had little influence on his general standing with Connecticut voters. Three Republican leaders who had been prominently identified with the school bus bill were not involved in the 1958 election. Charles W. Jewett, Nelson Brown, and Theodore Ryan did not seek renomination. Fred Pope, running for re-election to the State House of Representatives from the "safe" Republican town of Fairfield, was drowned in the Democratic tide.

The political status of these men following the 1958 election could not be said to be a consequence solely nor directly of their actions in connection with the school bus bill. Brown and Ryan had

* The extent of the Democratic victory was tellingly revealed in Democratic State Headquarters a few hours after the polls closed. The very first reports by television and radio foretold a sizable Democratic triumph. A climax was reached when Democratic State Chairman John Bailey hung up the telephone and announced dryly, "We carried Scotland." The happy headquarters workers may have felt for a moment that the Democratic tide was going to sweep the British Isles. However, the Chairman was reporting the results from the small town, traditionally Republican, in eastern Connecticut.

stepped aside for personal reasons, and Pope's defeat was but one of many Republican losses. Jewett's departure seemed motivated by little enthusiasm for political life. This enthusiasm may have been further reduced by his experience with the school bus bill, but it is significant that this was the only issue on which he took a strong public stand.[51]

The 1958 election results suggested that the school bus issue and Protestant-Catholic competition or conflict were subordinate influences on the Connecticut voter. However, the conduct of the state nominating conventions, the prevalence of the "balanced ticket" philosophy, revealed the concern of Republican and Democratic politicians about those influences. Religion was still a significant factor in the minds of Connecticut politicians even if the voter did not, apparently, give it much weight in making his decision in the voting booth.

ACCOMMODATION AND LITIGATION

On the eve of the 1959 session of the General Assembly it seemed likely that the school bus issue would be revived. Immediately following the passage of the school bus bill in 1957, the House had adopted a resolution proposing a constitutional amendment limiting direct or indirect aid for non-public schools to transportation only. In accordance with Connecticut procedure, that resolution would be brought up for another vote in the 1959 session. Here would be another occasion for religious partisans to clash.

The clash was avoided.

Catholic and Protestant members of the NCCJ "round table" did not want a repetition of the 1957 conflict. At their November meeting they discussed the pending resolution. It soon transpired that priest, minister, and rabbi were opposed to the measure. Catholic opposition was based on the fact that the amendment treated transportation as an aid to the school. This was contrary to their reasoning. Furthermore, the proposal also seemed to prohibit health services to non-public school pupils. The ministers and rabbis did not want the provision for school bus service written into the state constitution. The clergymen decided that they would seek a private meeting with legislative leaders.

Charles Benham, NCCJ Hartford executive, was asked to invite Republican and Democratic legislative leaders to the next "round table" on December 18, 1958. The legislators were surprised but relieved to learn that the clergy of the three faiths were agreed in their opposition to the proposed amendment. They told the clergymen that if all three religious groups were opposed to it, the resolution "didn't have a chance." The meeting was cordial, and the legislators expressed their appreciation for the opportunity to meet with the clergymen and talk informally. They much preferred to handle such matters without a public fight.[52]

On February 18, 1959, there was a public hearing on the proposed constitutional amendment.[53] Representatives of Catholic and Protestant groups briefly expressed their opposition, and the hearing was closed. It was clear that the amendment would not provoke a repetition of the 1957 Protestant-Catholic struggle. The resolution died in committee.

The opponents of the school bus law decided to take their fight to the courts rather than to the legislature. The new organization Citizens for the Connecticut Constitution appealed for support in many Connecticut towns. Francis Snyder of Newtown, chairman of the group, made addresses in Protestant churches in about seventy Connecticut towns in the year following the Newtown referendum. In these speeches he appealed for funds to finance a court test of the school bus law. He was aided in this fund-raising effort by Dr. Worley, who also spoke in several towns. There was strong response to the request for contributions. Many Protestants were still opposed to the school bus law and were interested enough in challenging its constitutionality to give money for the purpose. Opponents of the law were determined to press the case all the way to the Supreme Court of the United States, if necessary.[54]

The case was argued before the Connecticut Supreme Court of Errors on February 2, 1960.

The school bus law was upheld by a four-to-one decision of the Supreme Court of Errors on June 13, 1960.[55] The majority relied on the *Everson* case and the child-benefit theory. Chief Justice Raymond Baldwin said that the Court majority followed the United States Supreme Court and other state courts in holding:

> . . . that public transportation to private schools aids the parents, who are under compulsion of law to send their children to school; that it is a measure to promote the safety of the children; and that therefore it helps the parent and the child and not the school.

Decisions by courts of other states where such service was found to be unconstitutional were based, Justice Baldwin said, "on the peculiar language of the [other states'] constitutional provision" or on different circumstances.*

Article seventh of the Connecticut Constitution ("No person shall by law be compelled to join or support any congregation, church or religious association"), declared Justice Baldwin, had the same effect as the First Amendment of the federal constitution in prohibiting government establishment of or assistance to religion. He quoted in full Justice Black's minimal definition, which had been presented

---

* This was not entirely correct. Seven times in six states, courts in rejecting the child-benefit theory had found transportation an aid to the school and therefore an unconstitutional assistance to sectarian education. [*State ex. rel. Traub v. Brown*, 36 Del. 181 (1934); *Judd v. Board of Education*, 278 N.Y. 200 (1938); *Gurney v. Ferguson*, 190 Okla. 254 (1942); *Sherrard v. Jefferson County Board of Education*, 249 Ky. 469 (1942); *Mitchell v. Consolidated School District*, 17 Wash. 2d 261 (1943); *Visser v. Nooksack Valley School District*, 33 Wash. 2d 699 (1949); *Zellers v. Huff*, 55 N. Mex. 501 (1951).]

In contrast, five times in four states, courts had accepted the child-benefit theory and had held school transportation to be an aid to the child, not the school, and therefore not an unconstitutional aid to religion. [*Board of Education v. Wheat*, 174 Md. 314 (1938); *Adams v. County Commissioners*, 180 Md. 550, 556 (1942); *Nichols v. Henry*, 301 Ky. 434 (1944); *Bowker v. Baker*, 73 Cal. App. 2d 653 (1946); *Everson v. Board of Education*, 132 N.J.L. 98 (1944).]

The *Judd* case in New York was followed by a constitutional amendment which permitted the state legislature to provide for transportation of non-public school pupils (see p. 222). After the *Sherrard* case in Kentucky the state legislature authorized such transportation to be paid for out of general county funds rather than school funds; subsequently, in the *Nichols* case, this was found to be a proper exercise of the state's police power "for the protection of children."

in both the *Everson* and *McCollum* cases.[56] The school bus law did none of the things prohibited by that definition of the First Amendment. The Connecticut statute was:

> . . . consistent with the present-day policy of gathering children into modern schools for better educational opportunities. It primarily serves the public health, safety and welfare and fosters education. In the light of our history and policy, it cannot be said to compel support of any church. . . . It comes up to, but does not breach, the "wall of separation" between church and state.

The majority did uphold the plaintiff's contention that money from the "school fund" and from the "town deposit fund" could be used only for "the common or public schools." These special funds had been placed under specific constitutional and statutory restriction. These restrictions, however, did not apply to the general revenues of the state.

The dissenting member, Justice Mellitz, held that the single issue was: "Does the payment by the town for the transportation of pupils to or from St. Rose's School constitute support of the school" as prohibited by article seventh of the Connecticut Constitution? He quoted from decisions of New York and Delaware courts to contend that "the purpose of transportation is to promote the interests of the private school or religious or sectarian institution." [57] He rejected the contention that such an expenditure, because it furthered the public welfare, was not proscribed by the constitutional restriction.

> The majority opinion does not question that where transportation is required to enable a child to attend school, it is an integral part of the operation of the school, and that payment of the expense of transportation is an expenditure in support of the school. The opinion professes to draw a distinction between a form of support which is proscribed and a form which is constitutionally permissible. In my view all compulsory support is proscribed, and the only questions to be resolved are whether the expenditure involved constitutes "support" and, if it does, whether the beneficiary of the support is a "congregation, church or religious association." . . . Here, the existence of both elements is established.

Justice Mellitz described as "not relevant to the question before us" the discussion by the majority "of the exemption of the property of religious organizations from taxation."

The majority opinion had reviewed the history of tax exemption in Connecticut to throw light "on the meaning and intent of article seventh." Since such tax exemption had been granted in earliest colonial days and had been re-enacted immediately following adoption of the 1818 state constitution, the majority asserted that the "support" prohibited by the constitution did not mean every form of governmental assistance to religious organizations. In his dissent from this "irrelevant" discussion, Justice Mellitz declared:

> We have consistently recognized that the statutes . . . merely state a rule of nontaxability . . . in pursuance of the "principle that property necessary for the operation of State and municipal governments, and buildings occupied by those essential supports of government, public education and public worship, ought not to be the subject of taxation. . ." *Yale University* v. *New Haven*, 71 Conn. 316, 332, 42 A. 87.

In upholding the school bus law the Connecticut Supreme Court of Errors followed the child-benefit theory and the reasoning of the United States Supreme Court in the *Everson* case. Transportation was found to be a service to the child and to the parent, not to the school. But the illustrative argument concerning church tax exemption, the equating of such exemption with an appropriation of public funds, suggested that there was a kind of government encouragement of religion that the majority viewed as constitutionally permissible. This view was supported by Justice Mellitz in his dissent when he ascribed church tax exemption to the fact that public worship was one of the "essential supports of government." * Such a view is hardly in accord with the declaration of Justice Black, quoted in the

---

* Basing church tax exemption on the fact that public worship is a support of government has obvious ominous implications. It might well follow that a state could decide to impose taxes on a church which was deemed to be not an "essential support" of government.

majority opinion, that neither a state nor the federal government "can pass laws which aid one religion, aid all religions, or prefer one religion over another." The Connecticut justices, like those who had argued this issue elsewhere, selected from the opinions of the United States Supreme Court those statements which supported their conclusions but ignored those which did not.

After the decision by the Connecticut court, the Catholic Archdiocese of Hartford had no comment in response to news reporters' inquiries. The opponents of the school bus law announced they would appeal to the United States Supreme Court.[58]

The Connecticut decision on the *Newtown* case came at a time— June, 1960— when Catholic Democrat Senator John F. Kennedy was completing a long campaign for his party's presidential nomination. The "Catholic" issue in politics, therefore, was receiving much public discussion. If a petition were to be brought in any Connecticut town for bus service for Catholic school pupils, the referendum campaign would be conducted among voters already made more conscious of Protestant-Catholic divisions in politics. Connecticut could not be sure that there might not be in some towns a repetition of the conflicts of 1956 and 1957.

VIII:

CONCLUSION

THE DECISION on the school bus bill by the 1957 General Assembly provided a climax but not a conclusion in the religious-political struggles in Connecticut.

The Supreme Court of the United States had developed three guides—church-state separation, church-state cooperation, and the child-benefit theory—which caused conflict on the Court and did not resolve conflict in Connecticut. In the *Everson, McCollum,* and *Zorach* opinions the Court majorities emphasized they were following the principle of separation. But this principle was coupled with that of child benefit in the *Everson* decision and with the cooperation doctrine in the *Zorach* decision. Although the first two principles—separation and child benefit—were not necessarily in conflict, they did, in application, raise difficult problems of definition. Justice Black in the *Everson* opinion tried, not too successfully, to show the distinction between permissible government service to a child and prohibited government aid to a religious school. Black's reasoning was sound but his exposition was inadequate.

The key phrase in Black's explanation of the principle of separation as embodied in the First Amendment was his declaration that government could not "aid all religions." [1] Clergymen and others who regard religion as vital to the public welfare sometimes have found it difficult to accept the Court's prohibition of nonpreferential aid to religion by government. Indeed the Court itself, in the *Zorach* decision, tried to get away from the restrictions of the *Everson* opinion with an exposition of the cooperation principle. Justice Douglas tried to expound and reconcile the principles of separation and of cooperation. He succeeded only in emphasizing the conflict between them.

The complexity of the Court's views on church-state relations resulting from the combination of the three principles was compounded by the strong and numerous minority opinions. The effect of the Court's decisions was to leave the people of Connecticut (and other states) free to decide on programs of auxiliary services and some kinds of cooperation between government agencies and religious groups. The Court's inclination to leave these questions to state decision crucially diminished the First Amendment's prohibition of religious establishment, however defined, as a federal constitutional principle effective in all parts of the nation.

The debates in Connecticut revealed that participants did look to the Supreme Court for authoritative definition of the national Constitution and for guidance in the determination of public policy when a constitutional question was involved. The Connecticut debaters rapidly became familiar with the various opinions of the Court, or at least with those sections which appeared to support the policy they were advocating. The Court's majority and minority opinions provided partisans on both sides with abundant material to use as "quotations" in the contests over local or state policy on auxiliary services.

The debaters quoted most frequently from the *Everson* opinions. In that decision the Court had made it clear that the national Constitution did not restrict a state from providing a general transportation program for school children, including those in parochial schools. The Court, however, did not follow the line of reasoning on which its decision was based. Transportation was defined as a welfare service, but the Court did not recognize that "equal protection of the laws" prohibited unreasonable discrimination against some children. On the contrary, it suggested that a state could so discriminate. The Court avoided following the logic of the child-benefit theory. The deficient logic of the *Everson* majority opinion contributed to the confusion of arguments in the Connecticut struggles.

The controversies in Connecticut during 1956 and 1957 were not relieved by the ambiguous provisions of the state Constitution and statutes nor by the refusal of the state Attorney General to give an opinion to guide local boards of education. The State Board of Education would go no further than to pass the question on to the local school boards and to the legislature.

The four local disputes and the legislative struggle recounted above provide a basis for analysis of the arguments employed by supporters and opponents of public services for parochial school pupils. Conclusions may also be drawn about the roles played by political and religious leaders.

PROVISIONS OF THE SCHOOL BUS LAW

The bill as amended and adopted was devised to win support of a legislative majority rather than to follow consistently the logic of the child-benefit theory. The bill's supporters would say that it was the best that could be done. It contained the four features suggested by majority leader Pope; it was permissive, it was limited to bus service, it provided for a referendum, and it limited the service to local schools.[2] The bill, therefore, accepted the same contradictions that had been accepted by the Supreme Court of the United States. It was advanced on the contention that transportation was not an educational service but a welfare service. As such, it could be given to parochial school children and still not constitute "an establishment of religion." But this was only half the logic. If school transportation was a welfare service to the child, on what basis might a state or a town exclude him from such service? The child's age, his physical ability, the distance to school, and the hazards en route were all factors which might reasonably be held to affect his need for transportation. Discriminating among children according to such factors could not be regarded as a denial of due process or equal treatment of the laws. But what legal or logical basis was there for

denying the child a welfare service (and transportation was so described by the bill's supporters as well as by the Supreme Court)
because his school was operated for profit or because a majority of
his classmates were from outside the town? The law did discriminate
against children who attended profit schools or schools where a
majority of the pupils were from outside the town. The logic of the
child-benefit theory was relaxed for the sake of the legislative purpose.
No one was willing to champion the cause of pupils in expensive
preparatory schools or schools operated for profit merely for the
sake of logical consistency.

The "home-rule" provision was an essential feature of the bill.
In Connecticut, one of the cradles of the town meeting, the phrase
"home rule" carries great appeal. Supporters of this provision could
also cite the opinion of Supreme Court Justice Jackson about the
importance of local control.[3] The controversy over auxiliary services
was brought to the General Assembly because of the variety of local
practices and uncertainties about the law. The General Assembly answered the question by giving it back to the towns to decide by local
referendum. But, again, why should the welfare benefits received by a
child be dependent upon the religious affiliation of the townspeople?
The practical effect of the "home rule" provision was to declare that
Catholic school children in "Catholic" towns could ride, but those
in "Protestant" towns must walk. Do not Catholic school children
in New Canaan have the same right to welfare services as those in
Danbury?

Since the legislature decided on "home rule" on this question,
it was probably wiser to vest the decision in all the voters of the
town than in one of the municipal agencies. The provision for a
referendum may be the major contribution made by the school bus
law to restrained decision-making about transportation for parochial
school pupils in Connecticut. By giving authority to the voters, the
General Assembly established an orderly procedure. Instead of pressure exerted on local officials, appeal must be made to a majority of
the town's voters. In towns with Catholic schools whose pupils are
not yet given transportation, the majority of the population will

most likely be Protestant. The extremist tactics of Father Baker or Father Davey will not persuade the Protestant voter; they will be more likely to alienate him. The indirect approach of Father Leahy or the tentative measures of Father Daniel will in all probability be more successful in winning majority support of transportation for Catholic school pupils.

There will be a temptation for militant Protestants to emphasize arguments aimed at the "divisiveness" of the non-public school or at the dangers of what they may describe as the growing political power of the Catholic Church. Such contentions may inspire counter-charges of bigotry and anti-Catholicism. This kind of argument could produce an explosive local atmosphere. Local tensions may be increased if state or national religious leaders or organizations direct their efforts toward influencing a town referendum on transportation for non-public school pupils.

It seems likely that the local decision will be much influenced by the general standing of the Catholic school in the town. Where the school is accepted as part of the community, where the Catholic clergymen and other Catholic leaders have cordial relations with non-Catholic residents, where religious affiliation has been minimized as a factor in the politics of the community, it is probable that many voters will see the question as one of protection for, or service to, all the children of the town.

The adoption of the school bus bill was regarded as a victory by advocates of auxiliary services in Connecticut. In reality, the law did not decide the question of the extension of auxiliary services or even of transportation to non-public school pupils. It simply trans-ferred that decision to voters in towns with non-public schools.

THE ARGUMENTS

Most of the arguments used by both sides in the local disputes and in the legislative debates could be found in the opinions of justices of the United States Supreme Court. Supporters of auxiliary services repeatedly said they were seeking welfare services for children.

They often cited the *Cochran* and *Everson* cases. Opponents of services held that the services sought, particularly transportation, constituted public aid to religious education and as such violated the principle of separation of church and state. The child-benefit theory and the principle of church-state separation were usually employed in argument without being defined. Definitions, however, were strongly implied if not spelled out.

The principle of church-state separation as used by Protestants in Connecticut meant primarily prohibition of public financial aid or services for parochial schools or their pupils. This interpretation was applied to transportation despite the Supreme Court's holding that transportation was a welfare service, not an unconstitutional aid to religion. No opposition was expressed in Connecticut to the school lunch and school milk programs supported by public funds and extended to both public and parochial school children. Little objection was made, outside of Castleton, to the health services provided in thirty-three towns to parochial school pupils. These services were generally accepted as benefits to the child rather than aid to the school. No one objected that the school lunch and school milk programs were administered according to procedures which measured the need of the school rather than the need of the child.

Although the separation principle was employed by Protestants to oppose auxiliary services for Catholic schools, it was almost never interpreted as prohibiting the use of the public schools for the promotion of religion. Protestant school board members in High Hills opposed transportation for Catholic school pupils but made church attendance a condition of employment for their superintendent of schools. Protestants on the Castleton school board viewed dental services at public expense for parochial school pupils as a violation of church-state separation but voted in favor of the distribution of Gideon Bibles in the public schools. They could invoke simultaneously the principle of separation against Catholic aspirations and the principle of cooperation in support of Protestant desires.

The principle of separation of church and state was not ignored by all advocates of auxiliary services. The Reverend Joseph V. King distinguished between services for children and aid to non-public schools. Children had a constitutional right to services, Father King said, but aid to the school in the form of buildings or religious textbooks would be an unconstitutional aid to religion.

For many supporters of auxiliary services, the child-benefit theory was subsidiary to the major thesis that parochial schools were performing a public service and hence were deserving of public support. The *Cochran* and *Everson* decisions were cited to show constitutional sanction of auxiliary services for parochial school pupils, but some advocates of services extended the logic of the child-benefit theory far beyond the specifics of books and bus service. Richard Joyce Smith did not limit his argument to auxiliary services but called for public funds to pay the tuition of private school pupils and to construct extensions to existing parochial schools. His argument was consistent with the position of the Catholic bishops of the United States. They wanted recognition of independent schools as an integral part of the nation's educational system. Their argument seemed to rely more on the public purpose of the non-public school than on the need of the non-public school child.

Many advocates of auxiliary services for parochial school pupils in Connecticut made use of the "tax savings" argument. The assertion that parochial schools reduced the tax burden was used as frequently as, if not more often than, the child-benefit theory. Often the two arguments were used in combination, despite their inherent contradiction. After saying that transportation was a service to the child, the advocate would contend that parochial schools were deserving of this help because they made for substantial tax savings.

Connecticut opponents of auxiliary services, in addition to invoking the church-state separation principle, frequently protested against public services for parochial schools on the grounds that they were divisive. Sigmund Adler called any religious division of our people "un-Christian and undemocratic." Dr. Worley objected to using public money to foster religious segregation. A resolution adopted by the governing board of the Christian Science Church in High Hills held that school segregation by religion was as undemocratic as segregation by race or color. Such arguments were aimed not merely against services but against non-public schools or against "authoritarianism."

The "wedge" argument was presented repeatedly by opponents of auxiliary services. The pamphlet "The Bus Wedge," by Paul Blanshard, was given wide distribution. At the public hearing and in the floor debate, opponents quoted the *America* article by Richard Joyce Smith to show the logical consequences of accepting public responsibility for parochial school bus service.

Proponents of auxiliary services did not give much attention to the wedge argument in their debate. Some of them, like Senator Ryan, regarded this argument as implying a Catholic conspiracy to undermine the public schools. Such anti-Catholic contentions were regarded as unworthy of a reply. At the public hearing, the Reverend Harold Keir had asked seriously that the proponents of auxiliary services state their aims specifically and provide an "authoritative" statement renouncing other public aid or services. The apprehensions of some opponents might have been partially allayed if Archbishop O'Brien had announced that he agreed with Archbishop Cushing; that he was not seeking government aid for parochial school construction but wanted to see Catholic school children receive health services, transportation, and school lunches on an equal basis with public school children. Father King had expressed such views on the radio program sponsored by the Connecticut Citizens for the Public Schools, but this was three months before the public hearing and the statement was not further publicized. No official of the Hartford Archdiocese replied to Mr. Keir's question.

Some Protestant apprehensions about Catholic ambitions were supported by the statements of Richard Joyce Smith, the *Catholic World* editorial, and the statements of the Catholic bishops of the United States. Protestant concern about the possible use of transportation as a precedent for far more extensive services could not, in fairness, be dismissed simply as anti-Catholicism. An authoritative rejection of the contentions of Richard Joyce Smith would have helped to dissipate some opposition to the school bus bill.

Senator Ryan attempted to meet the wedge argument by amending the Kopacz bill to specify "medical, dental nursing and transportation" services instead of "health, welfare and safety" services. This was late in the struggle, however, and the wedge argument, supported by quotations from the Blanshard pamphlet and the *America* article, had been long unanswered. By the time the Ryan amendment was presented to the Senate, the House leaders had already concluded that the bill would have to be limited to transportation to have any chance at all for passage. Indeed, the Republican House caucus had already voted, 99 to 90, against even such a limited proposal. It was ironic that health services, which were not strongly opposed in local disputes, were the object of so much criticism in the legislature. It is possible that the wide publicity given the *America* article—which stressed health services, facilities, and buildings—was more effective in generating opposition than the Blanshard pamphlet "The Bus Wedge."

In general, debaters on both sides set forth principles or cited Supreme Court decisions to support a policy conclusion. The principles were not followed consistently in the argument of those who proclaimed them, nor did those who cited Supreme Court decisions accept the full decision they cited. Most of the debaters turned to Court opinions for weapons rather than for enlightenment. Principles were instruments rather than convictions. The divisions so manifest on the Supreme Court in the *Everson, McCollum,* and *Zorach* cases were reflected in the conflicts in Connecticut.

RELIGIOUS LEADERS AND GROUPS

In the final House debate on the school bus bill, a point of order was made that remarks about the Catholic Church were not germane. The intention of this move was, obviously, to place some restraint on a discussion that seemed likely to become a bitter religious dispute. The point of order was upheld by the Speaker but rejected by the House members. They recognized the religious connections and were not afraid to permit discussion of them.

In an editorial following the public hearing and in the news story reporting the final debate on the bill, the *Catholic Transcript* criticized those who saw the division over the bill as a Protestant-Catholic conflict. Opponents of the bill were described as clouding the issue by attempts "to bind the Catholic Church to the bill." [4] In the light of the history of the measure, such comments by the *Transcript* were disingenuous, to say the least.

The religious division could hardly be doubted. In the final week of the legislative struggle, the political activities of the Protestant and Catholic clergy had reached a crescendo in a cacophonous symphony which had begun a year earlier. The *Transcript's* trumpeting of Richard Joyce Smith's call for public aid to independent schools was, for the executive committee of the Connecticut Council of Churches, a signal to prepare for battle. Preludes to this discordant theme of Protestant against Catholic had been played in a number of towns. Clergymen as well as school board members had divided along religious lines on auxiliary services. The legislative struggle began with a bill prepared by the legal counsel for the Archdiocese and Monsignor Robert Doyle. Opposition had been mobilized by a Methodist minister, Dr. Loyd Worley, acting for a committee of the Connecticut Council of Churches. The editorials of the *Transcript* put the weight of the Catholic Church publicly on the side of the bill. The sermons, church newsletters, and public statements of ministers were all directed against the bill. The whole story of the struggle for auxiliary services in Connecticut was filled with conflicts of Protestant against Catholic.

Neither the Protestant nor the Catholic clergy consulted the membership of their churches before committing their groups to a position on auxiliary services. In Parkville, High Hills, and Diamond City, the Catholic clergy took a public stand and looked to their church members to support that stand. In High Hills, Protestant ministers, without any policy action by their congregations, actively opposed the request for bus service. Protestant school board member

William Manners received no answer when he asked his minister, "Why did you stick your nose in?"

In the legislative struggle, too, church groups were committed by their religious leaders without policy action by the membership. The decision to press for a bill on auxiliary services in the 1957 legislature, Monsignor Doyle said, was made by the Archbishop.[5] On the Protestant side, the decision to oppose any such bill was made by the executive committee of the Connecticut Council of Churches. On this political issue the Protestant leaders did not consult the Protestant membership, nor did the Archbishop put the question to Connecticut's Catholics. The position of the churches on this public policy matter was established by the religious leaders, not by the membership.

Once their positions were taken, the Protestant and Catholic clergy made use of techniques familiar in the influencing of legislative action. They stimulated their sympathizers to write, telephone, or meet with legislators. Protestant ministers distributed literature of Protestants and Other Americans United. Monsignor Doyle, for the Archdiocese, distributed information about the *Everson* decision. Protestant ministers made use of their church newsletters, and the *Transcript* spoke for the Catholic clergy. The newsletters did not have the impact of the *Transcript*. No comment in any church newsletter received attention in the daily press; the *Transcript's* editorials did. It is not clear, however, whether this helped or hindered the progress of the school bus bill. Republican Chairman Baldwin estimated that the *Transcript's* editorial "Rule or Ruin" lost twenty votes of members who, but for that editorial, would have supported the bill. There was a shock value resulting from the *Transcript's* declarations, however, that could not be denied. If they offended some legislators, they surely made others more conscious of the numbers of the Catholic voters in their towns. The *Transcript* was completely blunt in its forecast of the consequences facing a legislator who opposed the school bus bill; his action would be "corrected at the polls."

The obvious assumption behind the *Transcript's* statement was that Catholic voters would reach the same political conclusions as the official newspaper of the Archdiocese. This assumption was evident in the *Transcript's* entire coverage of the 1956–1957 conflict in Connecticut. This legislative proposal was treated as though it was, for Catholics, not debatable like any other public policy question, but a matter of dogma. There was never any suggestion in the editorial or news columns that a Catholic could be opposed to the paper's position on auxiliary services. Representative Quinlan's statement that he opposed the school bus bill although he sent his own children to a Catholic school was reported in the *Hartford Courant* but not in the *Catholic Transcript*.[6]

The tactics of the Protestant clergy, although less strident than those of the *Transcript*, were based on similar assumptions. They assumed that their religious followers held the same political views as the clergy. The impression given by the ministers' statements was that the aggressive Catholics would expand their political power still further unless Connecticut Protestants were alerted to rise up in wrathful opposition. It was the gambling issue and the birth-control issue in different form. It was Protestant against Catholic.

The Protestant-Catholic conflict was not relieved by the *Transcript's* repeated description of opponents of auxiliary services as "bigots." The Reverend Payson Miller's retort was "dogmatic arrogance." It could hardly be expected that the emotional contests experienced in Connecticut would be entirely free from irrationalism and prejudice, but such epithetical argumentation served only to intensify the religious division.

During the legislative struggle the Catholic clergy used the pulpit to speak about the school bus bill only once—to deliver the letter of the bishops on the Sunday before the final vote on the measure. Some Protestant ministers made frequent use of their pulpits to oppose the bill. The ministers did not have a weekly newspaper, and access to the letters columns of the Hartford newspapers was limited. Nor did the Protestant clergy have the complete hierarchical organization that is an inherent feature of the Catholic Church. Those ministers who strongly opposed the school bus bill may have felt that their pulpit was their only platform. Yet they were shocked and offended when the bishops employed the same means.

It is unlikely that the editorials of the *Transcript* influenced Protestant public opinion or that sermons of Protestant ministers influenced any Catholics. The political pronouncements of the Protestant and Catholic clergy convinced leaders of Jewish groups that Jews would only suffer by participation in the conflict. It would do a Jew little good to get caught in this fight between Christian forces. Protestant and Catholic tactics effectively silenced the Jews.

In some of the local disputes clergymen exploited their office for political purposes. Father Davey in High Hills and Father Baker in Diamond City went so far as to denounce from the pulpit Catholics who, as school board members, took a political position different from that of the Catholic clergy. Father Baker with his fiery demand for political action under his leadership, and Mr. Esty with his inconsistent, contradictory plea for moderation and understanding, were both aware that their sermons were intended to provide not spiritual solace for their congregations but political guidance for the community. Hence, before being delivered in church, the sermons were delivered to the newspaper office.

In contrast, Father Daniel in Parkville did not exploit his church office beyond making the formal request of the school board for bus service. In Castleton the clergy did not get involved in the question of health services. Neither Parkville nor Castleton was afflicted with the dissensions experienced by High Hills and Diamond City.

The "pulpit politics" of Father Baker and Father Davey stirred resentment among townspeople. Catholic, Protestant, and Jew generally felt that the church was not the proper forum for political oratory. But the resentment was given no public expression. While Mrs. Kant was so offended by Father Davey's political sermons that she began attending a Catholic church in another town, she was alone in this act of protest. The religious superiors of Fathers Baker and Davey, however, were not indifferent to the effect of their political sermonizing on the community. Father Leahy, named to succeed Father Davey, was apparently instructed to repair the breach. Mon-

signor Bradley acted to restrain Father Baker indirectly through
the meeting of Catholic clergy and Catholic public officials. Politically, a religious leader may offend deeply his own church members
and the community at large without experiencing the restraint of
public criticism or retort.

In the local disputes Monsignor Bradley and a few other clergymen demonstrated a regard for other goals than the immediate one
of approval or rejection of the request for transportation. The Monsignor acted politically as a non-clerical community leader might act.
He went to the school board as a community leader exercising his
influence in the political arena, not in the sanctuary of his church.
While he argued that there was virtue on his side, he did not claim
that the Deity favored his position. Father Leahy in High Hills and
Father Daniel in Parkville were concerned not solely with the question of school transportation but also with the general standing of
their churches in the communities. Mr. Esty in Diamond City appealed for moderation and understanding.

Locally, some clergymen were conscious of the undesirable social
consequences of political conflict on religious lines. During the legislative struggle, only Mr. Keir among the clergy made any gesture
toward compromise and reasonable discussion of differences. His
request at the public hearing for a statement of the specific services
being sought so that each might be discussed on its merits was futile.
His was a lone voice in a storm of controversy, and he went unheard.
Never in the four local disputes nor in the long legislative contest
on the state level did a Protestant minister and a Catholic priest sit
down together to discuss their differences. Christian principles of
brotherhood, it seemed, were not operative in this controversy.

After the battle was over there seemed to be a growing recognition
among Connecticut citizens, clergy and laymen, that the bitterness
it had generated was shameful. There was a consciousness that a
serious climax had occurred in Connecticut life. The once-dominant
Yankee Protestant learned during the conflict that he had lost
dominant status. At least one minister recognized this change and
commented, "We are a minority acting like a majority." The bold-

ness and assurance of earlier years would have to be put aside now for an attitude of accommodation and adjustment. "Catholics are tired of being treated like an unimportant minority," said a priest. And in some instances they had behaved with the belligerence of a long-downtrodden group fighting desperately for equality. Now that the Catholics had demonstrated their political potential, that belligerence would have to be put aside. There was a need now for the greater sense of responsibility that should come with influence.

The Protestant and Catholic clergy had had their fight. The conflict had relieved some tension. Once the issue had been settled, non-clerical groups began to move to bring minister and priest together. The breach revealed in the school bus battle had to be healed. Clerical conflict would create strains in many other areas of Connecticut life.

The experience of the school bus battle, and the conferences promoted by non-clerical groups to bring the clergymen of various faiths together to discuss their political differences, were instrumental in making some of Connecticut's clergymen more mature politically. They learned that informal discussion of differences could sometimes bring agreement on a course of action where there was not a uniformity of viewpoint. They had different views on the constitutional amendment concerning school bus service, but they could agree that they were opposed to it.

Although the clergy were becoming politically more mature, there was no clear indication that they were becoming politically more responsible. The decision to oppose the constitutional amendment was made by a conference of clerical leaders. The issue was not considered by Protestant and Catholic citizens nor by a representative assembly. Protestant and Catholic influence was exerted by clergymen who assumed they were acting in the interests of their religious adherents. This assumption was accepted by the legislative leaders with whom the clergy conferred. The legislators were probably confident that there would be no serious denominational conflict without the support of the clergy. If the clergy did not want a political battle, there would be none.

After the *Newtown* case was initiated, no petition was filed in any town for a referendum on transportation. It seemed to be agreed that the issue had moved into the judicial field, at least temporarily. When in June, 1960, the law was upheld by the Supreme Court of Errors, speculation began as to whether petitions would be started in some towns. It had been three years since the law was passed; would the truce continue until the United States Supreme Court acted?

LEGISLATORS, PARTY LEADERS, AND PUBLIC OFFICIALS

No political body or official is happy to be handed a "hot potato." The most difficult political issues, however, usually find their way to the legislature. When other agencies of government are unable to resolve satisfactorily differences between strongly contending interests, the legislature is likely to be called on to mediate the conflict. This was the function that the 1957 Connecticut General Assembly was called on to perform in the dispute over auxiliary services. No other government agency or officer or non-governmental body was able to resolve the differences or serve as a satisfactory forum where differences could be considered. This potato was too hot.

Local school boards had handled the issue promptly, but in none of the towns was the decision accepted as the final one. Questions of constitutionality and of statutory authority caused uncertainties. School board members and others looked to the legislature for a decision.

State officials and political leaders were under pressures to take sides in the dispute. Some simply avoided it. The Attorney General gave a decision which placed the responsibility on local school boards and town counsels. The State Board of Education took no stand other than asking for "clarification" of the law. The Democratic Governor held himself apart from the controversy. These state authorities, like the local school boards, looked to the legislature to handle the issue.

The responsibility for the action of the legislature was felt most directly by the Republican leadership. Their party had won overwhelming control of both houses in 1956. There could be no doubt that the fate of the school bus bill would be decided by the Republicans. The Republican legislative policy committee members knew they were facing "a tough one," but they agreed to support the bill. This decision was taken without consultation with the Republican legislators. The leaders, thinking of a statewide constituency, responded to Hurley's persuasion and their estimate of Catholic interest. They gave early support to the bill and provided the decisive impetus for its passage. The House members, too, largely reflected constituency interest. But they represented a local constituency.

The Republican leaders faced a problem familiar to legislators, the accommodation of a particular interest to the general interest. By successful exercise of the influence and authority of their position, they achieved both goals.

After the initial decision by the Republican legislative policy committee to support the bill, the opposing forces in the legislature became manifest and there began the usual processes of mediation, testing of strength, maneuver, discussion, and attempts at compromise. Out of concern for reducing tension, majority leader Pope and state chairman Baldwin avoided direct pressure on House members. Mr. Hurley's suggestion to use local bills as currency to buy votes for the bus bill was rejected. The leaders pressed for the school bus bill without generating animosities which affected other legislation. Mr. Pope's expressed concern for the entire legislative program rather than the fate of one bill obviously was the wiser policy.

Possibly the leadership's main contribution was less in exercising pressure than in keeping open the channels of discussion. They maintained an atmosphere in which obstacles could be removed. There were plenty of obstacles; a badly drawn bill, a committee opposed to it, a series of parliamentary tangles, and a compromise offer that might have sidetracked the measure. While there were strong differences about the bill and deep resentments at pressures exerted from outside the legislature, the Republican leadership did not give potential animosities within the legislature any cause to grow. Until the very last day, leaders on both sides were willing to discuss some means of compromise.

Most legislators would have welcomed some compromise agreement. The suggestion of a House resolution proposing a constitutional amendment offered what seemed to some a means of getting the Republican Party "off the hook." The practice of local option on auxiliary services could continue. Who could object to putting the issue to the voters of the state to decide as a constitutional question? For the Republican leaders this must have offered some attractions. But to supporters of the bill outside of the legislature it might have looked as simply a delaying action. And it was a course that was still open if the House defeated the bill. The House leaders, wisely, in the light of their aims, decided to debate the measure. This was not what a majority of the House members wanted, but it did result in the passage of the bill. Only the determination of the supporters of the bill forced the legislature to a decision. That decision was made reluctantly and the question was passed off for definitive reply by local referendum. The Assembly's action was not so much an answer as a transfer of jurisdiction.

This church-connected legislative division the lawmakers and the politicians found especially difficult and distasteful. When it was done with, they said they wanted no more such struggles. Yet the following year both parties fashioned their state tickets, as they had for earlier campaigns, in a way calculated to offer candidates with special appeal for the several religious and nationality groups. While they complained about intense religious identification with legislative purposes, they remained willing to exploit religious identification to win votes.

Politicians were aware of the political importance of religious affiliation as they were of other group interests, geographic, nationalistic, and economic. They could deal with these various factors in a convention hall or a legislative assembly. They understood the rules and restrictions to be observed in working out solutions for the political demands of these various interests. They shared assumptions about the political process and could differ intensely without permanently alienating one another.

The clerical partisans did not share these assumptions about the political process. When they found their aims were different, they did not discuss their differences with each other. They sought not a mediation table but a battleground. The clerical conflict in the public arena made the problem more difficult to resolve inside the legislature.

Religious groups in a dispute over public policy tend to behave as crusaders seeking victory for a righteous cause. Political bodies search for a compromise. A political crusade between strongly polarized, uncompromising belligerents imposes severe strains on the legislative process. Such belligerents, pressing a difficult political question with determination, may compel a legislative answer, but that answer is likely to be reluctant and evasive.

THE EFFECT OF THE CONFLICT

The conflict which produced the reluctant legislative decision of 1957 had a marked effect on Connecticut politics generally and on the Republican Party in particular. Divisions within the legislature were minimized and were largely repaired afterward. This was not true outside of the legislature.

The Republican Party leaders tried to do something desired by the Catholic clergy of Connecticut and, it was presumed, by many Catholic voters. The school bus bill was passed, but the consequences for the Republican Party were not clear after the General Assembly adjourned. The Republican leaders had demonstrated their awareness of and sympathy for Catholic legislative interests. The struggle over the bill, however, dramatized the strong opposition to Catholic interests within the Republican Party. There was no such opposition revealed within the Democratic Party. A majority of the Republican representatives on the birth-control bill, the Speaker's ruling, and the school bus bill, voted in opposition to Catholic interest. The Democrats in the General Assembly had demonstrated much more support for the school bus bill and more opposition to the birth-control bill.

In spite of the passage of the school bus bill and in spite of the "overbalancing" of its state ticket, the Republican Party in 1958 went down to its greatest defeat in Connecticut history. The religious issue was, after all, only one factor in Connecticut politics. Nevertheless, it was indisputably on record that the Republican leaders had proved responsive to Catholic interests. A Connecticut Catholic might now feel less of a stranger in the Republican Party. But increased emphasis on religion in politics may make the position of a Catholic Republican politician in Connecticut similar to that of a Southern Democrat in national politics. Because of assumed continuing support by a particular segment of the voters, he may wield significant legislative and party influence. But his close identification with that segment of the voters may well reduce his acceptance by other groups. This identification may seriously hamper his nomination for the chief executive position.

The most serious effect of the conflict over the school bus bill was its inhibition of the normal extralegislative activities in the democratic lawmaking process. The fear of extreme internal division prevented multisectarian groups from considering the issue. Important civic organizations, therefore, failed to take part in the opinion-forming process. Public policy statements were made only by spokesmen for religious groups. Reluctance to contribute to community division and fear of economic retaliation reduced the newspapers' discussion of the question.

The seriousness of these effects was amplified by the methods followed by the clergy in reaching public policy decisions. Their methods in the school bus conflict were leader-oriented rather than member-oriented. Questions of public policy were not submitted to the membership but were likely to be made by the executive group or the ecclesiastical head. These policies were not first subjected to the tempering of group discussion. Church members who did not agree with the proclaimed policy were in general unwilling to oppose publicly their religious leaders and their coreligionists.

When group leaders approach a problem of public policy by refusing to discuss differences and by holding positions which they declare are beyond compromise, they strongly modify the legislative process. Instead of discussion, determination of areas of agreement and disagreement, and compromise of differences, the contest becomes a test of strength accompanied by the threat of political or even economic reprisals against opponents. This uncompromising approach by theologians is understandable. Accustomed to seeking or expounding the "good" in terms of moral absolutes or eternal verities, they may easily regard their opponents as advocates of immoral doctrines. How can a man of God compromise with the forces of evil? This approach to a public policy question is not likely to lead to a solution which will win the acquiescence of the minority. The decision, when it comes, will be regarded not as a solution to a problem in public law, but as a triumph or a defeat in a battle for righteousness; and the loser will vow to carry on the war.

This is not the making of public policy but a struggle for the control of the state.

Can our political system remain democratic if religious leaders make such use of the influence of their church groups? How long can our political parties perform their roles as mediators, adjusting special demands to the general public interest, if other moderating influences are driven out of the political arena and two inflexible opponents concentrate their blows on the arbiter?

The 1957 experience with religious pressure groups was clearly an unhappy one for local and state officials and political leaders. At the end of the struggle in the General Assembly, the issue was returned to the towns, where religious groups could exercise their will in the places where they predominated. When that decision was made in 1957 there was little indication that there would be any more charity displayed by religious groups in local disputes than they had shown in the state contest.

The distinctive feature of the 1957 legislative battle over the school bus bill was a great irony. The qualities esteemed by religious standards—persuasion, moderation, patience, respect for the demands of another's conscience, forgivingness, a spirit of brotherhood that persists despite strong differences of opinion—these qualities were displayed by the politicians. The same, alas, could not be said for the clergy. This regrettable lack shocked the public, the politicians, and the clergy themselves.

However, there were on the state level some clergymen and laymen who realized that measures could be taken to prevent a repetition of the religious-political division Connecticut had suffered. In the local disputes one or two clergymen had shown a concern for values other than their immediate political purpose. The promotion of better understanding among clergymen of the several faiths was the first and essential step to be taken. The agreement that avoided a conflict in the 1959 legislature suggested that some advance had been made.

In that instance, however, both sides were opposed to the resolution for a constitutional amendment. Greater tests of the political maturity of the Connecticut clergy would come in different fashion. How would they react when there was a severe division along denominational lines on whether a bill should be approved? How would they behave in future local disputes on such issues? Would they be able to differ and still avoid the extremes of 1957? Would the "round-table" meetings lead to broader communication and a greater feeling of confidence and respect among the clergy? Would sectarian competition for legal dominance be exchanged for more charitable attitudes and a spirit of brotherhood?

The answers to such questions could not be drawn with any certainty two years after the Connecticut school bus battle. It was evident, however, that many people on both sides of that conflict looked back on some of the events with regret and regarded the possibility of a new contest with distaste. Some other approach was needed for religious-political differences. If that approach were to be based on a feeling of fraternity instead of antagonism, on accommodation instead of competition, the change would depend in large part on the behavior of the clergy.

There was reason to hope that the school bus battle and the 1958 election results would have some beneficial results on Connecticut's politics. Political leaders might become more conscious that a popular candidate and a vigorous campaign were more likely to be successful than calculated appeals to religious or nationality groups. Perhaps they might even ask of the clergy, as other groups were asked, that some effort be made to reconcile differences before an appeal was brought for legislative action. Religious leaders might become more conscious that weapons did not persuade and that political goals, like any others, were colored by the means employed to achieve them. In time the clergy and other religious partisans might more fully appreciate that the doctrines taught in their sacred writings could be successfully applied in working for their political goals.

APPENDIX I

Bills Relating to Public Services for Non-Public School Pupils Introduced in 1957 Connecticut General Assembly

PUBLIC ACT NUMBER 547

(Senate Bill 872, introduced by Senator Benjamin Kopacz and amended by Senate Amendment Schedule A and Senate Amendment Schedule B offered by Senator Theodore Ryan. This is the "school bus bill" signed into law by Governor Abraham Ribicoff on May 29, 1957.)

AN ACT CONCERNING SERVICES THAT MAY BE FURNISHED PRIVATE SCHOOL CHILDREN WHEN SUCH SCHOOLS ARE NOT CONDUCTED FOR A PROFIT.

Section 1. Any town, city, borough or school district may provide, for its children attending private schools therein, not conducted for profit, when a majority of the children attending such school are from such municipality, any transportation services provided for its children attending public schools. Any such municipality, which on the effective date of this act is providing such services, may continue to furnish the same until an official determination to the contrary is voted under the provisions of section 2 of this act.

Section 2. The chief executive authority of any such municipality shall, upon petition of at least five per cent of the electors as determined by the last-completed registry list, submit the question of determining whether the services specified in section 1 of this act may be so provided to a vote of the electors of such municipality at a special meeting called for such purpose within twenty one days after the receipt of such petition. Such petition shall contain the street addresses of the signers and shall be submitted to the municipal clerk, who shall certify thereon the number of names of electors on such petition, which names are on the last-completed registry list. Each page of such petition shall contain a statement, signed under penalties of perjury, by the person who circulated the same, that each person whose name appears on such page signed the same in person and that the circulator either knows each such signer or that the signer satisfactorily identified himself to the circulator. The warning for such meeting shall state that the purpose of such meeting is to vote on determining whether the services may be provided. Such vote shall be taken and the results thereof canvassed and declared in the same manner as is provided for the election of officers of such municipality, except that absentee voting shall not be permitted. The vote on such determination shall be taken by voting machine and the designation of the question on the voting machine ballot label shall be "For transportation of children attending private schools, YES" and "For transportation for children attending private schools, NO" and such ballot label shall be provided for use in accordance with the provisions of section 727d. If, upon the official determination of the result of such vote, it appears that the majority of all the votes so cast are in approval of such question, the provision of said section shall take effect at the beginning of the next fiscal period of such municipality.

Senate Bill 872, introduced by Senator Benjamin Kopacz.

AN ACT CONCERNING SERVICES THAT MAY BE FURNISHED PRIVATE SCHOOL CHILDREN WHEN SUCH SCHOOLS ARE NOT CONDUCTED FOR A PROFIT.

Any town which provides any municipal services for the children of the town attending public schools may provide similar services to any child of said town attending private school not conducted for profit in said town.

STATEMENT OF PURPOSE: To make it permissive for towns to provide services for private school children.

Senate Bill 898, introduced by Senator Benjamin Kopacz.

AN ACT AMENDING THE CHARTER OF THE CITY OF MERIDEN CONCERNING TRANSPORTATION OF SCHOOL CHILDREN.

Section 72 of special act number 413 of the 1921 session of the general assembly is amended to read as follows: (1) The court of common council shall have the power, by the vote of a majority of its members and subject to the veto power of the mayor, to provide by resolutions, ordinances or by-laws for the transportation of elementary school children to and from schools other than public schools located within the city of Meriden, provided attendance at such schools has been approved by the state board of education, whenever transportation to and from such schools is reasonable, desirable and consistent with the health, safety and welfare of such school children; and the court of common council may enact regulations and enter into contracts for such transportation. (2) The board of apportionment and taxation shall have the power to make appropriations to pay the cost of such transportation.

STATEMENT OF PURPOSE: To make it permissive for the council to provide transportation to children attending schools other than public schools.

Senate Bill 900, introduced by Senator Benjamin Kopacz.

AN ACT PROVIDING FOR TRANSPORTATION OF SCHOOL CHILDREN ATTENDING OTHER THAN PUBLIC SCHOOLS IN MERIDEN.

Section 37 of the special acts, number 413, of the 1921 regular session of the general assembly is amended by adding the following to said section; The board of education of said city shall provide to any child attending a private school, not conducted for profit, in said city the same transportation services as provided by said city for those attending public schools and the board of apportionment and taxation shall make the appropriation to the board of education for such purpose.

STATEMENT OF PURPOSE: To make it mandatory for the board of education to provide same transportation services to children attending non-profit schools as those attending private schools. [The last words of the final sentence are obviously in error. They should read "non-profit, private schools as those attending public schools."]

House Bill 870, introduced by Representative Louis J. Padula.

AN ACT CONCERNING MUNICIPAL SERVICES FOR SCHOOL CHILDREN.

Any town or school district which provides any municipal services for the children of such town or school district attending public schools therein may provide similar services for any child residing in such town or school district and attending a private school, not conducted for profit, in such town or school district.

STATEMENT OF PURPOSE: To allow towns and school districts supplying municipal services to pupils in its public schools to provide similar services for pupils resident within the town or district and attending private, non-profit schools therein.

House Bill 880, introduced by Representatives David J. Dickson, Jr., and Benito Muzio.

AN ACT CONCERNING TRANSPORTATION FOR STUDENTS OF PAROCHIAL SCHOOLS.

[Italics indicate amendment to an existing statute proposed by bill.]

Section 1 . . . All towns having, according to the 1930 United States census, a population of less than six thousand, may be reimbursed by the state for one-half the cost of transportation of children to and from elementary schools, *including parochial schools of elementary grade level,* such reimbursement not to exceed twenty dollars per pupil, annually. . . .

Section 2 . . . Each town shall furnish, by transportation or otherwise, school accommodations so that each child over six and under sixteen years of age may attend school as required in section 1445, *transportation to be provided for children who attend parochial school as well as public school* . . .

Section 3 . . . Any town in which a high school is not maintained shall pay the reasonable and necessary cost of transportation of any pupil who resides with his parents or guardian in such town and who, with the written consent of the board of education, attends any high school [provided such high school be] approved by the state board of education or *any parochial school of high school grade level* . . .

STATEMENT OF PURPOSE: To provide transportation to school for students of parochial schools.

[The amendment of section 3 would appear to be unnecessary under the ruling of the office of the Attorney General in 1945. See above, Chapter III.]

APPENDIX II

The Influence of Constituency

The vote on Senate Bill 872 in the 1957 Connecticut House of Representatives; the vote of members from towns with Catholic schools compared with the vote of members from towns without Catholic schools.

The Vote on Passage of Senate Bill 872
(A "yea" vote favored the "school bus bill.")

	Number of Towns	Total Votes	Abs.	Yea	Nay
Towns with Catholic schools	50	103	1	79	23
Towns without Catholic schools	119	176	11	55	110

Towns with Catholic Schools

Town and Member (Democrats in *italic*)	Vote on Passage of S.B. 872 Yea	Nay	Town and Member (Democrats in *italic*)	Vote on Passage of S.B. 872 Yea	Nay
Ansonia			Bristol		
Pepe, P. A.	Y		Krawiecki	Y	
Palmer, E. F.		N	Fitzgerald	Y	
Bloomfield			Danbury		
Bitzer		N	Keane	Y	
Carpenter, S. B.		N	Novaco	Y	
Bridgeport			Deep River		
Arnold	Y		LaPlace		N
D'Amicol	Y		Larson		N

Towns with Catholic Schools

Town and Member (Democrats in *italic*)	Vote on Passage of S.B. 872 Yea	Nay	Town and Member (Democrats in *italic*)	Vote on Passage of S.B. 872 Yea	Nay
Derby			Naugatuck		
Pepe, F. H.	Y		Ratkeivich	Y	
Caldwell	Y		Rosa	Y	
East Hartford			New Britain		
Burke	Y		*Googel*	Y	
Warren, L. B.	Y		*Badolato*	Y	
Enfield			New Canaan		
Crombie	Y		Cunningham		N
Javorski	Y		Hall, C. W.	Y	
Fairfield			New Hartford		
Pope	Y		Eddy	Y	
James		N	Goldbeck	Y	
Greenwich			New Haven		
Douglass		N	Cook		N
Matthews		N	Tomasino	Y	
Griswold			New London		
Gwiazdowski	Y		Cushman	Y	
Liberty	Y		Dreyfus	Y	
Hamden			New Milford		
Hyde		N	Ambler	Y	
Kielwasser	Y		Noble	Y	
Hartford			Norwalk		
Kerrigan	Y		Padula	Y	
Girouard	Y		Shostak	Y	
Killingly			Norwich		
Kesaris		N	Dugas	Y	
Sorel	Y		Mackenzie	Y	
Manchester			Plainfield		
Warren, R. S.	Y		*DeMuth*	Y	
Rogers		N	*Mopsik*	Y	
Meriden			Pomfret		
Austin	Y		Bosworth	Y	
Femia	Y		Howe	Y	
Middletown			Portland		
Bouteiller	Y		*O'Brien*	Y	
Cleary	Y		Watson	Y	
Milford			Putnam		
Elker		N	Lewis	Y	
Toulson		N	Shepard	Abs.	

Towns with Catholic Schools

Town and Member (Democrats in *italic*)	Vote on Passage of S.B. 872		Town and Member (Democrats in *italic*)	Vote on Passage of S.B. 872	
	Yea	Nay		Yea	Nay
Ridgefield			Wallingford		
Draper	Y		Bennett	Y	
Keeler	Y		Farnam		N
Shelton			Waterbury		
Taylor		N	Grize	Y	
Winnick	Y		Jones		N
Sprague			Watertown		
Papineau	Y		Russell	Y	
Stafford			Tyler	Y	
Dickson	Y		West Hartford		
Muzio	Y		Sheehan	Y	
Stamford			Schwolsky		N
Clarke	Y		West Haven		
Givens	Y		Gilhuly	Y	
Stonington			Swanson	Y	
Allyn		N	Westport		
Perry		N	Ferne	Y	
Stratford			Mackie		N
Prokop	Y		Winchester		
Smyth, W. J.	Y		Hutton	Y	
Thompson			O'Connor	Y	
Blanchette	Y		Windham		
La Fleur	Y		Hanna	Y	
Torrington			Kucharski	Y	
Fahey	Y		Windsor Locks		
Piscitelli	Y		Gragnolati	Y	
Trumbull			Greene	Y	
Blackman	Y				
Eielson	Y				
Vernon					
Welles	Y				
Bateman		N			

	Abs.	Yea	Nay
Totals			
103 votes	1	79	23

Towns without Catholic Schools

Town and Member (Democrats in *italic*)	Vote on Passage of S.B. 872		Town and Member (Democrats in *italic*)	Vote on Passage of S.B. 872	
	Yea	Nay		Yea	Nay
Andover			Canterbury		
Covell		N	Frink		N
Ashford			Grab	Abs.	
Bartok	Y		Canton		
Zambo	Y		Sweeton		N
Avon			Chaplin		
August		N	*Lucas*	Y	
Barkhamsted			Cheshire		
Lavieri	Y		Andrews	Y	
Roberts	Y		Suarez	Y	
Beacon Falls			Chester		
O'Shea	Y		Watrous		N
Berlin			Clinton		
Clapp		N	Elliott		N
Ellsworth	Y		Colchester		
Bethany			*Cohen*	Y	
Turner		N	Standish	Y	
Bethel			Colebrook		
Reed		N	Pruyn	Y	
Streaman	Y		Smith, E. W.	Y	
Bethlehem			Columbia		
Hunt		N	Williams, L. H.		N
Bolton			Cornwall		
Gagliardone	Y		Calhoun		N
Bozrah			Clark, H. L.		N
Winchester		N	Coventry		
Branford			Miller		N
Hammer		N	Smith, R. F.		N
Young	Abs.		Cromwell		
Bridgewater			Anderson		N
Hambrock	Y		Darien		
Brookfield			Farmer		N
Pinney		N	Frate	Y	
Brooklyn			Durham		
Strunk		N	*Murray*	Y	
Burlington			Newton		N
Hogan	Y		Eastford		
Canaan			Piper		N
Davies		N			

TOWNS WITHOUT CATHOLIC SCHOOLS

Town and Member (Democrats in *italic*)	Vote on Passage of S.B. 872 Yea	Nay	Town and Member (Democrats in *italic*)	Vote on Passage of S.B. 872 Yea	Nay
East Granby			Guilford		
Seymour		N	Dudley	Y	
East Haddam			McAdam		N
Ballek	Y		Haddam		
Hatfield	Y		Carpenter, L. T.		N
East Hampton			VonHagen		N
Blankenbiller	Y		Hampton		
Hallberg	Y		Stone		N
East Haven			Hartland		
Croumey		N	Hall, J. B.	Y	
Mauttey	Y		Martin, L. B.	Y	
East Lyme			Harwinton		
Manwaring		N	Bentley		N
Easton			Delay		N
Svihra		N	Hebron		
East Windsor			Links		N
Stolle		N	Smith, E. H.		N
Woolam		N	Kent		
Ellington			Cady		N
Wraight		N	Killingworth		
Essex			Carlson, G. A.		N
Comstock		N	Saglio		N
Farmington			Lebanon		
Noyes		N	Nourse		N
Robotham		N	Pultz		N
Franklin			Ledyard		
Kingsley		N	Rowley		N
Glastonbury			Lisbon		
Barnett		N	Maynard	Y	
Goodhue	Abs.		Litchfield		
Goshen			Lester		N
Conlon	Abs.		Marsters		N
Vaill	Abs.		Lyme		
Granby			Beebe		N
Allison	Y		Brevillier		N
Wolcott	Y		Madison		
Groton			Cairns		N
Brown	Y				
Wood		N			

Towns without Catholic Schools

Town and Member (Democrats in *italic*)	Vote on Passage of S.B. 872 Yea	Nay	Town and Member (Democrats in *italic*)	Vote on Passage of S.B. 872 Yea	Nay
Mansfield			Old Saybrook		
Richards		N	Fairbank		N
Smith, E. O.		N	Orange		
Marlborough			Martin, E. W.		N
Lord	Y		Wright		N
Middlebury			Oxford		
Gray		N	Maybury		N
Middlefield			Plainville		
Lombardo	Y		Koskoff		N
Monroe			*Villardi*	Y	
Kissam		N	Plymouth		
Montville			Oelschlegel	Y	
Radgowski	Y		Pratt		N
Morris			Preston		
Ives		N	Fleming		N
New Fairfield			Mansfield		N
Baggs		N	Prospect		
Newington			Harrison	Y	
Benson		N	Redding		
Mortensen	Y		Carlson, A.		N
Newtown			Marsh		N
Curtis, S. F.	Y		Rocky Hill		
Terrell		N	Little	Abs.	
Norfolk			Rust	Y	
Robertson		N	Roxbury		
Zanobi	Y		Beatty		N
North Branford			Salem		
Williams, S. T.	Abs.		*Ploszaj*	Y	
North Canaan			Salisbury		
May		N	Nash		N
North Haven			Paavola		N
Cipriano	Y		Scotland		
North		N	Moseley		N
North Stonington			Seymour		
Lee		N	Driscoll	Y	
White		N	Fosdick		N
Old Lyme			Sharon		
Patterson		N	Luce		N
			Pearson	Y	

TOWNS WITHOUT CATHOLIC SCHOOLS

Town and Member (Democrats in *italic*)	Vote on Passage of S.B. 872		Town and Member (Democrats in *italic*)	Vote on Passage of S.B. 872	
	Yea	Nay		Yea	Nay
Sherman			Washington		
Osborn		N	Kennedy	Y	
Simsbury			Quinlan		N
Gerston	Y		Waterford		
Wallace	Y		Bascom		N
Somers			McCartin	Y	
Phillips		N	Westbrook		
Strekas		N	Schlossbach	Abs.	
Southbury			Weston		
Platt		N	Lupton		N
Southington			Wethersfield		
Curtiss, E. F.		N	Budd		N
Parliman		N	Wilcox		N
South Windsor			Willington		
Buckland	Abs.		Hall, G. H.	Abs.	
Sterling			Repko		N
Arcand	Y		Wilton		
Suffield			Donaldson	Y	
Kuras	Y		Windsor		
Prout		N	D'Addario	Y	
Thomaston			Gustafson		N
Innes		N	Wolcott		
Tolland			Mattson	Y	
Clough		N	Woodbridge		
Metcalf		N	Vestal		N
Union			Woodbury		
Pallanck	Abs.		Cowles		N
Plusnin		N	Cronk		N
Voluntown			Woodstock		
Palmer, B. G.	Y		Peshmalyan		N
Warren			Pitt		N
Angevine		N			

	Abs.	Yea	Nay
Totals			
176 votes	11	55	110

NOTES

INTRODUCTION

1. *Hartford Courant*, March 13, 1957; *Hartford Times*, March 12, 1957.
2. *Catholic Transcript*, March 14, 1957. (Cited hereafter as *Transcript*.)
3. *Hartford Courant*, March 17, 1957.
4. *Hartford Times*, March 19, 1957.

I: THE GENERAL SETTING

1. This summary is digested from the detailed account in Mary Paul Mason, *Church-State Relationships in Education in Connecticut, 1633–1953* (Washington, D.C.: Catholic University of America Press, 1953).
2. *Ibid.*, p. 232.
3. He was borrowing from Kenneth W. Underwood, *Protestant and Catholic* (Boston: Beacon Press, 1957).
4. The child-benefit theory was widely discussed following *Everson* v. *Board of Education*, 330 U.S. 1 (1947). This line of argument was followed by the United States Supreme Court in *Cochran* v. *Louisiana State Board of Education*, 281 U.S. 370 (1930). See Chapter II.
The child-benefit theory has also been argued in a number of cases before state courts. It was rejected by a New York appellate court in *Smith* v. *Donahue*, 195 N.Y. Supp. 715 (1922), the earliest judicial consideration of the theory. The phrase "child-benefit theory" was apparently coined by the New Jersey Supreme Court in *Everson* v. *Board of Education of Township of Ewing*, 132 N.J. L. 98 (1944).
5. Leo Pfeffer, *Church, State and Freedom* (Boston: Beacon Press, 1950), pp. 119–20, quoting Jefferson's letter to the Danbury Baptists Association.
6. For a summary of this debate and an analysis of the argument, see Pfeffer, Chapter V, "The Meaning of the Principle," pp. 115–159.
7. Clark Spurlock, *Education and the Supreme Court* (Urbana: University of Illinois Press, 1955), p. 76.
8. James B. Conant, "Unity and Diversity in Secondary Education," *Leadership for American Education* (Official Report of American Association of School Administrators: Washington, 1952), pp. 239–241.
9. *New York Times*, July 4, 1952.
10. *Transcript*, April 24, 1952.
11. *Ibid.*, April 17, 1952.
12. *New York Times*, June 19, 1949.

13. Pfeffer, pp. 487–488, citing *New York Times, Religious News Service, Brooklyn Tablet, Christian Century, Churchman,* and *America.* See esp. *New York Times,* June 27, 1949.

14. *New York World-Telegram,* June 23, 1949.

15. *Ibid.,* July 8 and July 15, 1949.

16. *New York Times,* July 23, 1949.

17. *New York Times,* July 24 and July 26, 1949.

18. *New York Times,* July 28, 1949.

19. *Ibid.,* August 6, 1949.

20. *U.S. News and World Report,* December 2, 1955, pp. 102–104.

21. *Ibid.,* pp. 104–105.

22. *Ibid,* December 23, 1955, p. 67.

23. *New York Times,* November 21, 1948.

24. *Transcript,* November 20, 1952.

25. Pfeffer, p. 308, quoting from "The American Tradition and the Relation between Religion and Education," *Religion and Public Education.* American Council on Education Studies, IX, No. 22. Washington, D.C., February, 1945.

26. *Ibid.,* pp. 298–299, quoting Agnes E. Meyer, "The Clerical Challenge to the Schools," *Atlantic Monthly,* March, 1952, p. 46.

27. Neil G. McCluskey, *Catholic Viewpoint on Education* (Garden City, N.Y.: Hanover House, 1959), pp. 50–52.

28. See Chapter II.

29. They included Edwin McNeill Poteat, President, Colgate-Rochester Divinity School; G. Bromley Oxnam, Bishop, the Methodist Church, New York Area; and John A. Mackay, President, Princeton Theological Seminary. Copies of the manifesto are available in pamphlet form from Protestants and Other Americans United, 1633 Massachusetts Avenue, N.W., Washington 6, D.C.

30. McCluskey, p. 183, citing the *New York Times,* January 26, 1948.

31. Pfeffer, pp. 435–438.

32. John C. Murray, "For Freedom and Transcendance of the Church," *American Ecclesiastical Review,* January, 1952, pp. 28–49. See vigorous response, Francis J. Connell, "Reply to Father Murray," *ibid.,* pp. 49–59. See also V. R. Vanitelli, "Church-State Anthology: The Work of Father Murray," *Thought,* March, 1952, pp. 6–42; Robert J. Welch, "The Catholic Church and American Democracy," *The Christian Family,* June, July–August, September, 1956. See George W. Shea, "Catholic Orientations on Church and State," *American Ecclesiastical Review,* December, 1951, pp. 405–416; and "The Theory of the Lay State," *ibid.,* July, 1951, pp. 7–18, for views contrary to those of Fathers Murray and Welch.

33. Joseph C. Fenton, "The Status of a Controversy," *American Ecclesiastical Review,* 124 (June, 1951) p. 452.

34. John C. Bennett, "A Reply to Dr. Pearson," *The Christian Century,* 74 (January 2, 1957), p. 14.

35. McCluskey, pp. 168–176.

36. *Ibid.,* pp. 181–182.

37. Pfeffer, pp. 438–442.

38. Such disturbances are not always widely reported in the daily press but receive ample attention in sectarian periodicals. Partisans in these disputes, there-

fore, are generally familiar with similar conflicts in other areas. See "News from the Field: Question of Welfare Benefits," *The Catholic Educational Review,* 55 (February, 1957), pp. 132–134, for a review of controversies over health services and transportation for non-public school pupils in New York, New Jersey, Pennsylvania, Wisconsin, and Vermont.

39. *New York Times,* December 17, 1956.
40. *Ibid.,* December 24, 1956.
41. *Ibid.,* February 4, 1957.
42. *New York Times,* December 30, 1956.
43. *Ibid.,* January 3 and January 4, 1957.
44. *Ibid.,* March 10, 1957.
45. *Christian Register: Unitarian,* April, 1957, p. 31.
46. *New York Times,* December 28, 1956.
47. Mimeographed copy of sermon, First Unitarian Congregational Society of Hartford.
48. *New York Times,* December 20, 1956.
49. *Ibid.,* March 2, 1957.
50. *Hartford Times,* March 4, 1957.
51. *New York Times,* March 3, 1957.
52. *Hartford Courant,* March 11, 1957.
53. *New York Times,* March 10, 1957.
54. Obviously, a long euphemism for "Jews elected from cities."
55. Connecticut Yankee," by A. H. O. [Alan H. Olmstead], *Manchester* (Connecticut) *Evening Herald,* December 11, 1956.

II: THE SUPREME COURT

1. *Pierce* v. *Society of Sisters of the Holy Name of Jesus and Mary* and *Pierce* v. *Hill Military Academy,* 268 U.S. 510 (1925); *Cochran* v. *Louisiana State Board of Education,* 281 U.S. 370 (1930); *Everson* v. *Board of Education,* 330 U.S. 1 (1947); *Illinois ex rel. McCollum* v. *Board of Education,* 333 U.S. 203 (1948); *Zorach* v. *Clauson,* 343 U.S. 306 (1952).
2. 268 U.S. 510 (1925).
3. Pfeffer, p. 429. For a more detailed discussion of the *Pierce* case, see McCluskey, pp. 129–136.
4. 281 U.S. 370 (1930).
5. 330 U.S. 1 (1947).
6. 333 U.S. 203 (1948).
7. 343 U.S. 306 (1952).
8. 333 U.S. 203 (1948).
9. 343 U.S. 306 (1952).

III: THE LEGAL SETTING IN CONNECTICUT

1. *Everson* v. *Board of Education of the Township of Ewing.* 132 N.J. L. 98 (1944).

2. *City of New Haven* v. *Town of Torrington,* 132 Conn. 194 (1945).

3. Connecticut, State Department of Education, *Laws Relating to Education,* 1959. Compiled by Theodore Powell. Cited hereafter as *Laws.*

4. *New Britain Trust Co.* v. *Stoddard,* 120 Conn., 123, 127.

5. *Laws,* p. 4.

6. *Ibid.,* p. 10.

7. *Ibid.,* p. 9.

8. Keith W. Atkinson, *Public School Law in Connecticut,* State Department of Education Bulletin 51 (Hartford: 1951), pp. 23–46.

9. *Laws,* p. 80.

10. *Ibid.,* pp. 28, 29, 38, 74–79, and *passim.*

11. *Ibid.,* p. 80.

12. *Ibid.,* p. 81.

13. *Ibid.,* pp. 68–69.

14. *Ibid.,* p. 70.

15. *Ibid.,* p. 10.

16. *Ibid.,* p. 10.

17. Maurice J. Ross, *The Relationship of Public and Non-Public Schools in Connecticut* (Hartford: State Department of Education, 1956), pp. 32–57.

18. *Laws,* p. 83.

19. *Ibid.,* p. 83.

20. *Ibid.,* pp. 83–84.

21. *Ibid.,* p. 16.

22. *Laws,* p. 15.

23. *Ibid.,* p. 96.

24. Letter in files of Connecticut State Department of Education from Office of Attorney General to Roger M. Thompson, Director of Administration, State Department of Education, Hartford, December 14, 1945.

25. Letter in files of Connecticut State Department of Education from Office of Attorney General to Finis E. Engleman, Commissioner of Education, State Office Building, Hartford, December 15, 1952.

26. Atkinson, pp. 24–26.

27. Mason, p. 284.

28. Files of Connecticut State Department of Education.

29. *Ibid.*

30. *Ibid.*

31. Section 10–220. *Laws,* p. 80.

32. Files of Connecticut State Department of Education.

33. *Laws,* pp. 75–76.

34. *Ibid.,* pp. 75–76.

35. *Ibid.,* p. 76.

36. *Laws,* p. 78.

37. *Ibid.,* p. 78.

38. *Ibid.,* p. 78.

39. *Ibid.,* pp. 75–76.

40. Below, p. 160.

41. *Laws,* p. 79.

42. *Laws,* p. 8.

43. Public Law 396, 79th Congress.

44. Interviews with Mrs. Edith Cushman, School Lunch and Nutrition Consultant, Connecticut State Department of Education, August and September, 1956.

IV: THE PRELIMINARY STRUGGLE

1. *America*, November 10, 1956, p. 152.

2. Minutes of the State Board of Education, December 7, 1955, in the files of the State Department of Education, Hartford (cited hereafter as Minutes). The writer attended the meeting.

3. Maurice J. Ross, "The Relationship of Public and Non-Public Schools in Connecticut," Research Bulletin No. 6, State Department of Education, Hartford, 1956 (cited hereafter as Ross).

4. Interviews with Maurice J. Ross, January and February, 1956.

5. Ross, p. v.

6. Ross, Table I, "Enrollment in Connecticut Schools, 1900–1955," p. 3.

7. Ross, p. 5.

8. Connecticut, *Educational Directory of Connecticut, 1955–1956* (Hartford: State Department of Education, 1955), p. 29. These schools were approved as high schools by the State Board of Education for certification purposes and for the attendance of pupils whose tuition was to be paid from public funds.

9. Dr. Ross' report did not distinguish among types of non-public schools. The figure on Roman Catholic schools presented here was determined by examination of the basic data used by Dr. Ross.

10. Ross, p. 7.

11. Files of the State Department of Education.

12. Ross, p. 7.

13. Ross, p. 8.

14. Ross, p. 7.

15. Ross, p. v.

16. Minutes, May 9, 1956.

17. Below, pp. 96–101.

18. *Laws*, p. 9.

19. *Laws*, p. 69. The words "during such hours and terms" were deleted by The 1958 General Assembly.

20. Ross, p. 10.

21. Minutes, May 11, 1956.

22. *Laws*, p. 5.

23. Below, pp. 99, 100, and 196.

24. See the editorial pages of the *Hartford Times* and the *Hartford Courant*, May, June, and July, 1956.

25. *Hartford Times*, May 12, 1956.

26. *Hartford Times*, August 4, 1956. Presumably the letter writer meant that a case could be brought by a resident of one of the towns then giving auxiliary services to parochial school pupils.

27. *Transcript*, May 3, 1956.

28. *The Transcript* and Mr. Smith were wrong. The Supreme Court had not approved such services. See above, Chapter II.

29. *Transcript*, May 3, 1956.

30. Interview with Sigmund Adler, November 10, 1956.

31. *Transcript*, June 21, 1956.

32. Files of Sigmund Adler.

33. The writer was present at the conference.

34. "Better Schools," National Citizens Council for Better Schools, 9 East 40th Street, New York, June, 1957.

35. Interview with an officer of the Connecticut Association of Boards of Education, February 13, 1957.

36. Below, pp. 192–193.

37. Interview with Mrs. Ralph C. Lasbury, November 11, 1956.

38. "For Better Schools," WTIC, Hartford, December, 1956.

39. Minutes, March 7, 1956.

40. *West Hartford News*, May 17, 1956.

41. Minutes, May 29, 1956.

42. Mimeographed newsletter, Connecticut Council of Churches, January, 1957.

43. Minutes, November 7, 1956.

44. Richard Joyce Smith, "Aid To Private and Parochial Schools," *America*, November 10, 1956, pp. 152–57.

45. *Transcript*, November 8, 1956.

46. *Hartford Times*, November 15, 1956.

47. To this writer.

48. *West Hartford News*, November 15, 1956.

49. Minutes, December 5, 1956.

50. *Hartford Courant and Hartford Times*, December 6, 1956. For the wire story see, for example, "State Unit Bars Public Funds to Private Schools," Associated Press dispatch in *Manchester* (Connecticut) *Evening Herald*, December 6, 1956.

51. *West Hartford News*, December 13, 1956.

V: FOUR LOCAL DISPUTES

1. *Hartford Times.*

2. Connecticut, "Weekly Health Bulletin," State Department of Health, Hartford.

3. As reported by the 1950 census.

4. *Ross*, p. 18.

5. Interview with superintendent of schools and chairman of the Parkville Board of Education, the Reverend John Paul, March, 1957.

6. Interview with superintendent of schools in Parkville, March, 1957.

7. Based on interviews with superintendent of schools, the Reverend John Paul, and other Board members cited below.

8. Interview with David Coy, July, 1957 (telephone).

9. Interview with the Reverend John Paul.
10. Interview with Frank Martin, July, 1957 (telephone).
11. Interview with the Reverend John Paul.
12. *Ibid.*
13. Interview with Frank Martin.
14. *Hartford Times* and interview with Father Albert Daniel, March, 1957.
15. Interview with Father Albert Daniel.
16. Based on interviews cited above.
17. Connecticut, "Weekly Health Bulletin."
18. Connecticut, *Register and Manual*, 1956 (Hartford: Secretary of State).
19. As reported by 1950 census.
20. Interview with superintendent of schools Gerald Masters, April, 1957.
21. Ross, p. 18.
22. Interview with Mayor Anthony Carmello, April, 1957.
23. Based on interviews with superintendent of schools and board members cited below.
24. Minutes of meeting of Diamond City Board of Education and *Diamond City Star.*
25. *Diamond City Star.*
26. *Ibid.*
27. Interview with school board chairman Patrick McDowell, April, 1957.
28. Interviews with superintendent of schools, Mayor Carmello, and school board members.
29. Interview with Mayor Carmello.
30. *Diamond City Star.*
31. *Diamond City Star.*
32. *Ibid.*
33. *Diamond City Chronicle.*
34. Interviews with Patrick McDowell, Monroe Green, and John Bernard, April, 1957.
35. *Diamond City Star.*
36. *Ibid.* and minutes of meeting of Diamond City Council.
37. *Diamond City Star* and *Diamond City Chronicle.*
38. *Diamond City Star.*
39. Interviews with Patrick McDowell and Mayor Anthony Carmello.
40. *Diamond City Star.*
41. Interview with Mayor Anthony Carmello.
42. Minutes of meeting of Diamond City Council.
43. *Ibid.* and *Diamond City Star.*
44. Interview with Patrick McDowell.
45. Interview with John Bernard and minutes of Diamond City Board of Education.
46. Interview with Monroe Green.
47. *Diamond City Star* and minutes of Diamond City Board of Education.
48. Interviews with Patrick McDowell, Monroe Green, and John Bernard.
49. *Diamond City Star* and minutes of Diamond City Board of Education.
50. Interview with superintendent of schools Gerald Masters.
51. Minutes of Diamond City Board of Education.

52. A. C. Spectorsky, *The Exurbanites* (Philadelphia: J. B. Lippincott Company, 1955).

53. As reported by 1950 census and Connecticut "Weekly Health Bulletin."

54. Records of Connecticut State Department of Education.

55. Interviews with Superintendent of Schools John Gavin and school board members cited below.

56. Records of High Hills Board of Education.

57. Interviews with Father Everett Davey, October, 1956, and records of High Hills Board of Education.

58. Records of High Hills Board of Education.

59. Interview with Father Everett Davey.

60. Interview with Harold Chain, October, 1956.

61. Interview with Superintendent of Schools John Gavin, October, 1956.

62. Interview with Father Everett Davey.

63. Interview with Dr. Wallace Doan, October, 1956.

64. Records of High Hills Board of Education.

65. Connecticut, *Register and Manual*, 1956.

66. Records of High Hills Board of Education.

67. *Ibid.* and *High Hills News* and other newspapers.

68. This writer attended the meeting.

69. Interview with Dr. Wallace Doan.

70. This report of the executive session is based on interviews with Superintendent of Schools John Gavin, Board chairman Charles Ford, and Board members Harold Chain, William Manners, and Dr. Anthony Pinza.

71. Interview with William Manners, April, 1957.

72. Interview with Dr. Wallace Doan.

73. Interview with Charles Ford, November, 1956.

74. Interview with Dr. Anthony Pinza, December, 1956.

75. Interview with William Manners.

76. Interview with Father Everett Davey.

77. Interview with William Manners.

78. Comments given in interviews with Board members cited above.

79. Interview with Dr. Anthony Pinza.

80. Interview with Charles Ford, April, 1957.

81. Interview with Mrs. Martha McNulty, May, 1957.

82. Interview with William Manners, April, 1957.

83. This is the statement attributed to Mr. Manners by Mrs. McNulty in an interview with this writer.

84. Interview with William Manners.

85. Interview with Mrs. Martha McNulty.

86. Interview with William Manners.

87. Interviews with Mr. and Mrs. William Manners, April, 1957, and Charles Ford, April, 1957.

88. Interview with John Gavin, April, 1957.

89. Interview with Dr. Wallace Doan, March, 1957.

90. Interview with Charles Ford and Mrs. Martha McNulty.

91. Interview with Charles Ford.

92. Interview with William Manners.

93. Interview with Charles Ford.

94. Interviews with Charles Ford and William Manners.

95. Interview with John Gavin.

96. Interviews with Charles Ford and William Manners.

97. Interview with Charles Ford.

98. Interview with Mrs. Martha McNulty.

99. The political and religious affiliations of school board members were determined in interviews cited above.

100. Interview with Horton Churchill, chairman of Castleton Board of Education, February, 1957.

101. Connecticut, *Register and Manual*, 1956.

102. Ross, p. 18.

103. As reported by 1950 census and Connecticut, "Weekly Health Bulletin."

104. Connecticut, *Register and Manual*, 1956, and interviews with Board members cited below.

105. The political and religious affiliations of members of the Castleton Board of Education were determined in the interviews cited below.

106. Interviews with Horton Churchill and with school board member Dennis Doherty, January, 1957.

107. *Ibid.* The meeting was reported in some Hartford area newspapers.

108. *Ibid.*

109. *Ibid.*

110. Interview with Horton Churchill.

111. Interview with George Lord Speaker, III, February, 1957.

112. Interview with Aaron Booker, February, 1957.

113. Interview with Dennis Doherty.

114. Interview with Warren Sales, February, 1957.

115. Interview with Mrs. Ruth Fast, February, 1957.

116. The meeting was reported in some Hartford area newspapers.

117. *Ibid.*

VI: THE LEGISLATIVE STRUGGLE

1. 1957 *Connecticut General Assembly* (Hartford: Legislative Service Bureau).

2. Above, pp. 30–31.

3. Interview with Monsignor Robert W. Doyle, August 23, 1957.

4. Interview with Senator Benjamin Kopacz, July 25, 1957.

5. Interview with John Hurley, August 7, 1957.

6. Above, pp. 88–91.

7. Interview with the Reverend Loyd Worley, August 19, 1957.

8. *Ibid.*

9. Interview with Senator Benjamin Kopacz.

10. Connecticut, *Legislative Record Index* (Final Edition) No. 19, General Assembly, January Session, 1957), p. 76.

11. Interview with John Hurley.

12. Interview with Clarence Baldwin, August 16, 1957.

13. Interviews with John Hurley and Clarence Baldwin.

14. Interview with Clarence Baldwin.

15. The account of this meeting is based on interviews with several of those who were present.

16. Interview with Senator Theodore Ryan, July 30, 1957.

17. Interviews with several of those present at the meeting.

18. For texts of the bills, see Appendix I.

19. Interview with Representative E. O. Smith, June 19, 1957.

20. Interview with Frederick Pope, July 18, 1957.

21. Interview with Nelson Brown, September 10, 1957.

22. Interview with Frederick Pope.

23. Connecticut, *Legislative Record Index*, pp. 76 and 121.

24. Connecticut, Legislative Bulletin No. 25, 1957, General Assembly, January session, pp. 19–20.

25. Paul Blanshard's pamphlet "The Bus Wedge" is available from Protestants and Other Americans United for Separation of Church and State, 1633 Massachusetts Avenue, N.W., Washington, D.C.

26. Connecticut, *Legislative Bulletin No. 25*, 1957, General Assembly, January session, pp. 19–20.

27. Interview with the Reverend Loyd Worley.

28. Interview with Monsignor Robert W. Doyle.

29. Interview with Father William J. Daly, Hamden, Connecticut, March 21, 1957.

30. Interview with John Hurley.

31. Interview with Clarence Baldwin.

32. *Hartford Times*, March 7, 1957.

33. Interviews with Clarence Baldwin and Frederick Pope.

34. This account of the public hearing is based on the writer's observation, supplemented by the record in the files of the Joint Committee on Education of the Connecticut General Assembly and by reports in the *Hartford Courant*, March 13, 1957, *Hartford Times*, March 12, 1957, and the *Catholic Transcript*, March 14, 1957, and by interviews as cited.

35. Telephone interview with Joseph Cooney, August 7, 1957.

36. Below, Appendix I.

37. *Ibid.*

38. The practice of a sponsor submitting a substitute bill at the public hearing was not unusual in the Connecticut General Assembly and caused little complication when a committee was favorably disposed toward the proposed legislation. On this controversial issue, the Education Committee was not disposed to report out any bill favorably and certainly would not accommodate the sponsor by raising in committee a bill in accordance with his suggested substitute.

39. The legislators were assumed to have other legislative business elsewhere and therefore were heard first.

40. Ross.

41. The Committee for the White House Conference on Education reported: "Under our system of school finance, nonpublic schools must obtain virtually all of their revenues from private sources. The Committee recommends that all children, regardless of whether they be enrolled in public or nonpublic

schools, receive basic health and safety services at public expense; the extent to which 'basic health and safety services' should go and the question of whether public school funds or other public funds should be used to provide them, must be determined at the State and community levels to reflect existing laws and desires." *A Report to the President* (Washington: U.S. Government Printing Office, 1956), p. 60.

42. *Chance v. Mississippi State Textbook Board*, 190 Miss. 453 (1941).

43. Below, pp. 192–193.

44. *Chance v. Mississippi Text Book Rating and Purchasing Board*, 190 Miss. 453 (1941).

45. When an attempt was made later for a mandatory bill it was quickly dismissed. Below, p, 231.

46. Interview with Samuel Googel, February 7, 1958.

47. *Hartford Times*, March 16, 1957.

48. *Ibid.*

49. *Hartford Courant*, April 9, 1957.

50. *Ibid.*, April 14, 1957.

51. *New London Evening Day*, April 24, 1957.

52. This writer was present at the convention.

53. *Transcript*, March 14, 1957.

54. *Hartford Times*, March 25, 1957.

55. Mimeographed copy of sermon from the Reverend Payson Miller, "Dogmatic Arrogance versus Journalism."

56. Monthly Communication of the Minister to the People, June, 1957.

57. Files of the Reverend Loyd Worley.

58. March 16, 1957.

59. This argument is similar to that expressed in the resolution of the American Jewish Congress reported in a letter to the *Hartford Times*. Above, p. 83.

60. *Manchester Herald*, April 18, 1957.

61. *Bridgeport Herald*, April 7, 1957.

62. *Hartford Times*, April 24, 1957.

63. *Hartford Courant*, April 5, 1957.

64. Interviews with Nelson Brown, Clarence Baldwin, and Frederick Pope.

65. Interview with Meade Alcorn, July 14, 1957.

66. Interview with Clarence Baldwin.

67. *Hartford Times*, April 19, 1957.

68. Ross.

69. *New Haven Register*, April 21, 1957.

70. Interview with James Mutrie, April 23, 1957.

71. Interviews with John Hurley and Clarence Baldwin.

72. Interview with Frederick Pope.

73. Interview with Clarence Baldwin.

74. *Hartford Times*, May 4, 1957.

75. *Ibid.*, May 7, 1957.

76. Interviews with Mrs. Lucy Hammer, July 19, 1957, and E. O. Smith.

77. This account of the Republican caucus is based on the writer's observation (from outside the Hall), interviews with several Republican leaders, and accounts in the *Hartford Courant* and *Hartford Times*, May 9, 1957.

78. *Hartford Times*, May 9, 1957.

79. This account of the Senate debate is based on the writer's observation, supplemented by reports in the *Hartford Courant*, May 14, 1957, and the *Hartford Times*, May 14, 1957.

80. Another qualifying clause, "not conducted for profit," was obviously intended to apply to the school, but the section was misplaced so that it applied to the municipality; i.e., "Any town, city, borough, or school district not conducted for profit . . ."

81. Interviews with Theodore Ryan. The second section of the amended bill was prepared by Representative Rodney Eielson, who was well informed about referendum procedures.

82. Interview with Theodore Ryan.

83. Interviews with Theodore Ryan, Nelson Brown, and Frederick Pope.

84. Connecticut, "Senate Journal," May 21, 1957. The misplaced clause was relocated so that the bill referred to "private schools therein not conducted for profit when a majority of the children attending such school are from such municipality."

85. Connecticut, *Pocket Manual: Roll, Committees and Rules of the General Assembly of Connecticut*, 1957, pp. 88, 114.

86. Interviews with Clarence Baldwin and Frederick Pope.

87. This account of the debate about the Speaker's ruling is based on the writer's observation supplemented by reports in the *Hartford Courant*, May 23, 1957, and the *Hartford Times*, May 22, 1957.

88. *Hartford Courant*, May 23, 1957.

89. Interview with Monsignor John Kennedy.

90. *Hartford Courant*, May 19, 1957.

91. *Transcript*, May 23, 1957.

92. Interview with Clarence Baldwin.

93. Interview with Frederick Pope.

94. Interview with John Hurley.

95. Interviews with Theodore Ryan and Benjamin Kopacz.

96. Interview with Clarence Baldwin.

97. *Hartford Courant*, May 24, 1957.

98. *Hartford Times*, May 24, 1957.

99. Interview with Mrs. Lucy Hammer, secretary to and a member of the Education Committee.

100. This account of the opposition of Protestant ministers is obtained largely from the files of the Reverend Loyd Worley.

101. Interviews with Clarence Baldwin and Joseph Cooney.

102. *Hartford Courant*, May 26, 1957.

103. Indeed, courts in three states have ruled subsequent to the *Everson* case that under the state constitution bus service could not be given to parochial school pupils (*Visser* v. *Nooksack Valley School District*, 33 Washington 2nd [1949]; *Zellers* v. *Huff*, 55 New Mexico 501 [1951]; *McVey* v. *Hawkins*, 365 Missouri 44 [1953]).

104. *Hartford Courant*, May 26, 1957.

105. Interview with Theodore Ryan.

106. Interview with Benjamin Kopacz.

107. In conversation with this writer.

108. *Hartford Courant*, May 26, 1957.

109. *Hartford Times*, May 28, 1957.

110. *Ibid.*

111. Interview with Robert Cairns, July 19, 1957.

112. Interviews with Mrs. Lucy Hammer, Clarence Baldwin, and Meade Alcorn.

113. Interviews with Mrs. Ralph C. Lasbury and E. O. Smith.

114. Interview with E. O. Smith. Representing the opponents of the bill on the committee were Representatives E. O. Smith, Lucy Hammer, Robert Cairns, Searle Pinney, and Theodore V. Marsters. Representing the supporters were Representatives Erving Pruyn, Louis J. Padula, George M. Bennett, Rodney S. Eielson, and Anthony E. Wallace.

115. Interviews with E. O. Smith, Clarence Baldwin, and Mrs. Lucy Hammer.

116. Interview with E. O. Smith.

117. *Ibid.*

118. Interview with Frederick Pope.

119. Interview with E. O. Smith.

120. *Hartford Times*, May 29, 1957.

121. *Hartford Times*, May 30, 1957.

122. *Manchester Evening Herald*, May 29, 1957.

123. This account of the debate and action on the bill, S.B. 872, is based on the writer's observation supplemented by reports in the *Hartford Times* and *Hartford Courant*, May 30, 1957, the *Transcript*, June 6, 1957, and interviews as cited.

124. *Adams et al.* v. *County Commissioners of St. Mary's County*, 26 Atl. 377, Maryland (1942); *Nichols, et al.* v. *Henry*, 301 Kentucky 434 (1945); *Bowker* v. *Baker*, 73 Cal. App. 2d 653 (1946). In conversation later Mr. Pope reported that he had no citation for a court decision in Massachusetts. Arguing for the bill on the floor of the House, he did not mention that state courts in Washington, Missouri, and New Mexico subsequent to the *Everson* decision had declared the practices in violation of their states' constitutions. See note 103 above.

125. Interview with Frederick Pope and Clarence Baldwin.

126. Interviews with Representatives Richard Sheehan, July 5, 1957, and Samuel Googel.

127. Appendix II.

128. Connecticut, *Register and Manual*, 1955, p. 459.

VII: AFTERMATH

1. Interview with Mrs. Lucy Hammer.

2. Interview with Samuel Googel.

3. "Connecticut Yankee," by A. H. O. [Alan H. Olmstead], *Manchester Evening Herald*, June 8, 1957.

4. May 31, 1957.

5. Interview with Meade Alcorn.

6. Interview with Clarence Baldwin.

7. Interview with Theodore Ryan.

8. Interview with Benjamin Kopacz.

9. Interview with John Hurley.

10. Interviews with Mrs. Hammer, Mr. Cairns, and Mr. E. O. Smith.

11. Interviews with Clarence Baldwin and Meade Alcorn.

12. *Manchester Evening Herald*, June 1, 1957.

13. *Ibid.*, June 3, 1957.

14. *Transcript*, June 6, 1957.

15. Files of Mr. Worley.

16. Monthly Communication of the Minister to the People, July–August, 1957.

17. *Hartford Times*, May 30, 1957.

18. Files of Dr. Worley

19. John S. Kennedy, "Opposition to a Bus Bill," *America*, September 7, 1957.

20. *Hartford Times*, January 19, 1958, and "Monthly Communication . . . ," November, 1957.

21. *Manchester Evening Herald*, May 31, 1957.

22. *Hartford Times*, June 22, 1957.

23. Records of State Department of Education.

24. *Hartford Courant*, June 2, 1957.

25. This writer attended the luncheon and served as host for the television series.

26. Interviews with the Reverend William Bradley, November 26, 1959, and the Reverend Harold Keir, February 1, 1960.

27. Files of Mr. Keir. The notice was signed by Gordon Lee Burke of East Hartford, who described himself as a Mason and a Methodist. Mr. Keir did not attend the meeting and did not accept the invitation to join the new chapter.

28. *Ibid.*

29. *Hartford Times*, January 10, 1958.

30. See above, p. 177.

31. *Hartford Courant*, January 10, 1958.

32. *Transcript*, January 16, 1958.

33. This account of the conflict within the Connecticut Council of Churches is based largely on the files of the Reverend Harold Keir, supplemented by interviews with Mr. Keir and the Reverend William Bradley.

34. Minutes of the Meeting of the Board of Directors, Connecticut Council of Churches, January 28, 1958. Files of Mr. Keir.

35. Interview with Mr. Keir.

36. Mimeographed copy of sermon, "Paul Blanshard—Religious Scholar," by the Reverend Payson Miller, Unitarian Meeting House, Hartford, March 2, 1958. Files of Mr. Keir.

37. *Hartford Courant* and *Hartford Times*, April 29, 1958, and files of Mr. Keir.

38. *Transcript*, May 1, 1958.

39. "Religion and Freedom," report by Donald McDonald on the Seminar, 1958, is available from the Fund for the Republic, New York City. This writer took part in the Seminar.

40. Remarks of Father Raymond T. Bosler, McDonald, p. 38.

41. Remarks of Norman St. John-Stevas, *ibid.*, p. 48.

42. Remarks of Theodore Powell, "Religion in a Free Society," *Christianity Today*, May 26, 1958, p. 39.

43. This writer participated in the conference.

44. This account of the Brookfield and Newtown referenda is based on an interview with Paul S. Smith, editor of the *Newtown Bee*, and on reports carried by that newspaper in July, August, and September, 1958.

45. This was not the heaviest vote in Newtown history, although it was close to it. A zoning ordinance referendum the year before drew a total vote of 2650, just 189 more votes than were cast on the school bus issue. The ordinance was defeated by two votes. A short time earlier a bond issue for a junior high school was approved by only three votes, 1094 to 1091. Newtown voters were accustomed to being evenly divided on local political issues.

46. *Hartford Courant* and *Hartford Times*, June 18, 1958.

47. "Connecticut Yankee," by A. H. O. [Alan H. Olmstead], *Manchester Evening Herald*, July 8, 1958. For a detailed account of the fight in the Democratic convention over the choice of a candidate for congressman at large, and for candid comments about the influence of nationality and religion, see "Candidate," Joseph P. Lyford, *Case Studies in Practical Politics* (New York, Henry Holt & Co., 1959).

48. Connecticut, *Register and Manual*, 1959, pp. 544–619.

49. *Hartford Courant* and *Hartford Times*, November 5, 1958.

50. The Republicans had placed one Jew on their state ticket, Simon Cohen, candidate for attorney general.

51. "Leader Who Might Have Been," by Eric Sandahl, *Bridgeport Herald*, March 2, 1958.

52. Interviews with the Reverend Harold Keir, the Reverend William Bradley, and Monsignor Robert W. Doyle, May 10, 1960.

53. *Hartford Courant*, February 19, 1959.

54. Interview with Dr. Loyd Worley, January 29, 1960.

55. *Snyder v. Newtown, Connecticut Law Journal*, June 14, 1960.

56. See above, pp. 38–39.

57. *Judd v. Board of Education*, 278 N.Y. 200 (1938); *State ex. rel. Traub v. Brown*, 36 Del. 181 (1934).

58. *Hartford Courant*, June 14, 1960.

VIII: CONCLUSION

1. See above, Chapter II.

2. Appendix II.

3. See above, Chapter II.

4. *Transcript*, June 6, 1957.

5. Interview with Monsignor Robert W. Doyle, August 23, 1957.

6. Cf. *Hartford Courant*, May 30, 1957, and *Transcript*, June 6, 1957.

BIBLIOGRAPHY

BOOKS

Brady, Joseph A., *Confusion Twice Confounded: The First Amendment and the Supreme Court.* South Orange, New Jersey: Seton Hall University Press, 1954.

Howe, Mark A. DeWolfe, *Cases on Church and State in the United States.* Cambridge, Massachusetts: Harvard University Press, 1952.

Lockard, Duane, *New England State Politics.* Princeton, New Jersey: Princeton University Press, 1959.

Mason, Mary Paul, *Church-State Relationships in Education in Connecticut, 1633–1953.* Washington: Catholic University of America Press, 1953.

McCluskey, Neil G., *The Catholic Viewpoint on Education.* Garden City, New York: Hanover House, 1959.

McCollum, Vashti, *One Woman's Fight.* New York: Doubleday & Company, 1951.

O'Neill, James M., *Catholicism and American Freedom.* New York: Harper & Brothers, 1952.

Pfeffer, Leo, *Church, State and Freedom.* Boston: Beacon Press, 1950.

Spectorsky, A. C., *The Exurbanites.* Philadelphia: J. B. Lippincott Co., 1955.

Spurlock, Clark, *Education and the Supreme Court.* Urbana, Illinois: University of Illinois Press, 1955.

Stokes, Anson Phelps, *Church and State in the United States.* 3 vols. New York: Harper & Brothers, 1950.

Underwood, Kenneth W., *Protestant and Catholic.* Boston: Beacon Press, 1957.

GOVERNMENT DOCUMENTS AND PUBLICATIONS

Connecticut

Atkinson, Keith, *Public School Law in Connecticut.* Hartford: State Department of Education, 1951.

Connecticut, State of, Constitution.
Educational Directory of Connecticut, 1955–1956. Hartford: State Department of Education.
"House Journal," General Assembly, January Session, 1957.
Legislative Bulletin No. 25. General Assembly, January Session, 1957.
Legislative Record Index No. 19. General Assembly, January Session, 1957.
Minutes of the State Board of Education, 1955–1957.
Pocket Manual: Roll, Committees and Rules of the General Assembly of Connecticut, 1957.
Powell, Theodore (compiler), *Laws Relating to Education.* Hartford: State Department of Education, 1959.
Register and Manual. Hartford: Secretary of State, 1955–1957.
Ross, Maurice J., "The Relationship of Public and Non-Public Schools in Connecticut." Hartford: State Department of Education, 1956.
"Senate Journal," General Assembly, January Session, 1957.
Stuart, Patricia, *Handbook for Connecticut Boards of Education.* Storrs: Institute of Public Opinion, University of Connecticut, 1956.
Weekly Health Bulletin. Hartford: State Department of Health, 1956–1957.

United States

Committee for the White House Conference on Education, *A Report to the President.* Washington: Government Printing Office, 1956.
Congress, Public Law 396, Seventy-ninth Congress, 1945–1946.

LEGAL CASES

Adams et al. v. *County Commissioners of St. Mary's County,* 26 Atl. 2nd 377, Maryland (1942).
Bowker v. *Baker,* 73 Cal. App. 2nd 653 (1946).
City of New Haven v. *Town of Torrington,* 132 Conn. 194 (1945)
Cochran v. *Louisiana State Board of Education,* 281 U.S. 370 (1930).
Everson v. *Board of Education,* 330 U.S. 1 (1947).
Everson v. *Board of Education of Township of Ewing,* 132 N.J.L. 98 (1944).
Heisey v. *County of Alameda et al.,* 352 U.S. 921 (1957).
Illinois ex. rel. McCollum v. *Board of Education,* 333 U.S. 203 (1948).
McVey v. *Hawkins,* 365 Mo. 44 (1953).
Nichols et al. v. *Henry,* 301 Ky. 434 (1945).

Pierce v. *Society of Sisters of the Holy Name of Jesus and Mary,* 268
U.S. 510 (1925).
Smith v. *Donahue,* 195 N.Y. Supp. 715 (1922).
Visser v. *Nooksack Valley School District,* 33 Wash. 2nd (1949).
Zellers v. *Huff,* 55 N.M. 501 (1951).
Zorach v. *Clauson,* 343 U.S. 306 (1952).

PERIODICALS

Bennett, John C., "Reply to Dean Pearson," *Christian Century,* Jan-
uary 2, 1957.
Christian Century, "Religion in a Free Society," May 28, 1958.
Christian Register: Unitarian, April, 1957.
Connell, Francis J., "Reply to Father Murray," *American Ecclesiastical
Review,* January, 1952.
———, "Theory of the Lay State," *American Ecclesiastical Review,* July,
1951.
Fenton, Joseph C., "The Status of a Controversy," *American Ecclesias-
tical Review,* June, 1951.
Kennedy, John S., "Opposition to a Bus Bill," *America,* September 7,
1957.
Murray, John Courtney, "Contemporary Orientations of Catholic
Thought on Church and State in the Light of History," *Theological
Studies,* June, 1949.
———, "For Freedom and Transcendence of the Church," *American
Ecclesiastical Review,* January, 1952.
———, "On Religious Freedom, Some Recent Literature," *Theological
Studies,* September, 1949.
———, "The Problem of State Religion: A Reply to George W. Shea,"
Theological Studies, June, 1951.
Shea, George W., "Catholic Doctrine and the Religion of the State,"
American Ecclesiastical Review, September, 1950.
———, "Catholic Orientations of Church and State," *American Ecclesias-
tical Review,* December, 1951.
Smith, Richard Joyce, "Aid for Private and Parochial Schools," *America,*
November 10, 1956.
U.S. News and World Report, December 2, December 23, 1955.
Welch, Robert J., "The Catholic Church and American Democracy,"
The Christian Family, June, July–August, September, 1956.
Yanitelli, V. R., "Church-State Anthology, The Work of Father Murray,"
Thought, March, 1952.

NEWSPAPERS

Better Schools, National Citizens Council for Better Schools, 9 East 40th
  Street, New York, May, June, 1957.
Bridgeport Herald, April, 1957; March, 1958.
Catholic Transcript (Hartford), 1955–1960.
Hartford Courant, 1955–1960.
Hartford Times, 1955–1960.
Manchester (Connecticut) *Evening Herald*, 1956–1960.
New Haven Register, April, 1957.
New London Evening Day, April, 1957.
New York World-Telegram, June, July, August, 1949.
New York Times, 1948–1949, 1952, 1955–1957.
West Hartford News, May, November, December, 1956.

INTERVIEWS

Alcorn, Meade, Republican National Chairman, July 14, 1957.
Baldwin, Clarence, Republican State Chairman, August 16, 1957.
Bauer, Philip, state senator, October 29, 1957.
Bradley, Reverend William, November 26, 1959.
Brown, Nelson, Speaker of the Connecticut House of Representatives,
  September 10, 1957.
Cairns, Robert, state representative, July 19, 1957.
Cooney, Joseph, legal counsel to the Roman Catholic Archdiocese of
  Hartford, August 7, 1957 (telephone).
Cushman, Edith, School Lunch and Nutrition Consultant, Connecticut
  State Department of Education, August, September, 1956.
Doyle, Monsignor Robert W., Superintendent of Schools, Roman Catho-
  lic Archdiocese of Hartford, August 23, 1957, and subsequent dates.
Googel, Samuel, state representative and Minority (Democratic) Leader,
  Connecticut House of Representatives, February 7, 1958.
Hammer, Lucy, state representative, July 19, 1957.
Hurley, John, August 7, 1957.
Keir, Reverend Harold, February 1, 1960.
Kennedy, Monsignor John S., editor, *Catholic Transcript* (Hartford),
  July 15, 1957.
Kopacz, Benjamin, state senator, July 25, 1957.
Lasbury, Mrs. Ralph C., November 11, 1956, and June 9, 1957.
Mutrie, James, legislative reporter, *New Haven Register*, April 23, 1957.

Pope, Frederick, state representative and Majority (Republican) Leader, Connecticut House of Representatives, July 18, October 16, 1957.

Ross, Maurice J., Chief, Bureau of Research and Statistics, Connecticut State Department of Education, January, February, 1957.

Ryan, Theodore, state senator and Senate President *pro tempore*, July 30, 1957.

Sheehan, Richard, state representative, July 5, 1957.

Worley, Reverend Loyd, August 19, 1957, and January 29, 1960.

OTHER SOURCES

Conant, James B., "Unity and Diversity in Secondary Education," *Leadership for American Education*. Official report of the American Association of School Administrators, Washington, 1952.

"Focus," television program, WNBC–TV, West Hartford, March 16, 1957.

"For Better Schools," radio program, WTIC, Hartford, December 2, 1956.

Johnson, Joseph N., "The Development of Certain Legal Issues Concerning the Relationship Between Public and Sectarian Education." Unpublished doctoral dissertation, Graduate School, University of Pittsburgh, 1953.

Lyford, Joseph P., "Candidate," *Case Studies in Practical Politics*. New York: Henry Holt & Co., Inc., 1959.

McDonald, Donald, "Religion and Freedom." Report on a seminar sponsored by the Fund for the Republic, New York, 1958.

INDEX